Shakespeare's Book of Insults, Insights and Infinite Jests

Merry Christmas
to grandma
with Love,
Susan

Love,
David

Have a merry
Christmas!
Brad

Shakespeare's Book of Insults, Insights and Infinite Jests

from the collection of John W. Seder

Templegate Publishers
Springfield, Illinois

ISBN: 0-87243-128-2

Published by
Templegate Publishers
302 East Adams Street
P.O. Box 5152
Springfield, Illinois
62705

INTRODUCTION

The great Shakespeare scholar A.C. Bradley pointed out that in the surviving descriptions of the dramatist by his acquaintances, the word "civil" prevails oddly, as if the word was meant to have more than perfunctory meaning. Like most words, "civil" bore a more concrete sense in those days, because of its felt connection with its Latin root *civis* (citizen) and especially because, in Elizabethan England as in the Old West, elemental civility was by no means to be taken for granted.

It is trite to say that Shakespeare is the master of every effect available to the English language, but even so, it is almost shocking that from a body of work hardly longer than a meaty Dickens novel an entire anthology of insults could be collected. It is needless to say that in Mr. Seder's collection the English insult appears at its most robust.

The Elizabethan age is one of those periods that arouse intense nostalgia in those who didn't have to live through the bloody things. The Tudor succession was uncertain, England was deeply riven by religious differences, feudalism was giving way to something undefined (men hadn't yet learned to call it capitalism). All sorts of people were pouring into London, Shakespeare among them. It was a moment of flux, anxiety, and opportunity.

It was therefore a moment of what would now be called intense status competition. Men competed with words and with swords, and the word and the sword competed with each other: how many poets nowadays get the chance to see a man disembowelled?

An insult is a way of reducing another's status, effective to the extent that rank hasn't already been settled. Invective skill must have been something of a practical necessity in Shakespeare's London; yet the finer, "civil" nature of this well-bred provincial gent must have longed for surcease from brawling manners. At the same time, his wit must have relished the sheer sport of contumely.

Mr. Seder offers much more than insults. He has gathered an astounding assortment of sharp observations, signs of the deep interest in individual character typical of both Shakespeare and the Renaissance. If the social pageant has ever been more splendid than it was in England around 1600, it has never been recorded with such wit and color.

But the insults! Someone said that invective is the most readable form of literature, and Shakespeare's is innocent of any sense of uncharity, since the objects of his withering shafts are all imaginary. Here, truly, we may delight in victimless crime.

William F. Buckley, Jr.

i

FOREWORD

This book is for you if you had to read Shakespeare in high school or college and were turned off by improbable plots, by archaic language full of *thees* and *thous*, and by characters and situations that seemed remote from your experience.

You may have had a teacher who either didn't see or couldn't help you find the wisdom and the beauty—and the humor—that are here. Or who didn't understand that Shakespeare's world is *not* distant and remote from ours.

No, indeed. Shakespeare's world *is our world*, the world of today. He began writing in the 1580s and died in 1616, and yet he is here and now. He wrote about *us*—you and me, our friends, our families, the people we work with and play with and argue with and go to bed with, the characters we see on the evening news and elect to public office.

You will find yourself in Shakespeare—everybody does.

The master had an incredible gift for expressing the universals of emotion and experience that have been shared by human beings everywhere and throughout all time—the thoughts and feelings and dreams, the doubts and fears. He told us about the glorious victories of kings and empires, but also about the little successes, the small comforts and pleasures of ordinary mortals. The clashes of mighty armies and the murders, yes, but also the minor misdemeanors, the little confusions and accidents and embarrassments of everyday life.

Look around you at your family, your friends and neighbors. Shakespeare knew them all:

> For what is wedlock forced but a hell, an age of discord and continual strife?

> The whining schoolboy, with his satchel and shining morning face, creeping like snail unwillingly to school.

> He is given to sports, to wildness and much company.

> Teeth hadst thou in thy head when thou wast born, to signify thou camest to bite the world.

> Many a time and often I ha' dined with him, and told him on't . . . yet he would embrace no counsel, take no warning.

> . . . three-inch fool!

Do you remember the last party you went to? Shakespeare was there before you:

> I shall grow jealous of you shortly, if you thus get my wife into corners.

> For he's in the third degree of drink.

> . . . which of you will stop the vent of hearing when loud rumour speaks?

If ladies be but young and fair they have the gift to know it.

His garments are rich, but he wears them not handsomely.

. . . when every goose is cackling.

Think about your job and the people you work with and work for. Shakespeare knew them:

Where have you been all this while? When every thing is ended, then you come.

. . . the fashion of these times, where none will sweat but for promotion.

O, that men's ears should be to counsel deaf, but not to flattery.

We have some old crab trees here.

. . . a botcher's apprentice.

If you browse through this book, it may surprise you to find yourself laughing. Shakespeare is full of humor, not only the broad clowning of the likes of Falstaff, but the deft little jabs and needles, sly and subtle jests. You may miss them if you don't listen (or read) carefully, since he sometimes drops a comic line incongruously into a scene of blood and gore (as when Macbeth's hired murderer reports, "My lord, his throat is cut, that I did for him."):

This passion, and the death of a dear friend, would go near to make a man look sad.

With the help of a surgeon, he might yet recover, and prove an ass.

He hath much land, and fertile . . . spacious in the possession of dirt.

In his sleep he does little harm, save to his bedclothes about him.

But for these vile guns, he would himself have been a soldier.

You are undone, captain, all but your scarf, that has a knot on 't yet.

There lives not three good men unhanged in England, and one of them is fat and grows old.

It has been my special pleasure to pick out some of these "apt and gracious words." these marvelous descriptions of the frailties and faults of foolish mortals. I hope it will be your pleasure to browse among them.

And—very important—*don't work at it.* This book is to *enjoy.*

John W. Seder

Washington, D.C.
August, 1984

TABLE OF CONTENTS

1
POLITICIANS

A politician, . . . one that would circumvent God.
— Hamlet, Act 5, Sc. 1

The caterpillars of the commonwealth . . .
— Richard II, Act 2, Sc. 3

. . . almost all repent in their election.
— Coriolanus, Act 2, Sc. 3

For they pray continually to their saint, the commonwealth; or rather, not pray to her, but prey on her.
— Henry IV, Part I, Act 2, Sc. 1

Policy sits above conscience.
— Timon of Athens, Act 3, Sc. 2

A certain convocation of politic worms . . .
— Hamlet, Act 4, Sc. 3

I had thought I had had men of some understanding and wisdom of my council, but I find none.
— Henry VIII, Act 5, Sc. 3

You cloudy princes . . .
— Richard III, Act 2, Sc. 2

Thy sumptuous buildings and thy wife's attire have cost a mass of public treasury.
— Henry VI, Part II, Act 1, Sc. 3

I have bought golden opinions from all sorts of people.
— Macbeth, Act 1, Sc. 7

Am I politic? Am I subtle? Am I a Machiavel?
— Merry Wives of Windsor, Act 3, Sc. 1

But man, proud man, drest in a little brief authority, most ignorant of what he's most assured, his glassy essence, like an angry ape, plays such fantasic tricks before high heaven as make the angels weep.
— Measure for Measure, Act 2, Sc. 2

That trick of state was a deep envious one.
— Henry VIII, Act 2, Sc. 1

O, that estates, degrees and offices were not derived corruptly, and that clear honour were purchased by the merit of the wearer!

— *Merchant of Venice, Act 2, Sc. 9*

If the other two be brained like us, the state totters.

— *The Tempest, Act 3, Sc. 2*

Thy sale of offices and towns . . . , if they were known, as the suspect is great, would make thee quickly hop without thy head.

— *Henry VI, Part II, Act 1, Sc. 3*

Something he left imperfect in the state . . .

— *King Lear, Act 4, Sc. 3*

The insolence of office . . .

— *Hamlet, Act 3, Sc. 1*

Gold will . . . place thieves, and give them title, knee and approbation with senators on the bench.

— *Timon of Athens, Act 4, Sc. 3*

. . . although in glorious titles he excel.

— *Henry VI, Part I, Act 5, Sc. 5*

I charge and command that, of the city's cost, the pissing-conduit run nothing but claret wine this first year of our reign.

— *Part II, Act 4, Sc. 1*

A foe to citizens, one that still motions war and never peace.

— *Part I, Act 1, Sc. 3*

It was a mad fantastical trick of him to steal from the state.

— *Measure for Measure, Act 3, Sc. 2*

Look where the sturdy rebel sits, even in the chair of state.

— *Henry VI, Part III, Act 1, Sc. 1*

Thou cold sciatica, cripple our senators, that their limbs may halt as lamely as their manners.

— *Timon of Athens, Act 4, Sc. 1*

Consider you what services he has done for his country? — Very well, and could be content to give him good report for it, but that he pays himself with being proud.

— *Coriolanus, Act 1, Sc. 1*

I am whipp'd and scourged with rods, nettled and stung with pismires, when I hear of this vile politician.

— *Henry IV, Part I, Act 1, Sc. 3*

If such a one be fit to govern . . . — Fit to govern! No, not to live.
— *Macbeth, Act 4, Sc. 3*

Thou art a villain. — You are — a senator.
— *Othello, Act 1, Sc. 1*

. . . makes civil hands unclean.
— *Romeo and Juliet, Prologue*

O, he sits high in all the people's hearts; and that which would appear offence in us his countenance, like richest alchemy, will change to virtue and to worthiness.
— *Julius Caesar, Act 1, Sc: 3*

. . . behold the great image of authority; a dog's obeyed in office.
— *King Lear, Act 4, Sc. 6*

Madness in great ones must not unwatch'd go.
— *Hamlet, Act 3, Sc. 1*

You grave but reckless senators . . .
— *Coriolanus, Act 3, Sc. 1*

You yourself are much condemn'd to have an itching palm, to sell and mart your offices for gold to undeservers.
— *Julius Caesar, Act 4, Sc. 3*

. . . thy yawning mouth for swallowing the treasure of the realm.
— *Henry VI, Part II, Act 4, Sc. 1*

Fie, lords! that you, being supreme magistrates, thus contumeliously should break the peace!
— *Part I, Act 1, Sc. 3*

Do you your office, or give up your place . . .
— *Measure for Measure, Act 2, Sc. 2*

. . . set all hearts in the state to what tune pleased his ear.
— *The Tempest, Act 1, Sc. 2*

For if such actions may have passage free,
Bond-slaves and pagans shall our statesmen be.
— *Othello, Act 1, Sc. 2*

The commons hath he pill'd with grievous taxes, and quite lost their hearts.
— *Richard II, Act 2, Sc. 1*

Alas! how should you govern, . . . that know not . . . how to study for the people's welfare?
— *King Lear, Act 5, Sc. 3*

. . . in the gross and scope of my opinion, this bodes some strange eruption
to our state.
— *Hamlet, Act 1, Sc. 1*

Some certain edicts and some strait decrees that lie too heavy on the
commonwealth . . .
— *Henry IV, Part I, Act 4, Sc. 3*

. . . the body public be a horse whereon the governor doth ride.
— *Measure for Measure, Act 1, Sc. 2*

You have an exchequer of words, and, I think, no other treasure to give
your followers . . .
— *Two Gentlemen of Verona, Act 2, Sc. 4*

. . . a brace of unmeriting, proud, violent, testy magistrates, alias fools . . .
— *Coriolanus, Act 2, Sc. 1*

I do discharge you of your office; give up your keys.
— *Measure for Measure, Act 5, Sc. 1*

What's done in the Capitol; who's like to rise, who thrives and who
declines.
— *Coriolanus, Act 1, Sc. 1*

. . . to o'erthrow law and in one self-born hour to plant and o'erwhelm
custom.
— *Winter's Tale, Act 4, Sc. 1*

. . . idol of idiot-worshippers . . .
— *Troilus and Cressida, Act 5, Sc. 1*

Well, would I were gently put out of office, before I were forced out!
— *Timon of Athens, Act 1, Sc. 2*

Since thou wert king . . . the commonwealth hath daily run to wreck.
— *Henry VI, Part II, Act 1, Sc. 3*

Now does he feel his title hang loose about him, like a giant's robe upon a
dwarfish thief.
— *Macbeth, Act 5, Sc. 2*

Cries out upon abuses, seems to weep over his country's wrongs, and by
this face, this seeming brow of justice, did he win the hearts of all that he
did angle for.
— *Henry IV, Part I, Act 4, Sc.3*

. . . and then the hearts of all his people shall revolt from him.
— *King John, Act 3, Sc. 4*

For how can tyrants safely govern home, unless abroad they purchase great alliance?

— *Henry VI, Part III, Act 3, Sc. 3*

The devil knew not what he did when he made man politic; he crossed himself by it.

— *Timon of Athens, Act 3, Sc. 3*

. . . to busy giddy minds with foreign quarrels . . .

— *Henry IV, Part II, Act 4, Sc. 5*

Come, wife, let's in and learn to govern better . . .

— *Henry VI, Part II, Act 4, Sc. 9*

Why such daily cast of brazen cannon, and foreign mart for implements of war?

— *Hamlet, Act 1, Sc. 1*

Well, I perceive he was a wise fellow and had good discretion, that, being bid to ask what he would of the king, desired he might know none of his secrets . . .

— *Pericles, Act 1, Sc. 3*

Ill beseeming any common man, much more a knight, a captain and a leader.

— *Henry VI, Part I, Act 4, Sc. 1*

. . . to make a shambles of the parliament-house!

— *Part III, Act 1, Sc. 1*

Ye gods! It doth amaze me a man of such a feeble temper should so get the start of the majestic world and bear the palm alone.

— *Julius Caesar, Act 1, Sc. 2*

. . . unworthily thou wast installed in that high degree.

— *Henry VI, Part I, Act 4, Sc. 1*

A king of shreds and patches . . .

— *Hamlet, Act 3, Sc. 4*

Burn all the records of the realm; my mouth shall be the parliament . . .

— *Henry VI, Part II, Act 4, Sc. 7*

And did he not . . . levy great sums of money through the realm . . . ?

— *Act 3, Sc. 1*

2

GO AWAY!

Farewell; if I can remember thee, I will think of thee . . .
— *All's Well that Ends Well, Act 1, Sc. 1*

I'll steal away. — There's honour in the theft.
— *Act 2, Sc. 1*

Vanish, or I shall give thee thy deserving . . .
— *Antony and Cleopatra, Act 4, Sc. 12*

Turn thou no more to seek a living in our territory.
— *As You Like It, Act 3, Sc. 1*

I thank you for your company, but . . . I had as lief have been myself alone.
— *Act 3, Sc. 2*

Let's meet as little as we can.
— *Act 3, Sc. 2*

I do desire we may be better strangers.
— *Act 3, Sc. 2*

Hence, old goat! . . . Hence, rotten thing, or I shall shake thy bones out of thy garments.
— *Coriolanus, Act 3, Sc. 1*

Take up some other station; here's no place for you.
— *Act 4, Sc. 5*

Get thee to a nunnery.
— *Hamlet, Act 3, Sc. 1*

. . . must send thee hence with fiery quickness.
— *Act 4, Sc. 3*

You tread upon my patience.
— *Henry IV, Part I, Act 1, Sc. 3*

When we need your use and counsel, we shall send for you.
— *Act 1, Sc. 3*

We license your departure . . .
— *Act 1, Sc. 3*

You have good leave to leave us.

        — Henry IV, Part I, Act 1, Sc. 3

Poor Jack, farewell! I could have better spared a better man.

            — Act 5, Sc. 4

Discharge yourself of our company.

        — Part II, Act 2, Sc. 4

Will you shog off?

        — Henry V, Act 2, Sc. 1

Why do you stay so long, my lords . . . ?

            — Act 4, Sc. 2

Away, away . . . we grace the yeoman by conversing with him.

       — Henry VI, Part I, Act 2, Sc. 4

Thou baleful messenger, out of my sight!

        — Part II, Act 3, Sc. 2

He shall not breathe infection in this air but three days longer . . .

            — Act 3, Sc. 2

And so we'll leave you to your meditations how to live better.

       — Henry VIII, Act 3, Sc. 2

Hence! home, you idle creatures, get you home. Is this a holiday?

       — Julius Caesar, Act 1, Sc. 1

Take away this villain; shut him up.

       — Love's Labour's Lost, Act 1, Sc. 2

Will these turtles be gone?

        — Act 4, Sc. 3

Keep some state in thy exit, and vanish.

        — Act 5, Sc. 2

Let us not be dainty of leave-taking, but shift away.

       — Macbeth, Act 2, Sc. 3

Stand not upon the order of your going, but go at once.

        — Act 3, Sc. 4

For there is not one among them but I dote on his very absence.

       — Merchant of Venice, Act 1, Sc. 2

If I could bid the fifth welcome with so good a heart as I can bid the other
four farewell . . .
>   — *Merchant of Venice*, Act 1, Sc. 2

Vanish like hailstones, go.
>   — *Merry Wives of Windsor*, Act 1, Sc. 3

At a word, hang no more about me.
>   — *Act 2, Sc. 2*

You wrong me, sir, thus still to haunt my house.
>   — *Act 3, Sc. 4*

Trip away, make no stay.
>   — *Midsummer Night's Dream*, Act 5, Sc. 1

Farewell, thou pure impiety and impious purity!
>   — *Much Ado about Nothing*, Act 4, Sc. 1

I will leave you now to your gossip-like humour.
>   — *Act 5, Sc. 1*

I must discontinue your company.
>   — *Act 5, Sc. 1*

I have charged thee not to haunt about my doors.
>   — *Othello*, Act 1, Sc. 1

Marry, would the word 'farewell' have lengthen'd hours and added years to
his short banishment, he should have had a volume of farewells, but
since it would not, he had none of me.
>   — *Richard II*, Act 1, Sc. 4

Bid me farewell. — 'Tis more than you deserve.
>   — *Richard III*, Act 1, Sc. 2

Earth gapes, hell burns, fiends roar, saints pray,
To have him suddenly convey'd away.
>   — *Act 4, Sc. 4*

Graze where you will, you shall not house with me . . .
>   — *Romeo and Juliet*, Act 3, Sc. 5

The door is open, sir; there lies your way.
>   — *Taming of the Shrew*, Act 3, Sc. 2

Go ply your needle; meddle not . . .
>   — *Act 2, Sc. 1*

Am I your bird? I mean to shift my bush.
— *Taming of the Shrew, Act 5, Sc. 2*

Mend my company; take away thyself.
— *Timon of Athens, Act 4, Sc. 3*

Fare thee well, fare thee well. — Thou art a fool to bid me farewell twice
. . . Shouldst have kept one to thyself, for I mean to give thee none.
— *Act 1, Sc. 1*

Go, take him away, and hang him presently.
— *Titus Andronicus, Act 4, Sc. 4*

A good riddance.
— *Troilus and Cressida, Act 2, Sc. 1*

If you can separate yourself and your misdemeanors, you are welcome to
the house; if not . . . she is very willing to bid you farewell.
— *Twelfth Night, Act 2, Sc. 3*

Go off; I discard you . . .
— *Act 3, Sc. 4*

Vent thy folly somewhere else.
— *Act 4, Sc. 1*

. . . direct thy feet where thou and I henceforth may never meet.
— *Act 5, Sc. 1*

By and by intend to chide myself even for this time I spend in talking to
thee.
— *Two Gentlemen of Verona, Act 4, Sc. 2*

Away, I say! Stay'st thou to vex me here?
— *Act 4, Sc. 4*

3
STUPIDITY

Not Hercules could have knocked out his brains, for he had none.
— *Cymbeline*, Act 4, Sc. 2

Here will be an old abusing of God's patience and the king's English.
— *Merry Wives of Windsor*, Act 1, Sc. 4

This is the silliest stuff that ever I heard.
— *Midsummer Night's Dream*, Act 5, Sc. 1

Foolery, sir, does walk about the orb like the sun, it shines everywhere.
— *Twelfth Night*, Act 3, Sc. 1

He has not so much brain as ear-wax.
— *Troilus and Cressida*, Act 5, Sc. 1

Look, he's winding up the watch of his wit; by and by it will strike.
— *The Tempest*, Act 2, Sc. 1

In our last conflict four of his five wits went halting off, and now is the whole man governed with one.
— *Much Ado About Nothing*, Act 1, Sc. 1

I count it but time lost to hear such a foolish song.
— *As You Like It*, Act 5, Sc. 3

According to Fates and Destinies and such odd sayings, the Sisters Three and such branches of learning . . .
— *Merchant of Venice*, Act 2, Sc. 2

Are his wits safe? Is he not light of brain?
— *Othello*, Act 4, Sc. 1

Sir, if you spend word for word with me, I shall make your wit bankrupt.
— *Two Gentlemen of Verona*, Act 2, Sc. 4

More of your conversation would infect my brain.
— *Coriolanus*, Act 2, Sc. 1

Thou shouldst not have been old till thou hadst been wise.
— *King Lear*, Act 1, Sc. 5

Either you are ignorant, or seem so, craftily; and that's not good.
— *Measure for Measure*, Act 2, Sc. 4

There's many a man hath more hair than wit.
— *Comedy of Errors, Act 2, Sc. 2*

Either thou art most ignorant by age, or thou wert born a fool.
— *Winter's Tale, Act 2, Sc. 1*

. . . hath learned no wit by nature nor art . . .
— *As You Like It, Act 3, Sc. 2*

And will you credit this base drudge's words, that speaks he knows not what?
— *Henry VI, Part II, Act 4, Sc. 2*

There is no darkness but ignorance, in which thou art more puzzled than the Egyptians in their fog.
— *Twelfth Night, Act 4, Sc. 2*

. . . that never read so far to know the cause . . .
— *Taming of the Shrew, Act 3, Sc. 1*

Repair thy wit, good youth, or it will fall to cureless ruin.
— *Merchant of Venice, Act 4, Sc. 1*

To be now a sensible man, by and by a fool, and presently a beast!
— *Othello, Act 2, Sc. 3*

I will prove those verses to be very unlearned, neither savouring of poetry, wit, nor invention.
— *Love's Labour's Lost, Act 4, Sc. 2*

I will not praise thy wisdom . . .

— *Troilus and Cressida, Act 2, Sc. 3*

For I mine own gain'd knowledge should profane, if I would time expend with such a snipe . . .
— *Othello, Act 1, Sc. 3*

The fool doth think he is wise, but the wise man knows himself to be a fool.
— *As You Like It, Act 5, Sc. 1*

Here's a fellow frights English out of his wits.
— *Merry Wives of Windsor, Act 2, Sc. 1*

You would be another Penelope; . . . all the yarn she spun in Ulysses' absence did but fill Ithaca full of moths.
— *Coriolanus, Act 1, Sc. 3*

How prove you that, in the great heap of your knowledge?
— *As You Like It, Act 1, Sc. 2*

Why, this is very midsummer madness.
> — *Twelfth Night*, Act 3, Sc. 4

O, these deliberate fools! when they do choose, they have the wisdom by their wit to lose.
> — *Merchant of Venice*, Act 2, Sc. 9

Can you not see? or will ye not observe . . . ?
> — *Henry VI, Part II*, Act 3, Sc. 1

It is a tale told by an idiot, full of sound and fury, signifying nothing.
> — *Macbeth*, Act 5, Sc. 5

A very superficial, ignorant, unweighing fellow.
> — *Measure for Measure*, Act 3, Sc. 2

That handful of wit . . . it is a most pathetical nit.
> — *Love's Labour's Lost*, Act 4, Sc. 1

Bait the hook well; this fish will bite.
> — *Much Ado About Nothing*, Act 2, Sc. 3

But if you be afeard to hear the worst, then let the worst unheard fall on your head.
> — *King John*, Act 4, Sc. 2

More matter for a May morning.
> — *Twelfth Night*, Act 3, Sc. 4

Dull unfeeling barren ignorance . . .
> — *Richard II*, Act 1, Sc. 3

A plentiful lack of wit.
> — *Hamlet*, Act 2, Sc. 2

You cram these words into mine ears against the stomach of my sense.
> — *The Tempest*, Act 2, Sc. 1

I can't say your worships have delivered the matter well, when I find the ass in compound with the major part of your syllables.
> — *Coriolanus*, Act 2, Sc. 1

. . . highly fed and lowly taught.
> — *All's Well that Ends Well*, Act 2, Sc. 2

You are so without these follies that these follies are within you and shine through you . . .
> — *Two Gentlemen of Verona*, Act 2, Sc. 1

This is the very false gallop of verses; why do you infect yourself with them?

— *As You Like It, Act 3, Sc. 2*

You waste the treasure of your time with a foolish knight.

— *Twelfth Night, Act 2, Sc. 5*

How ill it follows, after you have laboured so hard, you should talk so idly!

— *Henry IV, Part II, Act 2, Sc. 2*

Ourselves and our children have lost, or do not learn for want of time, the sciences that should become our country, but grow like savages.

— *Henry V, Act 5, Sc. 1*

. . . some ten words long . . . but by ten words it is too long.

— *Midsummer Night's Dream, Act 5, Sc. 1*

In sooth, thou wast in very gracious fooling last night, when thou spokest of Pigrogromitus, of the Vaspians passing the equinoctial of Queubus; 'twas very good, i'faith.

— *Twelfth Night, Act 2, Sc. 3*

. . . heavy ignorance aloft.

— *Sonnet 78*

A kind of excellent dumb discourse.

— *The Tempest, Act 3, Sc. 3*

Wilt thou show the whole wealth of thy wit in an instant?

— *Merchant of Venice, Act 3, Sc. 5*

Your reasons are too shallow and too quick.

— *Richard III, Act 4, Sc. 4*

He that has and a little tiny wit . . .

— *King Lear, Act 3, Sc. 2*

Has Page any brains? hath he any eyes? hath he any thinking? Sure, they sleep; he hath no use of them.

— *Merry Wives of Windsor, Act 3, Sc. 2*

. . . his brain, which is as dry as the remainder biscuit after a voyage.

— *As You Like It, Act 2, Sc. 7*

What a lack-brain is this!

— *Henry IV, Part I, Act 2, Sc. 3*

But he's a tried and valiant soldier — So is my horse . . .

— *Julius Caesar, Act 4, Sc. 1*

The common curse of mankind, folly and ignorance, be thine in great revenue!
— *Troilus and Cressida, Act 2, Sc. 3*

Purse and brain both empty.
— *Cymbeline, Act 5, Sc. 4*

Sir, he hath never fed of the dainties that are bred in a book; he hath not eat paper, as it were; he hath not drunk ink; his intellect is not replenished.
— *Love's Labour's Lost, Act 4, Sc. 2*

. . . in the why and the wherefore is neither rhyme nor reason.
— *Comedy of Errors, Act 2, Sc. 2*

. . . should not be chronicled for wise.
— *Two Gentlemen of Verona, Act 1, Sc. 1*

Hard at hand comes the master and main exercise, the incorporate conclusion.
— *Othello, Act 2, Sc. 1*

Though there was no great matter in the ditty, yet the note was very untuneable.
— *As You Like It, Act 5, Sc. 3*

He doth indeed show some sparks that are like wit.
— *Much Ado about Nothing, Act 2, Sc. 3*

. . . these giddy loose suggestions.
— *King John, Act 3, Sc. 1*

Cogitation resides not in that man that does not think.
— *Winter's Tale, Act 1, Sc. 2*

Thy wit, that ornament to shape and love, misshapen in the conduct of them both.
— *Romeo and Juliet, Act 3, Sc. 3*

Such a deal of skimble-skamble stuff . . ..
— *Henry IV., Part I, Act 3, Sc. 1*

Our very eyes are sometimes like our judgements, blind.
— *Cymbeline, Act 4, Sc. 2*

I do know of those that . . . are reputed wise for saying nothing, when . . . if they should speak, would almost damn those ears, which, hearing them, would call their brothers fools..
— *Merchant of Venice, Act 1, Sc. 1*

This letter, being so excellently ignorant . . . It comes from a clodpole.
— *Twelfth Night, Act 3, Sc. 4*

14

. . . exsufflicate and blown surmises.

— Othello, Act 3, Sc. 3

Senseless speaking, or a speaking such as sense cannot untie.

— Cymbeline, Act 5, Sc. 4

. . . the yea and no of general ignorance . . .

— Coriolanus, Act 3, Sc. 1

. . . deficient, blind or lame of sense . . .

— Othello, Act 1, Sc. 3

Tongue and brain not . . .

— Cymbeline, Act 5. Sc. 4

His words are a very fantasical banquet, just so many strange dishes.

— Much Ado about Nothing, Act 2, Sc. 3

These are old fond paradoxes to make fools laugh i' the alehouse.

— Othello, Act 2, Sc. 1

You know neither me, yourselves nor any thing.

— Coriolanus, Act 2, Sc. 1

You prescribe to yourself very preposterously.

— Merry Wives of Windsor, Act 2, Sc. 2

There is, sure, another flood toward, and these couples are coming to the ark. Here comes a pair of very strange beasts, which in all tongues are called fools.

— As You Like It, Act 5, Sc. 4

. . . that little little less than little wit.

— Troilus and Cressida, Act 2, Sc. 3

I said, thou hadst a fine wit. "True," said she, "a fine little one." "No," said I, "a great wit." "Right," says she, "a great gross one."

— Much Ado about Nothing, Act 5, Sc. 1

Cannot take two from twenty . . . and leave eighteen.

— Cymbeline, Act 2, Sc. 1

There will little learning die then, that day thou art hang'd.

— Timon of Athens, Act 2, Sc. 2

All men were o' my mind. — (Aside) Wit would be out of fashion.

— Troilus and Cressida, Act 2, Sc. 3

. . . prince of dumbness . . .

— King Lear, Act 4, Sc. 1

15

4
LECHERY

Lechery, lechery; still, wars and lechery; nothing else holds fashion.
— *Troilus and Cressida*, Act 5, Sc. 2

. . . the beast with two backs.
— *Othello*, Act 1, Sc. 1

I will find you twenty lascivious turtles ere one chaste man.
— *Merry Wives of Windsor*, Act 2, Sc. 1

Quoth she, before you tumbled me, you promised me to wed.
— *Hamlet*, Act 4, Sc. 5

When flesh is cheap and females dear, and lusty lads roam here and there
so merrily . . .
— *Henry IV, Part II*, Act 5, Sc. 3

. . . Silken dalliance . . .
— *Henry V*, Act 2, Prologue

He will to his Egyptian dish again.
— *Antony and Cleopatra*, Act 2, Sc. 6

. . . she has been sluiced in 's absence and his pond fish'd by his next
neighbour.
— *Winter's Tale*, Act 1, Sc. 2

We shall buy maidenheads as they buy hob-nails, by the hundreds.
— *Henry IV, Part I*, Act 2, Sc. 4

Full many a lady I have eyed with best regard and many a time.
— *The Tempest*, Act 3, Sc. 1

. . . a bed, which . . . shall not speak of your pretty encounters.
— *Troilus and Cressida*, Act 3, Sc. 2

Lascivious, wanton, more than well beseems a man of thy profession and
degree.
— *Henry VI, Part I*, Act 3, Sc. 1

. . . tell a whispering tale in a fair lady's ear.
— *Romeo and Juliet*, Act 1, Sc. 5

. . . did the act of darkness with her.
— *King Lear*, Act 3, Sc. 4

We may account thee a whoremaster and a knave; which notwithstanding, thou shalt be no less esteemed.

— *Timon of Athens, Act 2, Sc. 2*

. . . front her, board her, woo her, assail her.

— *Twelfth Night, Act 1, Sc. 3*

. . . a speeding trick to lay down ladies.

— *Henry VIII, Act 1, Sc. 3*

'Leven widows and nine maids is a simple coming-in for one man.

— *Merchant of Venice, Act 2, Sc. 2*

How if your husband start some other where?

— *Comedy of Errors, Act 2, Sc. 1*

. . . paddling palms and pinching fingers.

— *Winter's Tale, Act 1, Sc. 2*

I will no more trust him when he leers than I will a serpent when he hisses.

— *Troilus and Cressida, Act 5, Sc. 1*

There's no bottom, none, in my voluptuousness; your wives, your daughters, your matrons and your maids, could not fill up the cistern of my lust.

— *Macbeth, Act 4, Sc. 3*

'Tis true I have gone here and there.

— *Sonnet 110*

These fellows of infinite tongue, that can rhyme themselves into ladies' favours, they do always reason themselves out again.

— *Henry V, Act 5, Sc. 2*

He is now in some commerce with my lady.

— *Twelfth Night, Act 3, Sc. 4*

Beauty provoketh thieves sooner than gold.

— *As You Like It, Act 1, Sc. 3*

His eye . . . unto a greater uproar tempts his veins.

— *Rape of Lucrece*

. . . solicits her in the unlawful purpose.

— *All's Well that Ends Well, Act 3, Sc. 5*

He wooes both high and low, both rich and poor, both young and old.

— *Merry Wives of Windsor, Act 2, Sc. 1*

Stray lower, where the pleasant fountains lie.

— *Venus and Adonis*

17

. . . way to the forfended place.
— *King Lear, Act 5, Sc. 1*

. . . an adulterous thief, an hypocrite, a virgin-violator.
— *Measure for Measure, Act 5, Sc. 1*

For several virtues have I liked several women.
— *The Tempest, Act 3, Sc. 1*

If you like elsewhere, do it by stealth.
— *Comedy of Errors, Act 3, Sc. 2*

Well, thou hast called her to a reckoning many a time and oft.
— *Henry IV, Part I, Act 1, Sc. 2*

. . . the night of our solemnities.
— *Midsummer Night's Dream, Act 1, Sc. 1*

He hath devoted and given up himself to the contemplation, mark and
denotement of her parts and graces.
— *Othello, Act 2, Sc. 3*

The triple pillar of the world transformed into a strumpet's fool.
— *Antony and Cleopatra, Act 1, Sc. 1*

. . . his plants in others' orchards grew.
— *Lover's Complaint*

. . . meddle with thy mistress.
— *Coriolanus, Act 4, Sc. 5*

I shall grow jealous of you shortly, if you thus get my wife into corners.
— *Merchant of Venice, Act 3, Sc. 5*

Strange fowl light upon neighbouring ponds.
— *Cymbeline, Act 1, Sc. 4*

I was as virtuously given as a gentleman need to be; virtuous enough,
swore little, diced not above seven times a week, went to a bawdy-
house not above once in a quarter — of an hour.
— *Henry IV, Part I, Act 3, Sc. 3*

. . . The loose encounters of lascivious men.
— *Two Gentlemen of Verona, Act 2, Sc. 7*

And his spirits . . . hunt after new fancies.
— *Othello, Act 3, Sc. 4*

He that doth naught with her, . . . were best he do it secretly alone.
— *Richard III, Act 1, Sc. 1*

Made old offences of affections new.

— Sonnet 110

Lady, shall I lie in your lap?

— Hamlet, Act 3, Sc. 2

. . . driven on by the flesh.

— All's Well that Ends Well, Act 1, Sc. 3

Groping for trouts in a peculiar river.

— Measure for Measure, Act 1, Sc. 2

What is a whoremaster, fool? — A fool in good clothes, and something like thee.

— Timon of Athens, Act 2, Sc. 2

Sweetheart, I were unmannerly to take you out, and not to kiss you.

— Henry VIII, Act 1, Sc. 4

Young blood doth not obey an old decree.

— Love's Labour's Lost, Act 4, Sc. 3

'Tis thought you have a goodly gift in horning.

— Titus Andronicus, Act 2, Sc. 3

And now you are metamorphosed with a mistress.

— Two Gentlemen of Verona, Act 2, Sc. 1

I from my mistress come to you in post; if I return, I shall be post indeed.

— Comedy of Errors, Act 1, Sc. 2

Tricks he hath had in him, which gentlemen have.

— All's Well that Ends Well, Act 5, Sc. 3

I'll canvass thee between a pair of sheets.

— Henry IV, Part II, Act 2, Sc. 4

. . . might scratch her where'er she did itch.

— The Tempest, Act 2, Sc. 2

She hath been colted by him.

— Cymbeline, Act 2, Sc. 4

Give up your body to such sweet uncleanness.

— Measure for Measure, Act 2, Sc. 4

. . . a dangerous and lascivious boy, who is a whale to virginity and devours up all the fry it finds.

— All's Well that Ends Well, Act 4, Sc. 3

You men will never tarry . . . I might have still held off, and then you
would have tarried.
                              — *Troilus and Cressida, Act 4, Sc. 2*

Stealing her soul with many vows of faith and ne'er a true one.
                              — *Merchant of Venice, Act 5, Sc. 1*

Study where to meet some mistress fine.
                              — *Love's Labour's Lost, Act 1, Sc. 1*

I had rather hear my dog bark at a crow than a man swear he loves me.
                              — *Much Ado about Nothing, Act 1, Sc. 1*

This drivelling love . . . that runs lolling up and down to hide his bauble in
a hole.
                              — *Romeo and Juliet, Act 2, Sc. 4*

He capers nimbly in a lady's chamber.
                              — *Richard III, Act 1, Sc. 1*

He did love her, sir, as a gentleman loves a woman . . . He loved her, sir,
and loved her not.
                              — *All's Well that Ends Well, Act 5, Sc. 3*

Loves for his own ends, not for you.
                              — *Macbeth, Act 3, Sc. 5*

. . . some Dick, that . . . knows the trick to make my lady laugh . . .
                              — *Love's Labour's Lost, Act 5, Sc. 2*

Come, mistress, now perforce we will enjoy that nice-preserved honesty of
yours.
                              — *Titus Andronicus, Act 2, Sc. 3*

Lovers break not hours, unless it be to come before their time.
                              — *Two Gentlemen of Verona, Act 5, Sc. 1*

To play with mammets and to tilt with lips.
                              — *Henry IV, Part I, Act 2, Sc. 3*

. . . youthful men, who give their eyes the liberty of gazing.
                              — *Comedy of Errors, Act 5, Sc. 1*

. . . rustling in unpaid-for silk.
                              — *Cymbeline, Act 3, Sc. 3*

For thus popp'd Paris in his hardiment.
                              — *Troilus and Cressida, Act 4, Sc. 5*

You have, as it appears to me, practiced upon the easy-yielding spirit of this woman, and made her serve your uses both in purse and in person.
— *Henry IV, Part II, Act 2, Sc. 1*

Alas, that love, so gentle in his view, should be so tyrannous and rough in proof!
— *Romeo and Juliet, Act 1, Sc. 1*

The anointed sovereign of sighs and groans.
— *Love's Labour's Lost, Act 3, Sc. 1*

To raise a spirit in his mistress' circle of some strange nature, letting it stand till she had laid it and conjured it down.
— *Romeo and Juliet, Act 2, Sc. 1*

Hath not else his eye stray'd his affection in unlawful love?
— *Comedy of Errors, Act 5, Sc. 1*

. . . win a lady at leapfrog . . .
— *Henry V, Act 5, Sc. 2*

Not politic in the commonwealth of nature to preserve virginity.
— *All's Well that End's Well, Act 1, Sc. 1*

. . . untimely claspings . . .
— *Pericles, Act 1, Sc. 1*

It is the manner of a man to speak to a woman.
— *Love's Labour's Lost, Act 1, Sc. 1*

When night-dogs run, all sorts of deer are chased.
— *Merry Wives of Windsor, Act 5, Sc. 5*

The poor Transylvanian is dead, that lay with the little baggage. — Ay, she quickly pooped him.
— *Pericles, Act 4, Sc. 2*

This gallant pins the wenches on his sleeve.
— *Love's Labour's Lost, Act 5, Sc. 2*

I'll make my heaven in a lady's lap . . .
— *Henry VI, Part III, Act 3, Sc. 2*

I'll unclasp my heart, and take her hearing prisoner with the force and strong encounter of my amorous tale.
— *Much Ado about Nothing, Act 1, Sc. 1*

Such is the simplicity of man to hearken after the flesh.
— *Love's Labour's Lost, Act 1, Sc. 1*

Beguiling virgins with the broken seals of perjury.
— *Henry V, Act 4, Sc. 1*

That's a fair thought to lie between maids' legs.
— *Hamlet, Act 3, Sc. 2*

. . . excellent in making ladies trip . . .
— *Pericles, Act 2, Sc. 3*

. . . conjunct and bosom'd with her . . .
— *King Lear, Act 5, Sc. 1*

Me they shall feel while I am able to stand.
— *Romeo and Juliet, Act 1, Sc. 1*

Is it not strange that desire should so many years outlive performance?
— *Henry IV, Part II, Act 2, Sc. 4*

It is too late to talk of love, and that's the mark I know you level at.
— *Pericles, Act 2, Sc. 3*

The wren goes to 't, and the small gilded fly does lecher in my sight.
— *King Lear, Act 4, Sc. 6*

Thou desirest me to stop in my tale against the hair.
— *Romeo and Juliet, Act 2, Sc. 4*

By my life, this is my lady's hand; these be her very C's, her U's and her T's.
— *Twelfth Night, Act 2, Sc. 5*

Why, then, it seems, some certain snatch or so would serve your turns.
— *Titus Andronicus, Act 2, Sc. 1*

All men have the like oaths; he had sworn to marry me when his wife's dead.
— *All's Well that End's Well, Act 4, Sc. 2*

If their daughters be capable, I will put it to them.
— *Love's Labour's Lost, Act 4, Sc. 2*

. . . wanton dalliance with a paramour.
— *Henry VI, Part I, Act 5, Sc. 1*

. . . please themselves upon her . . .
— *Pericles, Act 4, Sc. 1*

. . . go to hell for an eternal moment or so.
— *Merry Wives of Windsor, Act 2, Sc. 1*

And commit the oldest sins the newest kind of ways.
                    — *Henry IV, Part II, Act 4, Sc. 5*

Young men will do it, if they come to it, by cock . . .
                    — *Hamlet, Act 4, Sc. 5*

5
LIARS

Swearing by his honour, for he never had any.
— *As You Like It, Act 1, Sc. 2*

Let me have no lying; it becomes none but tradesmen.
— *Winter's Tale, Act 4, Sc. 4*

I do despise a liar as I do despise one that is false, or as I despise one that is not true.
— *Merry Wives of Windsor, Act 1, Sc. 1*

His evasions have ears thus long.
— *Troilus and Cressida, Act 2, Sc. 1*

He professes not keeping of oaths, in breaking 'em he is stronger than Hercules.
— *All's Well that Ends Well, Act 4, Sc. 3*

My vow was breath, and breath a vapour is.
— *Passionate Pilgrim*

. . . whose hearts are all as false as stairs of sand.
— *Merchant of Venice, Act 3, Sc. 2*

Honest in nothing but in his clothes.
— *Measure for Measure, Act 5, Sc. 1*

A very honest woman, but something given to lie; as a woman should not do, but in the way of honesty.
— *Antony and Cleopatra, Act 5, Sc. 2*

Why, sir, did I say you were an honest man? . . . I had lied in my throat, if I had said so.
— *Henry IV, Part II, Act 1, Sc. 2*

I do not greatly care to be deceived.
— *Antony and Cleopatra, Act 5, Sc. 2*

I do proclaim one honest man — mistake me not — but one; no more.
— *Timon of Athens, Act 4, Sc. 3*

Those lines that I before have writ do lie.
— *Sonnet 115*

Believe me not, and yet I lie not; I confess nothing, nor I deny nothing.
— *Much Ado about Nothing, Act 4, Sc. 1*

Stuffing the ears of men with false reports.

— *Henry IV, Part II, Induction*

Swore as many oaths as I spake words and broke them in the sweet face of heaven.

— *King Lear, Act 3, Sc. 4*

Thou smother'st honesty . . .

— *Rape of Lucrece*

This is the first truth that e'er thine own tongue was guilty of.

— *All's Well that Ends Well, Act 4, Sc. 1*

. . . register of lies.

— *Lover's Complaint*

Enough, . . . as this world goes, to pass for honest.

— *Winter's Tale, Act 2, Sc. 3*

Weigh oath with oath, and you will nothing weigh.

— *Midsummer Night's Dream, Act 3, Sc. 2*

Lord, Lord, how this world is given to lying!

— *Henry IV, Part I, Act 5, Sc. 4*

His promises fly so beyond his state that what he speaks is all in debt, he owes for every word.

— *Timon of Athens, Act 1, Sc. 2*

. . . stuff'd with protestations and full of new-found oaths, which he will break as easily as I do tear his paper.

— *Two Gentlemen of Verona, Act 4, Sc. 4*

As lying a gossip in that as ever . . . made her neighbours believe she wept for the death of a third husband.

— *Merchant of Venice, Act 3, Sc. 1*

Come, mistress, you must tell 's another tale.

— *Othello, Act 5, Sc. 1*

. . . hath done nothing but prate to me of the wildness of his youth, and the feats he hath done about Turnbull Street, and every third word a lie.

— *Henry IV, Part II, Act 3, Sc. 2*

At random from the truth . . .

— *Sonnet 147*

Vowing more than the perfection of ten, and discharging less than the tenth part of one.

— *Troilus and Cressida, Act 3, Sc. 2*

To be honest, as this world goes, is to be one man picked out of ten
thousand.

— Hamlet, Act 2, Sc. 2

And so to the Lie Circumstantial and the Lie Direct.

— As You Like It, Act 5, Sc. 4

These lies are like their father that begets them; gross as a mountain, open,
palpable.

— Henry IV, Part I, Act 2, Sc. 4

To things of sale a seller's praise belongs.

— Love's Labour's Lost, Act 4, Sc. 3

. . . old men of less truth than tongue.

— Sonnet 17

. . . indifferent honest . . .

— Hamlet, Act 3, Sc. 1

They say all lovers swear more performance than they are able.

— Troilus and Cressida, Act 3, Sc. 2

Neither true nor trusty.

— Passionate Pilgrim

For things are often spoke and seldom meant.

— Henry VI, Part II, Act 3, Sc. 1

. . . they are busied about a counterfeit assurance.

— Taming of the Shrew, Act 4, Sc. 4

Plain and not honest is too harsh a style.

— Richard III, Act 4, Sc. 4

What lies I have heard.

— Cymbeline, Act 4, Sc. 2

There is scarce truth enough alive to make societies secure.

— Measure for Measure, Act 3, Sc. 2

. . . the verity of it is in strong suspicion.

— Winter's Tale, Act 5, Sc. 2

. . . clap upon you two or three probable lies.

— All's Well that Ends Well, Act 3, Sc. 6

What time 'o day is it? — Time to be honest.

— Timon of Athens, Act 1, Sc. 1

That glib and oily art, to speak and purpose not.
— *King Lear, Act 1, Sc. 1*

I will pay you some, and, as most debtors do, promise you infinitely.
— *Henry IV, Part II, Epilogue*

That daily break-vow . . .
— *King John, Act 2, Sc. 1*

Well, I do nothing in the world but lie, and lie in my throat.
— *Love's Labour's Lost, Act 4, Sc. 3*

Breaking his oath and resolution, like a twist of rotten silk.
— *Coriolanus, Act 5, Sc. 6*

Your vows, put in two scales will even weigh, and both as light as tales.
— *Midsummer Night's Dream, Act 3, Sc. 2*

How subject we old men are to this vice of lying!
— *Henry IV, Part II, Act 3, Sc. 2*

Your falsehood shall become you well.
— *Two Gentlemen of Verona, Act 4, Sc. 2*

And as many lies as will lie in thy sheet of paper . . .
— *Twelfth Night, Act 3, Sc. 2*

There's no more faith in thee than in a stewed prune.
— *Henry IV, Part I, Act 3, Sc. 3*

Speaks brave words, swears brave oaths and breaks them bravely . . .
— *As You Like It, Act 3, Sc. 4*

. . . not at all a friend to truth.
— *Henry VIII, Act 2, Sc. 4*

You spotted snakes with double tongue.
— *Midsummer Night's Dream, Act 2, Sc. 2*

If I do lie, and do no harm by it, though the gods hear, I hope they'll
pardon it.
— *Cymbeline, Act 4, Sc. 2*

I have been fubbed off, and fubbed off, and fubbed off . . .
— *Henry IV, Part II, Act 2, Sc. 1*

Ay, but I fear you speak upon the rack, where men enforced do speak any
thing.
— *Merchant of Venice, Act 3, Sc. 2*

This knave's tongue begins to double.
— *Henry VI, Part II, Act 2, Sc. 3*

Go to, you're a dry fool, I'll no more of you; besides, you grow dishonest.
— *Twelfth Night, Act 1, Sc. 5*

Men should be what they seem . . .
— *Othello, Act 3, Sc. 3*

Your manner of wrenching the true cause the false way.
— *Henry IV, Part II, Act 2, Sc. 1*

There's no trust, no faith, no honesty in men; all perjured, all forsworn, all naught, all dissemblers.
— *Romeo and Juliet, Act 3, Sc. 2*

I never had honest men about me, I; all I kept were knaves.
— *Timon of Athens, Act 4, Sc. 3*

Your words and performances are no kin together.
— *Othello, Act 4, Sc. 2*

Having sworn too hard a keeping oath, study to break it.
— *Love's Labour's Lost, Act 1, Sc. 1*

For I can smooth, and fill his aged ear with golden promises . . .
— *Titus Andronicus, Act 4, Sc. 4*

An infinite and endless liar, an hourly promise-breaker.
— *All's Well that Ends Well, Act 3, Sc. 6*

. . . ever double both in his words and meaning.
— *Henry VIII, Act 4, Sc. 2*

. . . translated . . . out of honesty into English.
— *Merry Wives of Windsor, Act 1, Sc. 3*

I do perceive he is not the man that he would gladly make show to the world he is.
— *Henry V, Act 3, Sc. 6*

I could not with such estimable wonder overfar believe that.
— *Twelfth Night, Act 2, Sc. 1*

We need no grave to bury honesty; there's not a grain of it the face to sweeten of the whole dungy earth.
— *Winter's Tale, Act 2, Sc. 1*

. . . leave their false vows with him, like empty purses pick'd.
— *Timon of Athens, Act 4, Sc. 2*

Your oaths are words and poor conditions, but unseal'd, at least in my opinion.

— All's Well that Ends Well, Act 4, Sc. 2

. . . mouth-made vows, which break themselves in swearing.

— Antony and Cleopatra, Act 1, Sc. 3

Suits not in native colours with the truth.

— Henry V, Act 1, Sc. 1

Falser than vows made in wine.

— As You Like It, Act 3, Sc. 5

6

ARROGANCE

O, give me the spare men, and spare me the great ones.
— *Henry IV, Part II, Act 3, Sc. 2*

Upon what meat doth this our Caesar feed, that he is grown so great?
— *Julius Caesar, Act 1, Sc. 2*

If he swagger, let him not come here . . . I'll no swaggerers.
— *Henry IV, Part II, Act 2, Sc. 4*

He's poor in no one fault, but stored with all. — Especially in pride. — And topping all others in boasting.
— *Coriolanus, Act 2, Sc. 1*

Wilt thou reach stars, because they shine on thee?
— *Two Gentlemen of Verona, Act 3, Sc. 1*

I can call spirits from the vasty deep — Why, so can I, or so can any man; but will they come when you do call for them?
— *Henry IV, Part I, Act 3, Sc. 1*

For new-made honour doth forget men's names . . .
— *King John, Act 1, Sc. 1*

Let them obey that know not how to rule,
This hand was made to handle naught but gold.
— *Henry VI, Part II, Act 5, Sc. 1*

My lords, can ye endure to hear this arrogance? And from this fellow?
— *Henry VIII, Act 3, Sc. 2*

We charge you, that you have contrived . . . to wind yourself into a power tyrannical.
— *Coriolanus, Act 3, Sc. 3*

With what a majesty he bears himself, how insolent of late he is become, how proud, how peremptory . . .
— *Henry VI, Part II, Act 3, Sc. 1*

. . . the world too saucy with the gods incenses them to send destruction.
— *Julius Caesar, Act 1, Sc. 3*

Am I the master here, or you?
— *Romeo and Juliet, Act 1, Sc. 5*

And so he walks, insulting . . .
— Henry VI, Part III, Act 1, Sc. 3

It fits thee not to ask the reason why, because we bid it.
— Pericles, Act 1, Sc. 1

I, who never knew how to entreat, nor never needed that I should entreat . . .
— Taming of the Shrew, Act 4, Sc. 3

. . . he hath mused of taking kingdoms in.
— Antony and Cleopatra, Act 3, Sc. 13

Having his ear full of his airy fame.
— Troilus and Cressida, Act 1, Sc. 3

This top-proud fellow . . .
— Henry VIII, Act 1. Sc. 1

All pride is willing pride, and yours is so.
— Love's Labour's Lost, Act 2, Sc. 1

Who has a book of all that monarchs do, he's more secure to keep it shut . . .
— Pericles, Act 1, Sc. 1

. . . insolent, o'ercome with pride, ambitious past all thinking, self-loving.
— Coriolanus, Act 4, Sc. 6

For nothing can seem foul to those that win.
— Henry IV, Part I, Act 5, Sc. 1

His own opinion was his law.
— Henry VIII, Act 4, Sc. 2

O, it is excellent to have a giant's strength, but it is tyrannous to use it like a giant.
— Measure for Measure, Act 2, Sc. 2

The abuse of greatness is when it disjoins remorse from power.
— Julius Caesar, Act 2, Sc. 1

Wilt thou aspire to guide the heavenly car, and with thy daring folly burn the world?
— Two Gentlemen of Verona, Act 3, Sc. 1

. . . his soaring insolence.
— Coriolanus, Act 2, Sc. 1

You and I cannot be confined within the weak list of a country's fashion; we are the makers of manners.

— *Henry V, Act 5, Sc. 2*

I must not have you henceforth question me whither I go . . .

— *Henry IV, Part I, Act 2, Sc. 3*

'Tis pride that pulls the country down.

— *Othello, Act 2, Sc. 3*

When did he regard the stamp of nobleness in any person out of himself?

— *Henry VIII, Act 2, Sc. 3*

With half the bulk o' the world play'd as I pleased, making and marring fortunes.

— *Antony and Cleopatra, Act 3, Sc. 11*

Do you think that his contempt shall not be bruising to you when he hath power to crush?

— *Coriolanus, Act 2, Sc. 3*

Pride went before, ambition follows him.

— *Henry VI, Part II, Act 1, Sc. 1*

Being seldom seen . . . but like a comet I was wonder'd at.

— *Henry IV, Part I, Act 3, Sc. 2*

We are like to have biting statutes, unless his teeth be pulled out.

— *Henry VI, Part II, Act 4, Sc. 7*

As if the passage and whole carriage of this action rode on his tide.

— *Troilus and Cressida, Act 2, Sc. 3*

The laws are mine . . . who can arraign me for 't?

— *King Lear, Act 5, Sc. 3*

. . . over-proud and under-honest.

— *Troilus and Cressida, Act 2, Sc. 3*

The eagle suffers little birds to sing, and is not careful what they mean thereby, knowing that with the shadow of his wings he can at pleasure stint their melody.

— *Titus Andronicus, Act 4, Sc. 4*

It discolours the complexion of my greatness to acknowledge it.

— *Henry IV, Part II, Act 2, Sc. 2*

Yet in the number I do know but one that unassailable holds on his rank, unshaked of motion, and that I am he.

— *Julius Caesar, Act 3, Sc. 1*

Presumptuous vassals, are you not ashamed with this immodest clamorous outrage to trouble and disturb the king and us?

— *Henry VI, Part I, Act 4, Sc. 1*

. . . necessity so bow'd the state that I and greatness were compelled to kiss.

— *Henry IV, Part II, Act 3, Sc. 1*

I will not jump with common spirits and rank me with the barbarous multitudes.

— *Merchant of Venice, Act 2, Sc. 9*

Believe my words, for they are certain and unfallible.

— *Henry VI, Part I, Act 1, Sc. 2*

A man no mightier than thyself or me in personal action, yet prodigious grown and fearful, as these strange eruptions are.

— *Julius Caesar, Act 1, Sc. 3*

He that is proud eats up himself.

— *Troilus and Cressida, Act 2, Sc. 3*

The King is but a man, as I am, the violet smells to him as it doth to me . . . his ceremonies laid by, in his nakedness he appears but a man.

— *Henry V, Act 4, Sc. 1*

7

SHUT UP!

I love not many words. — No more than a fish loves water.
— *All's Well that Ends Well, Act 3, Sc. 6*

Thus he his special nothing ever prologues.
— *Act 2, Sc. 1*

Well said, that was laid on with a trowel.
— *As You Like It, Act 1, Sc. 2*

Pray you, no more of this; 'tis like the howling of Irish wolves against the moon.
— *Act 5, Sc. 2*

But it grows something stale with me.
— *Act 2, Sc. 4*

These jests are out of season; reserve them to a merrier hour than this.
— *Comedy of Errors, Act 1, Sc. 2*

There rest in your foolery.
— *Act 4, Sc. 3*

One of your great knowing should learn . . . forbearance.
— *Cymbeline, Act 2, Sc. 3*

Forbear sharp speeches . . .
— *Act 3, Sc. 5*

He hath not failed to pester us with message.
— *Hamlet, Act 1, Sc. 2*

Tying thine ear to no tongue but thine own.
— *Henry IV, Part I, Act 1, Sc. 3*

Come, come, no more of this unprofitable chat.
— *Act 3, Sc. 1*

Men of few words are the best men.
— *Henry V, Act 3, Sc. 2*

So! In the name of Jesu Christ, speak lower.
— *Act 4, Sc. 1*

But the saying is true, "The empty vessel makes the greatest sound."
— *Act 4, Sc. 4*

My lord, methinks, is very long in talk.
— *Henry VI, Part I, Act 1, Sc. 2*

. . . his lavish tongue . . .
— *Act 2, Sc. 5*

Let thy betters speak.
— *Part II, Act 1, Sc. 3*

He'll wrest the sense and hold us here all day.
— *Act 3, Sc. 1*

Particularities and petty sounds to cease!
— *Act 5, Sc. 2*

I cannot stay to hear these articles.
— *Part III, Act 1, Sc. 1*

Nay, stay not to expostulate.
— *Act 2, Sc. 5*

. . . as tedious as a twice-told tale, vexing the dull ear of a drowsy man.
— *King John, Act 3, Sc. 4*

What cracker is this same that deafs our ears with this abundance of superfluous breath?
— *Act 2, Sc. 1*

Zounds! I was never so bethump'd with words since I first call'd my brother's father dad.
— *Act 2, Sc. 1*

. . . these ill-tuned repetitions.
— *Act 2, Sc. 1*

Fare thee well; we hold our time too precious to be spent with such a brabbler.
— *Act 5, Sc. 2*

. . . more in word than matter.
— *King Lear, Act 3, Sc. 2*

He draweth out the thread of his verbosity finer than the staple of his argument.
— *Love's Labour's Lost, Act 5, Sc. 2*

The letter is too long by half a mile.
— *Act 5, Sc. 2*

. . . rein thy tongue.
> — *Love's Labour's Lost, Act 5, Sc. 2*

This will last out a night in Russia, when nights are longest there.
> — *Measure for Measure, Act 2, Sc. 1*

When every goose is cackling . . .
> — *Merchant of Venice, Act 5, Sc. 1*

He gives me the proverbs and the no-verbs.
> — *Merry Wives of Windsor, Act 3, Sc. 1*

I wonder that you will still be talking . . . nobody marks you.
> — *Much Ado About Nothing, Act 1, Sc. 1*

I cannot endure my Lady Tongue.
> — *Act 2, Sc. 1*

Cease thy counsel, which falls into mine ears as profitless as water in a sieve.
> — *Act 5, Sc. 1*

The general so likes your music that he desires you . . . to make no more noise with it . . . If you have any music that may not be heard, to 't again.
> — *Othello, Act 3, Sc. 1*

What needs this iteration?
> — *Act 5, Sc. 2*

This helpless smoke of words . . .

Deep sounds make lesser noise than shallow words.
> — *Rape of Lucrece*

Have done! for shame, if not for charity.
> — *Richard III, Act 1, Sc. 3*

Talkers are no good doers.
> — *Act 1, Sc. 3*

Will speak more in a minute then he will stand to in a month.
> — *Romeo and Juliet, Act 2, Sc. 4*

Be not so long to speak.
> — *Act 4, Sc. 1*

Peace, you mumbling fool! Utter your gravity o'er a gossip's bowl, for here we need it not.
> — *Act 3, Sc. 5*

. . . dressing old words new, spending again what is already spent.
— *Sonnet 76*

What strained touches rhetoric can lend.
— *Sonnet 82*

Nor are mine ears with thy tongue's tune delighted.
— *Sonnet 141*

To what end are all these words?
— *Taming of the Shrew, Act 1, Sc. 2*

You know, pitchers have ears . . .
— *Act 4, Sc. 4*

What a spendthrift is he of his tongue!
— *The Tempest, Act 2, Sc. 1*

. . . prate as amply and unnecessarily as this . . .
— *Act 2, Sc. 1*

My free drift halts not particularly.
— *Timon of Athens, Act 1, Sc. 1*

Come, sermon me no further.
— *Act 2, Sc. 2*

Leave these bitter deep laments . . .
— *Titus Andronicus, Act 3, Sc. 2*

Stop close their mouths, let them not speak a word.
— *Act 5, Sc. 2*

Lay thy finger on thy lips!
— *Troilus and Cressida, Act 1, Sc. 3*

Contain yourself, your passion draws ears hither.
— *Act 5, Sc. 2*

Words, words, mere words, no matter from the heart.
— *Act 5, Sc. 3*

Peace, you rogue, no more o' that.
— *Twelfth Night, Act 1, Sc. 5*

I will on with my speech in your praise . . . — Come to what is important in
it; I forgive you the praise.
— *Act 1, Sc.5*

Lips, do not move . . .
                                        — *Twelfth Night, Act 2, Sc. 5*

The time now serves not to expostulate.
                        — *Two Gentlemen of Verona, Act 3, Sc. 1*

Solicit me no more.
                                                — *Act 5, Sc. 4*

. . . leave this idle theme, this bootless chat.

Your treatise makes me like you worse and worse.

Then do they spend their mouths.

Their copious stories, oftentimes begun, End without audience and are
   never done.
                                        — *Venus and Adonis*

Why, what need we commune with you of this?
                                — *Winter's Tale, Act 2, Sc. 1*

Inform yourselves we need no more of your advice.
                                                — *Act 2, Sc. 1*

Here has been too much homely foolery already.
                                                — *Act 4, Sc. 4*

8

INCOMPETENCE

What men daily do, not knowing what they do!
— *Much Ado about Nothing, Act 4, Sc. 1*

. . . helping you to mar that which God made.
— *As You Like It, Act 1, Sc. 1*

. . . the wild-goose chase . . .
— *Romeo and Juliet, Act 2, Sc. 4*

. . . commit'st thy anointed body to the cure of those physicians that first wounded thee.
— *Richard II, Act 2, Sc. 1*

How cheerfully on the false trail they cry!
— *Hamlet, Act 4, Sc. 5*

Like a German clock, still a-repairing, ever out of frame, and never going aright . . .
— *Love's Labour's Lost, Act 3, Sc. 1*

He is not his craft's master; he doth not do it right.
— *Henry IV, Part II, Act 3, Sc. 2*

. . . how many fruitless pranks this ruffian hath botch'd up.
— *Twelfth Night, Act 4, Sc. 1*

That is the way to lay the city flat, to bring the roof to the foundation, and bury all . . . in heaps and piles of ruin.
— *Coriolanus, Act 3, Sc. 1*

The fashion of the world is to avoid cost, and you encounter it.
— *Much Ado about Nothing, Act 1, Sc. 1*

Mangle the work of nature . . .
— *Henry V, Act 2, Sc. 4*

. . . a botcher's apprentice.
— *All's Well that Ends Well, Act 4, Sc. 3*

The hardest knife ill-used doth lose his edge.
— *Sonnet 95*

How many actions most ridiculous hast thou been drawn to . . .
— *As You Like It, Act 2, Sc. 4*

Sir, you may thank yourself for this great loss.
— The Tempest, Act 2, Sc. 1

Alas, we bodged again . . .
— Henry VI, Part III, Act 1, Sc. 4

. . . a thing a little soil'd in the working.
— Hamlet, Act 2, Sc. 1

Striving to better, oft we mar what's well.
— King Lear, Act 1, Sc. 4

Here is such patchery, such juggling . . . !
— Troilus and Cressida, Act 2, Sc. 3

. . . we strut to our confusion.
— Antony and Cleopatra, Act 3, Sc. 13

The double gilt of this opportunity you let time wash off . . .
— Twelfth Night, Act 3, Sc. 2

Your abilities are too infant-like for doing much alone.
— Coriolanus, Act 2, Sc. 1

Men shall deal unadvisedly sometimes, which after hours give leisure to repent.
— Richard III, Act 4, Sc. 4

Botch and bungle up . . .
— Henry V, Act 2, Sc. 2

'Tis not well mended so, it is but botch'd.
— Timon of Athens, Act 4, Sc. 3

. . . goodly buildings left without a roof soon fall to ruin.
— Pericles, Act 2, Sc. 4

Any thing that's mended is but patched.
— Twelfth Night, Act 1, Sc. 5

. . . the confirmer of false reckonings.
— As You Like It, Act 3, Sc. 4

Confusion's cure lives not in these confusions.
— Romeo and Juliet, Act 4, Sc. 5

Those wounds heal ill that men do give themselves.
— Troilus and Cressida, Act 3, Sc. 3

I told ye all, when we first put this dangerous stone a-rolling, 'twould fall upon ourselves.

— *Henry VIII, Act 5, Sc. 3*

Smother'd in errors, feeble, shallow, weak . . .

— *Comedy of Errors, Act 3, Sc. 2*

To mar the subject that before was well.

— *Sonnet 103*

By Cheshu, I think a' will plow up all, if there is not better directions.

— *Henry V, Act 3, Sc. 2*

. . . did read by rote and could not spell.

— *Romeo and Juliet, Act 2, Sc. 3*

. . . with best meaning have incurred the worst.

— *King Lear, Act 5, Sc. 3*

. . . make a broken delivery of the business.

— *Winter's Tale, Act 5, Sc. 2*

Under some biting error.

— *Much Ado about Nothing, Act 4, Sc. 1*

. . . ridiculous and awkward action . . .

— *Troilus and Cressida, Act 1, Sc. 3*

Defect of judgement, to fail in the disposing of those chances which he was lord of.

— *Coriolanus, Act 4, Sc. 7*

. . . botch the words up fit to their own thoughts.

— *Hamlet, Act 4, Sc. 5*

Thus far, with rough and all unable pen, our bending author hath pursued the story . . .

— *Henry V, Epilogue*

The ringleader and head of all this rout.

— *Henry VI, Part II, Act 2, Sc. 1*

In all the play there is not one word apt, one player fitted.

— *Midsummer Night's Dream, Act 5, Sc. 1*

What fool hath added water to the sea . . .?

— *Titus Andronicus, Act 3, Sc. 1*

An unpractised swimmer plunging still with too much labour drowns for want of skill.

— *Rape of Lucrece*

'So so' is good, very good, very excellent good; and yet it is not, it is but so so.

— *As You Like It, Act 5, Sc. 1*

The mire . . . wherein thou stick'st up to the ears.

— *Romeo and Juliet, Act 1, Sc. 4*

Thou aimest all awry.

— *Henry VI, Part II, Act 2, Sc. 4*

If Troy not be taken till these two undermine it, the walls will stand till they fall of themselves.

— *Troilus and Cressida, Act 2, Sc. 3*

How camest thou in this pickle?

— *The Tempest, Act 5, Sc. 1*

. . . never broke any man's head but his own, and that was against a post when he was drunk.

— *Henry V, Act 3, Sc. 2*

So play the foolish throngs with one that swoons; come all to help him, and so stop the air by which he should revive.

— *Measure for Measure, Act 2, Sc. 4*

9

CONSPIRACY

Their hats are pluck'd about their ears, and half their faces buried in their cloaks.
> — *Julius Caesar*, Act 2, Sc. 1

Skulking in corners . . .
> — *Winter's Tale*, Act 1, Sc. 2

A pretty plot, well chosen to build upon.
> — *Henry VI, Part II*, Act 1, Sc. 4

Mark, how they whisper . . .
> — *King John*, Act 2, Sc. 1

See, to beguile the old folks, how the young folks lay their heads together!
> — *Taming of the Shrew*, Act 1, Sc. 2

I would to God thou and I knew where a commodity of good names were to be bought.
> — *Henry IV, Part I*, Act 1, Sc. 2

My purpose is, indeed a horse of that colour.
> — *Twelfth Night*, Act 2, Sc. 3

When rich villains have need of poor ones, poor ones may make what price they will.
> — *Much Ado about Nothing*, Act 3, Sc. 3

Affairs that walk . . . at midnight have in them a wilder nature than the business that seeks dispatch by day.
> — *Henry VIII*, Act 5, Sc. 1

I wonder men dare trust themselves with men. Methinks they should invite them without knives; Good for their meat, and safer for their lives.
> — *Timon of Athens*, Act 1, Sc. 2

. . . profited in strange concealments.
> — *Henry IV, Part I*, Act 3, Sc. 1

I have a jest to execute that I cannot manage alone.
> — Act 1, Sc. 2

And this man hath, for a few light crowns, lightly conspired.
> — *Henry V*, Act 2, Sc. 2

What were 't worth to know the secret of your conference?
                                    — *Henry VIII, Act 2, Sc. 3*

Masking the business from the common eye for sundry weighty reasons.
                                    — *Macbeth, Act 3, Sc. 1*

Every minute now should be the father of some stratagem.
                                    — *Henry IV, Part II, Act 1, Sc. 1*

Come, let us sup betimes, that afterwards we may digest our complots in some form.
                                    — *Richard III, Act 3, Sc. 1*

Excellent! I smell a device.
                                    — *Twelfth Night, Act 2, Sc. 3*

There was more than one confederate in the fact.
                                    — *Titus Andronicus, Act 4, Sc. 1*

I have operations which be humours of revenge.
                                    — *Merry Wives of Windsor, Act 1, Sc. 3*

Some villains of my court are of consent and sufferance in this.
                                    — *As You Like It, Act 2, Sc. 2*

And that's not suddenly to be perform'd, but with advice and silent secrecy.
                                    — *Henry VI, Part II, Act 2, Sc. 2*

I have some sport in hand wherein your cunning can assist me much.
                                    — *Taming of the Shrew, Induction, Sc. 1*

For if we meet in the city, we shall be dogged with company, and our devices known.
                                    — *Midsummer Night's Dream, Act 1, Sc. 2*

Then she plots, then she ruminates, then she devises . . .
                                    Merry Wives of Windsor, Act 2, Sc. 2

We will bind and hoodwink him so . . .
                                    — *All's Well that Ends Well, Act 3, Sc. 6*

That the time may have all shadow and silence in it.
                                    — *Measure for Measure, Act 3, Sc. 1*

. . . the secret treasons of the world.
                                    — *Henry VI, Part III, Act 5, Sc. 2*

. . . meet to plot, contrive or complot any ill 'gainst us . . .
                                    — *Richard II, Act 1, Sc. 3*

A rabble more of vile confederates.

— *Comedy of Errors, Act 5, Sc. 1*

Deep night, dark night . . . that time best fits the work we have in hand.

— *Henry VI, Part II, Act 1, Sc. 4*

What stratagems, how fell, how butcherly, erroneous, mutinous and unnatural.

— *Henry VI, Part III, Act 2, Sc. 5*

Craft against vice I must apply.

— *Measure for Measure, Act 3, Sc. 2*

Come home with me to supper, and I'll lay
A plot shall show us all a merry day.

— *Richard II, Act 4, Sc. 1*

O, conspiracy, . . . where wilt thou find a cavern dark enough to mask thy monstrous visage? Seek none, conspiracy, hide it in smiles and affability.

— *Julius Caesar, Act 2, Sc. 1*

Confederates in the deed that hath dishonour'd all our family.

— *Titus Andronicus, Act 1, Sc. 1*

. . . and bid suspicion double-lock the door.

— *Venus and Adonis*

A sort of naughty persons, lewdly bent . . .

— *Henry VI, Part II, Act 2, Sc. 1*

With whispering and most guilty diligence . . .

— *Measure for Measure, Act 4, Sc. 1*

And stop all sight-holes, every loop from whence the eye of reason may pry in upon us.

— *Henry IV, Part I, Act 4, Sc. 1*

You shall go near to call them both a pair of crafty knaves.

— *Henry VI, Part II, Act 1, Sc. 2*

At what ease might corrupt minds procure knaves as corrupt to swear against you? Such things have been done.

— *Henry VIII, Act 5, Sc. 1*

Good gentlemen, look fresh and merrily; let not our looks put on our purposes.

— *Julius Caesar, Act 2, Sc. 1*

There's a knot, a ging, a pack, a conspiracy against me . . .

— *Merry Wives of Windsor, Act 4, Sc. 2*

Seal up your lips, and give no words but mum; the business asketh silent secrecy.
— *Henry VI, Part II, Act 1, Sc. 2*

I fear I am attended by some spies.
— *Two Gentlemen of Verona, Act 5, Sc. 1*

Some dear cause will in concealment wrap me up awhile.
— *King Lear, Act 4, Sc. 3*

What mutter you, or what conspire you, lords?
— *Henry VI, Part III, Act 1, Sc. 1*

Who dares not stir by day must walk by night.
— *King John, Act 1, Sc. 1*

I will tell it softly; yon crickets shall not hear it.
— *Winter's Tale, Act 2, Sc. 1*

The fox barks not when he would steal the lamb.
— *Henry VI, Part II, Act 3, Sc. 1*

Like many clouds consulting for foul weather.
— *Venus and Adonis*

Not honestly, my lord, but so covertly that no dishonesty shall appear . . .
— *Much Ado about Nothing, Act 2, Sc. 2*

Now, if these men have defeated the law and outrun native punishment, though they can outstrip men, they have no wings to fly from God.
— *Henry V, Act 4, Sc. 1*

10
GLUTTONY

He hath eaten me out of house and home.
— *Henry IV, Part II, Act 2, Sc. 1*

. . . with a body fill'd and vacant mind.
— *Henry V, Act 4, Sc. 1*

To see meat fill knaves and wine heat fools.
— *Timon of Athens, Act 1, Sc. 1*

Bid them prepare for dinner. — That is done, sir, they all have stomachs.
— *Merchant of Venice, Act 3, Sc. 5*

Fat paunches have lean pates, and dainty bits make rich the ribs but bankrupt quite the wits.
— *Love's Labour's Lost, Act 1, Sc. 1*

Nothing but sit and sit, and eat and eat.
— *Taming of the Shrew, Act 5, Sc. 2*

Sir John Paunch . . .
— *Henry IV, Part I, Act 2, Sc. 2*

But doth not the appetite alter? A man loves the meat in his youth that he cannot endure in his age.
— *Much Ado about Nothing, Act 2, Sc. 3*

I am a great eater of beef and I believe that does harm to my wit.
— *Twelfth Night, Act 1, Sc. 3*

Thou shalt not gormandize . . . and sleep and snore, and rend apparel out.
— *Merchant of Venice, Act 2, Sc. 5*

The taste of sweetness, whereof a little more than a little is by much too much.
— *Henry IV, Part I, Act 3, Sc. 2*

Things sweet to taste prove in digestion sour.
— *Richard II, Act 1, Sc. 3*

He is a very valiant trencher-man; he hath an excellent stomach.
— *Much Ado about Nothing, Act 1, Sc. 1*

And mingle with the English epicures.
— *Macbeth, Act 5, Sc. 3*

Who riseth from a feast with that keen appetite that he sits down?
— *Merchant of Venice*, Act 2, Sc. 6

For soldiers' stomachs always serve them well.
— *Henry VI, Part I*, Act 2, Sc. 3

. . . full of supper and distempering draughts.
— *Othello*, Act 1, Sc. 1

. . . their thick breaths, rank of gross diet.
— *Antony and Cleopatra*, Act 5, Sc. 2

Thou seest I have more flesh than another man, and therefore more frailty.
— *Henry IV, Part I*, Act 3, Sc. 3

. . . a man of an unbounded stomach.
— *Henry VIII*, Act 4, Sc. 2

A huge feeder, . . . and he sleeps by day more than the wild-cat.
— *Merchant of Venice*, Act 2, Sc. 5

Gross, gross; fat, fat.
— *Love's Labour's Lost*, Act 5, Sc. 2

Come out of that fat room . . .
— *Henry IV, Part I*, Act 2, Sc. 4

Leave gormandizing.
— *Part II*, Act 5, Sc. 5

Then she bears breadth? — No longer from head to foot than from hip to hip.
— *Comedy of Errors*, Act 3, Sc. 2

A gross fat man . . . as fat as butter.
— *Henry IV, Part I*, Act 2, Sc. 4

Well, sir, I hope, when I do it, I shall do it on a full stomach.
— *Love's Labour's Lost*, Act 1, Sc. 2

They are as sick that surfeit with too much, as they that starve with nothing.
— *Merchant of Venice*, Act 1, Sc. 2

You should have fear'd false times when you did feast.
— *Timon of Athens*, Act 4, Sc. 3

In despite of his heart, he eats his meat without grudging.
— *Much Ado about Nothing*, Act 3, Sc. 4

I shall think the worse of fat men . . .
— *Merry Wives of Windsor, Act 3, Sc. 1*

My own searching eyes shall find him by his large and portly size.
— *Troilus and Cressida, Act 4, Sc. 5*

11
GOSSIP

The news abroad, I mean the whispered ones . . .
                                    — *King Lear, Act 2, Sc. 1*

For which of you will stop the vent of hearing when loud rumour speaks?
                                    — *Henry IV, Part II, Induction*

. . . evermore tattling.
                                    — *Much Ado about Nothing, Act 2, Sc. 1*

. . . whisper o'er the world's diameter.
                                    — *Hamlet, Act 4, Sc. 1*

Here comes Monsier Le Beau — with his mouth full of news — Which he
will put on us, as pigeons feed their young.
                                    — *As You Like It, Act 1, Sc. 2*

But you must be tittle-tattling before all our guests?
                                    — *Winter's Tale, Act 4, Sc. 4*

And thereby hangs a tale . . .
                                    — *Taming of the Shrew, Act 4, Sc. 1*

. . . coins slanders like a mint.
                                    — *Troilus and Cressida, Act 1, Sc. 3*

Report speaks goldenly of his profit.
                                    — *As You Like It, Act 1, Sc. 1*

A long-tongued babbling gossip . . .
                                    — *Titus Andronicus, Act 4, Sc. 2*

Marry, sir, they have comitted false report; moreover, they have spoken
untruths; secondarily, they are slanders; sixth and lastly, they have
belied a lady; thirdly, they have verified unjust things; and, to con-
clude, they are lying knaves.
                                    — *Much Ado about Nothing, Act 5, Sc. 1*

Many tales devised . . . by smiling pick-thanks and base newsmongers.
                                    — *Henry IV, Part I, Act 3, Sc. 2*

Hath the fellow any wit that told you this?
                                    — *Much Ado about Nothing, Act 1, Sc. 2*

And thence this slander, as I think, proceeds.
                                    — *Sonnet 131*

This carry-tale . . . that sometime true news, sometimes false doth bring.
— *Venus and Adonis*

His affairs come to me on the wind.
— *Antony and Cleopatra, Act 3, Sc. 6*

I shall tell you a pretty tale; it may be you have heard it.
— *Coriolanus, Act 1, Sc. 1*

His gift is in devising impossible slanders.
— *Much Ado about Nothing, Act 2, Sc. 1*

Where doth the world thrust forth a vanity . . . there's no respect how vile,
that is not quickly buzz'd into his ears?
— *Richard II, Act 2, Sc. 1*

. . . slander . . . whose breath rides on the posting winds.
— *Cymbeline, Act 3, Sc. 4*

. . . that only wounds by hearsay.
— *Much Ado about Nothing, Act 3, Sc. 1*

Where breath most breathes, even in the mouths of men.
— *Sonnet 81*

Heard you of nothing strange about the streets?
— *Antony and Cleopatra, Act 4, Sc. 3*

Foul whisperings are abroad . . .
— *Macbeth, Act 5, Sc. 1*

Shall we thus permit a blasting and scandalous breath to fall on him?
— *Measure for Measure, Act 5, Sc. 1*

What a strange infection is fall'n into thy ear!
— *Cymbeline, Act 3, Sc. 2*

I tell this tale vilely.
— *Much Ado about Nothing, Act 3, Sc. 3*

It is fit, what being more known grows worse, to smother it.
— *Pericles, Act 1, Sc. 1*

The report goes she has all the rule of her husband's purse.
— *Merry Wives of Windsor, Act 1, Sc. 3*

Mad slanderers by mad ears believed be.
— *Sonnet 140*

This from rumour's tongue I idly heard . . .
        — *King John, Act 4, Sc. 2*

. . . upon my tongues continual slanders ride . . .
        — *Henry IV, Part II, Induction*

Go to a gossip's feast, and go with me — With all my heart, I'll gossip at
this feast.
        — *Comedy of Errors, Act 5, Sc. 1*

Report is changeable . . .
        — *King Lear, Act 4, Sc. 7*

I can tell you strange news that you yet dreamt not of.
        — *Much Ado about Nothing, Act 1, Sc. 2*

. . . which I hear from common rumours.
        — *Timon of Athens, Act 3, Sc. 2*

Rumour is a pipe blown by surmises, jealousies, conjectures . . .
        — *Henry IV, Part II, Induction*

The world's loud tongue proclaims . . .
        — *Love's Labour's Lost, Act 5, Sc. 2*

The palace full of tongues, of eyes and ears . . .
        — *Titus Andronicus, Act 2, Sc. 1*

Stop the rumour and allay those tongues that durst disperse it.
        — *Henry VIII, Act 2, Sc. 1*

I understand, moreover, upon the Rialto . . .
        — *Merchant of Venice, Act 1, Sc. 3*

The injury of tongues . . .
        — *Winter's Tale, Act 1, Sc. 2*

Then speak again . . . but this one word, whether thy tale be true.
        — *King John, Act 3, Sc. 1*

Amongst the soldiers this is muttered . . .
        — *Henry VI, Part I, Act 1, Sc. 1*

And then 'twas fresh in murmur . . .
        — *Twelfth Night, Act 1, Sc. 2*

However these disturbers of our peace buzz in the people's ears.
        — *Titus Andronicus, Act 4, Sc. 4*

It is spoke freely out of many mouths . . .

        — *Coriolanus, Act 4, Sc. 6*

. . . reports but coarsely of her.

      — *All's Well that Ends Well, Act 3, Sc. 5*

But that slander, sir, is found a truth now; for it grows again fresher than e'er it was.

        — *Henry VIII, Act 2, Sc. 1*

Why, yet it lives there unchecked, that . . .

       — *Merchant of Venice, Act 3, Sc. 1*

They have been at a great feast of languages, and stolen the scraps.

      — *Love's Labour's Lost, Act 5, Sc. 1*

From rumour's tongues they bring smooth comforts false, worse than true wrongs.

       — *Henry IV, Part II, Induction*

What's the new news at the new court?

       — *As You Like It, Act 1, Sc. 1*

Please you to abrogate scurrility.

      — *Love's Labour's Lost, Act 4, Sc. 2*

Some carry-tale . . . some mumble-news.

        — *Act 5, Sc. 2*

What great ones do the less will prattle of . . .

       — *Twelfth Night, Act 1, Sc. 2*

12

AMBITION

. . . the fashion of these times, where none will sweat but for promotion.
— *As You Like It, Act 2, Sc. 3*

This jarring discord of nobility, this shouldering of each other in the court,
this factious bandying of their favourites . . .
— *Henry VI, Part I, Act 4, Sc. 1*

The next advantage will we take thoroughly.
— *The Tempest, Act 3, Sc. 3*

No man's pie is freed from his ambitious finger.
— *Henry VIII, Act 1, Sc. 1*

All kinds of natures, that labour on the bosom of this sphere to propagate
their states.
— *Timon of Athens, Act 1, Sc. 1*

And men may talk of kings, and why not I?
— *Henry VI, Part III, Act 3, Sc. 1*

Then every thing includes itself in power,
Power into will, will into appetite,
And appetite, an universal wolf,
So doubly seconded with will and power,
Must make perforce an universal prey,
And last eat up himself.
— *Troilus and Cressida, Act 1, Sc. 3*

Dost thou so hunger for mine empty chair that thou wilt needs invest
thee with my honours before thy hour be ripe?
— *Henry VI, Part II, Act 4, Sc. 5*

Since this earth affords no joy to me, but to command, to check, to
o'erbear such as are of better person than myself . . .
— *Part III, Act 3, Sc. 2*

But long I will not be Jack out of office.
— *Part I, Act 1, Sc. 1*

. . . like favourites, made proud by princes, that advance their pride
against that power that bred it.
— *Much Ado about Nothing, Act 3, Sc. 1*

Pride went before, ambition follows him.
— *Henry VI, Part II, Act 1, Sc. 1*

Caesar's ambition, which swell'd so much that it did almost stretch the sides o' the world.
— *Cymbeline, Act 3, Sc. 1*

Choked with ambition of the meaner sort . . .
— *Henry VI, Part I, Act 2, Sc. 5*

Such men as he be never at heart's ease whiles they behold a greater than themselves, and therefore are they very dangerous.
— *Julius Caesar, Act 1, Sc. 2*

But if it be a sin to covet honour, I am the most offending soul alive.
— *Henry V, Act 4, Sc. 3*

This holy fox, or wolf, or both — for he is equal ravenous as he is subtle.
— *Henry VIII, Act 1, Sc. 1*

You, brother mine, that entertain'd ambition, expell'd remorse and nature.
— *The Tempest, Act 5, Sc. 1*

While these do labour for their own preferment.
— *Henry VI, Part II, Act 1, Sc. 1*

I aim a mile beyond the moon.
— *Titus Andronicus, Act 4, Sc. 3*

By my troth and maidenhead, I would not be a queen. — I would, and venture maidenhead for 't, and so would you, for all the spice of your hypocrisy . . .
— *Henry VIII, Act 2, Sc. 3*

How he coasts and hedges his own way. But . . . all his tricks founder . . .
— *Act 3, Sc. 2*

God knows, my son, by what bypaths and indirect crook'd ways I met this crown.
— *Henry IV, Part II, Act 4, Sc. 5*

For yet I am not look'd on in the world.
— *Henry VI, Part III, Act 5, Sc. 7*

Fame, that all hunt after in their lives . . .
— *Love's Labour's Lost, Act 1, Sc. 1*

Counting myself but bad till I be best.
— *Henry VI, Part III, Act 5, Sc. 6*

From this swarm of fair advantages you took occasion . . .
— *Part I, Act 5, Sc. 1*

. . . vaulting ambition, which o'erleaps itself and falls on the other.
— *Macbeth, Act 1, Sc. 7*

I look to be either earl or duke, I can assure you.
— *Henry IV, Part I, Act 5, Sc. 4*

Go forward and be choked with thy ambition!
— *Henry VI, Part I, Act 2, Sc. 4*

Thou seek'st the greatness that will overwhelm thee.
— *Henry IV, Part II, Act 4, Sc. 5*

How holily he works in all his business! . . . He dives into the king's soul,
and there scatters dangers, doubts . . .
— *Henry VIII, Act 2, Sc. 2*

With powerful policy strengthen themselves.
— *Henry VI, Part III, Act 1, Sc. 2*

If thy thoughts were sifted, the king . . . is not quite exempt from the
envious malice of thy swelling heart.
— *Henry VI, Part I, Act 3, Sc. 1*

By devilish policy art thou grown great.
— *Part II, Act 4, Sc. 1*

The eagle-winged pride of sky-aspiring and ambitious thoughts, with rival-
hating envy . . .
— *Richard II, Act 1, Sc. 3*

I seek occasion how to rise . . .
— *Henry VI, Part III, Act 1, Sc. 2*

And, when I spy advantage, claim the crown, for that's the golden mark I
seek to hit.
— *Part II, Act 1, Sc. 1*

Surely, sir, there's in him stuff that puts him to these ends.
— *Henry VIII, Act 1, Sc. 1*

Nor did you think it folly to keep your great pretences veil'd till when they
needs must show themselves.
— *Coriolanus, Act 1, Sc. 2*

I'll make my heaven to dream upon the crown.
— *Henry VI, Part III, Act 3, Sc. 2*

For when the fox hath got in his nose, he'll soon find means to make the
body follow.
— *Act 4, Sc. 7*

. . . the plumed troop and the big wars that make ambition virtue!
— *Othello, Act 3, Sc. 3*

Does buy and sell his honour as he pleases, and for his own advantage.
— *Henry VIII, Act 1, Sc. 1*

. . . that reaches at the moon . . .
— *Henry VI, Part II, Act 3, Sc. 1*

It oft falls out, to have what we would have, we speak not what we mean.
— *Measure for Measure, Act 2, Sc. 4*

Well, say there is no kingdom then, . . . what other pleasure can the world afford?
— *Henry VI, Part III, Act 3, Sc. 2*

. . . thirsty after tottering honour . . .
— *Pericles, Act 3, Sc. 2*

But for a kingdom any oath may be broken . . .
— *Henry VI, Part III, Act 1, Sc. 2*

13
INCREDIBLE!

Is't real that I see?
— *All's Well that Ends Well*, Act 5, Sc. 3

There is nothing left remarkable beneath the visiting moon.
— *Antony and Cleopatra*, Act 4, Sc. 15

Mine eyes did sicken at the sight, and could not endure a further view.
— *Act 3, Sc. 10*

I sometimes do believe, and sometimes do not.
— *As You Like It*, Act 5, Sc. 4

What, are you mad, that you reason so?
— *Comedy of Errors*, Act 3, Sc. 2

Sleep I now, and think I hear all this?
— *Act 2, Sc. 2*

Am I in earth, in heaven or in hell? Sleeping or waking? Mad or well-advised?
— *Act 2, Sc. 2*

. . . and men of heart look'd wondering each at other.
— *Coriolanus*, Act 5, Sc. 6

There is something in this more than natural, if philosophy could find it out.
— *Hamlet*, Act 2, Sc. 2

O day and night, but this is wondrous strange!
— *Act 1, Sc. 5*

. . . amaze indeed the very faculties of eyes and ears.
— *Act 2, Sc. 2*

Tell me if you speak in jest or no.
— *Henry IV, Part I*, Act 2, Sc. 3

Is it fantasy that plays upon our eyesight? I prithee, speak, we will not trust our eyes without our ears.
— *Act 5, Sc. 4*

'Tis so strange that, though the truth of it stands off as gross as black and white, my eye will scarcely see it.
— *Henry V*, Act 2, Sc. 2

But thou, 'gainst all proportion, did bring in wonder. . .
— *Henry V, Act 2, Sc. 2*

A proper jest, and never heard before.
— *Henry VI, Part II, Act 1, Sc. 1*

O God, seest Thou this, and bearest so long?
— *Act 2, Sc. 1*

That would be ten days' wonder at the least.
— *Part III, Act 3, Sc. 2*

'Tis wondrous strange, the like yet never heard of.
— *Act 2, Sc. 1*

Like the owl by day, if he arise, be mocked and wonder'd at.
— *Act 5, Sc. 4*

Is this the honour they do one another?
— *Henry VIII, Act 5, Sc. 2*

Thou speakest wonders.
— *Act 5, Sc. 5*

There's two or three of us have seen strange sights.
— *Julius Caesar, Act 1, Sc. 3*

Wild amazement hurries up and down . . .
— *King John, Act 5, Sc. 1*

Who hath read or heard of any kindred action like to this?
— *Act 3, Sc. 4*

What think you? . . . or could you think? Or do you almost think, although you see, 'that you do see?
— *Act 4, Sc. 3*

Startles and frights consideration . . .
— *Act 4, Sc. 2*

As in a theatre, whence they gape and point . . .
— *Act 2, Sc. 1*

. . . a book where men may read strange matters.
— *Macbeth, Act 1, Sc. 5*

The attempt and not the deed confounds us.
— *Act 2, Sc. 2*

Can such things be, and overcome us like a summer's cloud, without
our special wonder?
                                          — *Macbeth, Act 3, Sc. 4*

Say from whence you owe this strange intelligence?
                                          — *Act 1, Sc. 3*

I' the name of truth, are ye fantastical, or that indeed which outwardly ye
show?
                                          — *Act 1, Sc. 3*

Were such things here . . . or have we eaten on the insane root that takes
the reason prisoner?
                                          — *Act 1, Sc. 3*

I have seen hours dreadful and things strange, but this sore night hath
trifled former knowings.
                                          — *Act 2, Sc. 4*

Did I tell this, who would believe me?
                                          — *Measure for Measure, Act 2, Sc. 4*

You have bereft me of all words . . .
                                          — *Merchant of Venice, Act 3, Sc. 2*

. . . past all expressing.
                                          — *Act 3, Sc. 5*

Thou almost makest me waver in my faith, to hold opinion with Pythag-
oras, that souls of animals infuse themselves into the trunks of men.
                                          — *Act 4, Sc. 1*

They do no more adhere and keep place together than the Hundredth
Psalm to the tune of Greensleeves.
                                          — *Merry Wives of Windsor, Act 2, Sc. 1*

I am so attired in wonder, I know not what to say.
                                          — *Much Ado about Nothing, Act 4, Sc. 1*

Is 't possible? Sits the wind in that corner?
                                          — *Act 2, Sc. 3*

. . . 'twas passing strange . . .
                                          — *Othello, Act 1, Sc. 3*

. . . most preposterous conclusions.
                                          — *Act 1, Sc. 3*

This cannot be, by no assay of reason.
                                          Act 1, Sc. 3

The heart and place of general wonder.

— Pericles, Act 4, Gower

Holy St. Francis, what a change is here!

— Romeo and Juliet, Act 2, Sc. 3

I am afeard . . . all this is but a dream, too flattering-sweet to be
substantial.

— Act 2, Sc. 2

Who will believe my verse in time to come?

— Sonnet 17

We, which now behold these present days, have eyes to wonder.

— Sonnet 106

Here is a wonder, if you talk of a wonder.

— Taming of the Shrew, Act 5, Sc. 2

Where did you study all this goodly speech?

— Act 2, Sc. 1

And wherefore gaze this goodly company, as if they saw some wondrous
monument, some comet or unusual prodigy?

— Act 3, Sc. 2

But is this true? or is it else your pleasure, like pleasant travellers, to
break a jest upon the company you overtake?

— Act 4, Sc. 5

Now I will believe that there are unicorns.

— The Tempest, Act 3, Sc. 3

These are not natural events; they strengthen from strange to stranger.

— Act 5, Sc. 1

If in Naples I should report this now, would they believe me?

— Act 3, Sc. 3

This is as strange a maze as e'er men trod . . . There is in this business more
than nature was ever conduct of.

— Act 5, Sc. 1

I'll show you how to observe a strange event.

— Timon of Athens, Act 3, Sc. 4

I know his lordship is but merry with me.

— Act 3, Sc. 2

I'll show thee wondrous things . . .

— *Titus Andronicus, Act 5, Sc. 1*

How, sir, are you in earnest then . . . ?

— *Act 1, Sc. 1*

If this were played upon a stage now, I could condemn it as an improbable fiction.

— *Twelfth Night, Act 3, Sc. 4*

I am ready to distrust mine eyes and wrangle with my reason.

— *Act 4, Sc. 3*

Such a deal of wonder is broken out within this hour, that ballad-makers cannot be able to express it.

— *Winter's Tale, Act 5, Sc. 2*

A notable passion of wonder . . .

— *Act 5, Sc. 2*

. . . more than history can pattern.

— *Act 3, Sc. 2*

14
GROUCHES

We have some old crab-trees here . . .

— *Coriolanus, Act 2, Sc. 1*

How tartly that gentleman looks! I never can see him but I am heart-burned
an hour after.

— *Much Ado about Nothing, Act 2, Sc. 1*

He receives comfort like cold porridge.

— *The Tempest, Act 2, Sc. 1*

Go, let him have a table by himself, for he does neither affect company,
nor is he fit for it indeed.

— *Timon of Athens, Act 1, Sc. 2*

The king hath on him such a countenance as he had lost some province.

— *Winter's Tale, Act 1, Sc. 2*

Another flap-mouthed mourner . . .

— *Venus and Adonis*

How is it that the clouds still hang on you?

— *Hamlet, Act 1, Sc. 2*

How now! Rain within doors . . .

— *Henry IV, Part II, Act 4, Sc. 5*

. . . high-proof melancholy . . .

— *Much Ado About Nothing, Act 5, Sc. 1*

How weary, stale, flat and unprofitable seem to me all the uses of the
world!

— *Hamlet, Act 1, Sc. 2*

To what purpose dost thou hoard thy words, that thou return'st no
greeting to thy friends?

— *Richard II, Act 1, Sc. 3*

You are so fretful, you cannot live long.

— *Henry IV, Part I, Act 3, Sc. 3*

The tartness of his face sours ripe grapes.

— *Coriolanus, Act 5, Sc. 4*

Nay, an you begin to rail on society once, I am sworn not to give regard to you.
                                        — *Timon of Athens, Act 1, Sc. 2*

. . . hath abjured the company and sight of men.
                                        — *Twelfth Night, Act 1, Sc. 2*

As she is now, she will but disease our better mirth.
                                        — *Coriolanus, Act 1, Sc. 3*

Thou crusty batch of nature.
                                        — *Troilus and Cressida, Act 5, Sc. 1*

I will not wish ye half my miseries, I have more charity.
                                        — *Henry VIII, Act 3, Sc. 1*

But wherefore do you droop?
                                        — *King John, Act 5, Sc. 1*

. . . so faint, so spiritless, so dull, so dead in look, so woe-begone.
                                        — *Henry IV, Part II, Act 1, Sc. 1*

Groan so in perpetuity . . .
                                        — *Cymbeline, Act 5, Sc. 4*

. . . melancholy malcontent . . .
                                        — *Venus and Adonis*

. . . the winter of our discontent . . .
                                        — *Richard III, Act 1, Sc. 1*

But were we burden'd with like weight of pain,
As much or more we should ourselves complain.
                                        — *Comedy of Errors, Act 2, Sc. 1*

And he will, after his sour fashion, tell you what hath proceeded worthy note today.
                                        — *Julius Caesar, Act 1, Sc. 2*

Leave me alone, for I must think of that which company would not be friendly to.
                                        — *Henry VIII, Act 5, Sc. 1*

As humorous as winter . . .
                                        — *Henry IV, Part II, Act 4, Sc. 4*

My lord leans wondrously to discontent.
                                        — *Timon of Athens, Act 3, Sc. 4*

Clear up . . . that cloudy countenance.

> — *Titus Andronicus*, Act 1, Sc. 1

. . . such a February face, so full of frost, of storm and cloudiness.

> — *Much Ado about Nothing*, Act 5, Sc. 4

Thou hast some crotchets in thy head.

> — *Merry Wives of Windsor*, Act 2, Sc. 1

. . . pouted in a dull disdain . . .

> — *Venus and Adonis*

Methinks you are too much of late in the frown.

> — *King Lear*, Act 1, Sc. 4

Why art thou thus attired in discontent?

> — *Rape of Lucrece*

Desiring this man's art and that man's scope,
With what I most enjoy contented least.

> — *Sonnet 29*

Sing, or express yourself in a more comfortable sort.

> — *Coriolanus*, Act 1, Sc. 3

Churlish as the bear . . .

> — *Troilus and Cressida*, Act 1, Sc. 2

You promised . . . to lay aside life-harming heaviness, and entertain a cheerful disposition.

> — *Richard II*, Act 2, Sc. 2

. . . sable-coloured melancholy . . .

> — *Love's Labour's Lost*, Act 1, Sc. 1

I at home starve for a merry look.

> — *Comedy of Errors*, Act 2, Sc. 1

. . . so forlorn, that his dimensions to any thick sight were invisible.

> — *Henry IV, Part II*, Act 3, Sc. 2

What is your cause of distemper?

> — *Hamlet*, Act 3, Sc. 2

. . . of such vinegar aspect, that they'll not show their teeth in way of smile.

> — *Merchant of Venice*, Act 1, Sc. 1

Thou shamest the music of sweet news by playing it to me with so sour
a face.
                                    — *Romeo and Juliet, Act 2, Sc. 5*

I am misanthropos, and hate mankind . . .
                                    — *Timon of Athens, Act 4, Sc. 3*

A better bad habit of frowning.
                                    — *Merchant of Venice, Act 1, Sc. 2*

You borrow not that face of seeming sorrow, it is sure your own.
                                    — *Henry IV, Part II, Act 5, Sc. 2*

What a frosty-spirited rogue is this!
                                    — *Part I, Act 2, Sc. 3*

. . . an irksome brawling scold.
                                    — *Taming of the Shrew, Act 1, Sc. 2*

Why rail'st thou on thy birth, the heaven and earth?
                                    — *Romeo and Juliet, Act 3, Sc. 3*

. . . heavy, sour, sad and much different from the man he was.
                                    — *Comedy of Errors, Act 5, Sc. 1*

...ye've got a humour there does not become a man.
                                    — *Timon of Athens, Act 1, Sc. 2*

. . . walk alone, like one that had the pestilence.
                                    — *Two Gentlemen of Verona, Act 2, Sc. 1*

They pass'd by me as misers do by beggars, neither gave to me good word
nor look.
                                    — *Troilus and Cressida, Act 3, Sc. 3*

. . . puts on outward strangeness, seems unkind.
                                    — *Venus and Adonis*

This is in thee a nature but infected; a poor unmanly melancholy . . .
                                    — *Timon of Athens, Act 4, Sc. 3*

I see your brows are full of discontent.
                                    — *Richard II, Act 4, Sc. 1*

. . . of churlish disposition and little recks to find the way to heaven by
doing deeds of hospitality.
                                    — *As You Like It, Act 2, Sc. 4*

He loves no plays, . . . he hears no music, seldom he smiles.
                                    — *Julius Caesar, Act 1, Sc. 2*

You must not look so sour. — It is my fashion, when I see a crab.
— *Taming of the Shrew, Act 2, Sc. 1*

If thou wert not sullen, I would be good to thee.
— *Timon of Athens, Act 1, Sc. 2*

Turn thy solemness out o' door . . .
— *Coriolanus, Act 1, Sc. 3*

Thou grumblest and railest every hour . . .
— *Troilus and Cressida, Act 2, Sc. 1*

. . . new lamenting ancient oversights . . .
— *Henry IV, Part II, Act 4, Sc. 5*

I am glad of your departure; adieu, good Monsieur Melancholy.
— *As You Like It, Act 3, Sc. 2*

Dost thou come here to whine?
— *Hamlet, Act 5, Sc. 1*

15
TRIVIA

A trifle, some eight-penny matter.
— *Henry IV, Part I, Act 3, Sc. 3*

The tears live in an onion that should water this sorrow.
— *Antony and Cleopatra, Act 1, Sc. 2*

Gratiano speaks an infinite deal of nothing . . . His reasons are as two
grains of wheat hid in two bushels of chaff; you shall seek all day ere
you find them, and when you have them, they are not worth the search.
— *Merchant of Venice, Act 1, Sc. 1*

Fold it over and over, 'tis three fold too little.
— *Two Gentlement of Verona, Act 1, Sc. 1*

Is the sun dimm'd, that gnats do fly in it?
— *Titus Andronicus, Act 4, Sc. 4*

Good lord, what madness rules in brainsick men, when for so slight and
frivolous a cause such factious emulations shall arise!
— *Henry VI, Part I, Act 4, Sc. 1*

That's neither here nor there.
— *Merry Wives of Windsor, Act 1, Sc. 4*

. . . admiring the nothing of it.
— *Winter's Tale, Act 4, Sc. 4*

Dainty and such picking grievances.
— *Henry IV, Part II, Act 4, Sc. 1*

They pass by me as the idle wind which I respect not.
— *Julius Caesar, Act 4, Sc. 3*

Nay, it makes nothing — If it mar nothing neither . . .
— *Love's Labour's Lost, Act 4, Sc. 3*

. . . give them thanks for nothing . . .
— *Midsummer Night's Dream, Act 5, Sc. 1*

Rings, gawds, conceits, knacks, trifles, nosegays . . .
— *Act 1, Sc. 1*

To find quarrel in a straw . . .
— *Hamlet, Act 4, Sc. 4*

. . . out of a great deal of old iron.

— *Henry VI, Part I, Act 1, Sc. 2*

Gnats are unnoted wheresoe'er they fly.

— *Rape of Lucrece*

Fractions . . . fragments, scraps, the bits and greasy relics . . .

— *Troilus and Cressida, Act 5, Sc. 2*

Thou thread, thou thimble, Thou yard, three-quarters, half-yard, quarter, nail! Thou flea, thou nit, thou winter-cricket thou! . . . Away thou rag, thou quantity, thou remnant . . .

— *Taming of the Shrew, Act 4, Sc. 3*

That's lesser than a little.

— *Coriolanus, Act 1, Sc. 4*

It was mere foolery; I did not mark it.

— *Julius Caesar, Act 1, Sc. 2*

. . . bird-bolts that you deem cannon-bullets.

— *Twelfth Night, Act 1, Sc. 5*

When you speak best unto the purpose, it is not worth the wagging of your beards.

— *Coriolanus, Act 2, Sc. 1*

Things base and vile, holding no quantity.

— *Midsummer Night's Dream, Act 1, Sc. 1*

A toy, a thing of no regard.

— *Henry VI, Part I, Act 4, Sc. 1*

O vain petitioner, beg a greater matter; thou now request'st but moonshine in the water.

— *Love's Labour's Lost, Act 5, Sc. 2*

Some petty and unprofitable dukedoms.

— *Henry V, Act 3, Prologue*

Let it not trouble you . . . think not on 't . . . let it not cumber your better remembrance.

— *Timon of Athens, Act 3, Sc. 6*

The sea being smooth, how many shallow bauble boats dare sail . . .

— *Troilus and Cressida, Act 1, Sc. 3*

. . . a snapper-up of unconsidered trifles.

— *Winter's Tale, Act 4, Sc. 3*

The smallest thread that ever spider twisted from her womb.
— *King John, Act 4, Sc. 3*

. . . unstable slightness.
— *Coriolanus, Act 3, Sc. 1*

Small to greater matters must give way. — Not if the small come first.
— *Antony and Cleopatra, Act 2, Sc. 2*

How low soe'er the matter, I hope in God for high words — A high hope
for a low heaven.
— *Love's Labour's Lost, Act 1, Sc. 1*

As thin of substance as the air.
— *Romeo and Juliet, Act 1, Sc. 4*

Uses a known truth to pass a thousand nothings with.
— *All's Well that Ends Well, Act 2, Sc. 5*

Done many things, some less, some more.
— *Coriolanus, Act 2, Sc. 3*

Every slight and false-derived cause, Yea, every idle, nice and wanton
reason . . .
— *Henry IV, Part II, Act 4, Sc. 1*

. . . abjects, orts and imitations.
— *Julius Caesar, Act 4, Sc. 1*

Some petty towns of no import.
— *Henry VI, Part I, Act 1, Sc. 1*

Why, 'tis a cockle or a walnut shell; a knack, a toy, a trick, a baby's cap.
— *Taming of the Shrew, Act 4, Sc. 3*

A grain, a dust, a gnat, a wandering hair, any annoyance.
— *King John, Act 4, Sc. 1*

A little gale will soon disperse that cloud, and blow it to the source from
whence it came . . . for every cloud engenders not a storm.
— *Henry VI, Part III, Act 5, Sc. 3*

Upon importance of so slight and trivial a nature.
— *Cymbeline, Act 1, Sc. 4*

Small lights are soon blown out.
— *Rape of Lucrece*

Currish thanks is good enough for such a present.
— *Two Gentlemen of Verona, Act 4, Sc. 4*

Many a thousand grains that issue out of dust.
                         — *Measure for Measure, Act 3, Sc. 1*

These things seem small and undistinguishable . . .
                         — *Midsummer Night's Dream, Act 4, Sc. 1*

Small things make base men proud.
                         — *Henry VI, Part II, Act 4, Sc. 1*

The fall of an ass, which is no great hurt.
                         — *Cymbeline, Act 1, Sc. 2*

Matter needless, of importless burden.
                         — *Troilus and Cressida, Act 1, Sc. 3*

. . . disdained scraps . . .
                         — *Rape of Lucrece*

I dare lay any money 'twill be nothing yet.
                         — *Twelfth Night, Act 3, Sc. 4*

Things small as nothing . . . he makes important.
                         — *Troilus and Cressida, Act 2, Sc. 3*

A little patch of ground that hath in it no profit but the name.
                         — *Hamlet, Act 4, Sc. 4*

I have heard it over, and it is nothing, nothing in the world.
                         — *Midsummer Night's Dream, Act 5, Sc. 1*

'Tis very clerkly done.
                         — *Two Gentlemen of Verona, Act 2, Sc. 1*

Is all our travail turned to this effect?
                         — *Henry VI, Part I, Act 5, Sc. 4*

In shape no bigger than an agate-stone on the forefinger of an alderman.
                         — *Romeo and Juliet, Act 1, Sc. 4*

Come, gentlemen, we sit too long on trifles, and waste the time . . .
                         — *Pericles, Act 2, Sc. 3*

The controversy of three-pence.
                         — *Coriolanus, Act 2, Sc. 1*

This idle theme, this bootless chat.
                         — *Venus and Adonis*

I had as lief you would tell me of a mess of porridge.
                         — *Merry Wives of Windsor, Act 3, Sc. 1*

71

This is nothing, fool. — Then 'tis like the breath of an unfee'd lawyer, you gave me nothing for it.
> — *King Lear*, Act 1, Sc. 4

. . . with a solemn earnestness, more than indeed belong'd to such a trifle.
> — *Othello*, Act 5, Sc. 2

. . . which is within a very little of nothing.
> — *All's Well that Ends Well*, Act 2, Sc. 4

What do you mean, to dote thus on such luggage?
> — *The Tempest*, Act 4, Sc. 1

This nothing that he so plentifully gives me . . .
> — *As You Like It*, Act 1, Sc. 1

. . . not worth the time of day.
> — *Pericles*, Act 4, Sc. 3

So far this shadow doth limp behind the substance.
> — *Merchant of Venice*, Act 3, Sc. 2

Are you such fools to square for this?
> — *Titus Andronicus*, Act 2, Sc. 1

. . . not worth a breakfast in the cheapest country.
> — *Pericles*, Act 4, Sc. 6

This passion, and the death of a dear friend, would go near to make a man look sad.
> — *Midsummer Night's Dream*, Act 5, Sc. 1

16

HOW THE MIGHTY HAVE FALLEN

Time is come round, and where I did begin, there shall I end.
— *Julius Caesar, Act 5, Sc. 3*

His eyes are humbler than they used to be.
— *Henry V, Act 4, Sc. 7*

What, is the old king dead? — As nail in door.
— *Henry IV, Part II, Act 5, Sc. 3*

All that lives must die, passing through nature to eternity.
— *Hamlet, Act 1, Sc. 2*

You are undone, captain, all but your scarf; that has a knot on 't yet.
— *All's Well that Ends Well, Act 4, Sc. 3*

An exhaled meteor . . .
— *Henry IV, Part I, Act 5, Sc. 1*

You see them great, and follow'd with the general throng and sweat of thousand friends; then in a moment, see how soon this mightiness meets misery.
— *Henry VIII, Prologue*

. . . and thus the whirligig of time brings in his revenges.
— *Twelfth Night, Act 5, Sc. 1*

Him that thou magnifiest with all these titles, stinking and fly-blown lies here at our feet.
— *Henry VI, Part I, Act 4, Sc. 7*

Time hath, my lord, a wallet at his back, wherein he puts alms for oblivion.
— *Troilus and Cressida, Act 3, Sc. 3*

. . . as he then was, mighty, . . . as he is now, nothing.
— *Henry VIII, Act 4, Sc. 2*

By medicine life may be prolong'd yet death will seize the doctor, too.
— *Cymbeline, Act 5, Sc. 5*

After summer evermore succeeds barren winter . . .
— *Henry VI, Part II, Act 2, Sc. 4*

Saint George, that swinged the dragon, and e'er since sits on his horse back
at mine hostess' door . . .
— *King John, Act 2, Sc. 1*

All the world's a stage.
And all the men and women merely players;
They have their exits and their entrances;
And one man in his time plays many parts,
His acts being seven ages. At first the infant,
Mewling and puking in the nurse's arms.
Then the whining school-boy, with his satchel
And shining morning face, creeping like snail
Unwillingly to school. And then the lover,
Sighing like furnace, with a woeful ballad
Made to his mistress' eyebrow. Then a soldier
Full of strange oaths, and bearded like the pard,
Jealous in honour, sudden and quick in quarrel,
Seeking the bubble reputation
Even in the cannon's mouth. And then the justice,
In fair round belly with good capon lined,
With eyes severe and beard of formal cut,
Full of wise saws and modern instances;
And so he plays his part. The sixth age shifts
Into the lean and slipper'd pantaloon,
With spectacles on nose and pouch on side,
His youthful hose, well saved, a world too wide
For his shrunk shank; and his big manly voice,
Turning again toward childish treble, pipes
And whistles in his sound. Last scene of all,
That ends this strange eventful history,
Is second childishness and mere oblivion,
Sans teeth, sans eyes, sans taste, sans every thing.
— *As You Like It, Act 2, Sc. 7*

I see thy glory like a shooting star, fall to the base earth from the firmament.
— *Richard II, Act 2, Sc. 4*

But kings and mightiest potentates must die, for that's the end of human
misery.
— *Henry VI, Part I, Act 3, Sc. 2*

All unavoided is the doom of destiny.
— *Richard III, Act 4, Sc. 4*

Cancelling your fame, blotting your names from books of memory . . .
— *Henry VI, Part II, Act 1, Sc. 1*

Today, unhappy day, . . . o'erthrows thy joys, friends, fortune and thy state.
— *Richard II, Act 3, Sc. 2*

The bright day is done, and we are for the dark.
— *Antony and Cleopatra, Act 5, Sc. 2*

So wise, so young, they say, do never live long . . .
— *Richard III, Act 3, Sc. 1*

Mean and mighty, rotting together, have one dust.
— *Cymbeline, Act 4, Sc. 2*

I have touch'd the highest point of all my greatness, and, from that full meridian of my glory, I haste now to my setting. I shall fall like a bright exhalation in the evening, and no man see me more.
— *Henry VIII, Act 3, Sc. 2*

Greatness, once fall'n out with fortune, must fall out with men, too.
— *Troilus and Cressida, Act 3, Sc. 3*

Where be the bending peers that flattered thee? Where be the thronging troops that followed thee?
— *Richard III, Act 4, Sc. 4*

These are stars, indeed, and sometimes falling ones.
— *Henry VIII, Act 4, Sc. 1*

Too famous to live long.
— *Henry VI, Part I, Act 1, Sc. 1*

I see the downfall of our house . . . I see, as in a map, the end of all.
— *Richard III, Act 2, Sc. 4*

My parks, my walks, my manors that I had, even now forsake me . . .
— *Henry VI, Part III, Act 5, Sc. 2*

You're shamed, you're overthrown, you're undone for ever!
— *Merry Wives of Windsor, Act 3, Sc. 3*

You are as a candle, the better part burnt out.
— *Henry IV, Part II, Act 1, Sc. 2*

The hope and expectation of thy time is ruin'd.
— *Part I, Act 3, Sc. 2*

A beggar, that was used to come so smug upon the mart.
— *Merchant of Venice, Act 3, Sc. 1*

Thus hath the course of justice wheel'd about, and left thee but a very prey to time.
— *Richard III, Act 4, Sc. 4*

To see a king transformed to a gnat!
— *Love's Labour's Lost, Act 4, Sc. 3*

Thy place is fill'd, thy sceptre wrung from thee, thy balm wash'd off wherewith thou wast anointed; no bending knee will call thee Caesar now.
— *Henry VI, Part III, Act 3, Sc. 1*

The end crowns all, and that old common arbitrator, Time, will one day end it.
— *Troilus and Cressida, Act 4, Sc. 5*

. . . to suffer a man of his place . . . to dance attendance on their lordships' pleasures, and at the door, too . . .
— *Henry VIII, Act 5, Sc. 2*

This was now a king, and now is clay?
— *King John, Act 5, Sc. 7*

To tumble down . . . from top of honour to disgrace's feet.
— *Henry VI, Part II, Act 1, Sc. 2*

The painful warrior famoused for fight,
After a thousand victories, once foil'd,
Is from the books of honour razed quite,
And all the rest forgot for which he toil'd.

— *Sonnet 25*

O mighty Caesar! Dost thou lie so low? Are all thy conquests, glories, triumphs, spoils, shrunk to this little measure?
— *Julius Caesar, Act 3, Sc. 1*

But even now worth this, and now worth nothing?
— *Merchant of Venice, Act 1, Sc. 1*

What, amazed at my misfortunes? Can thy spirit wonder a great man should decline?
— *Henry VIII, Act 3, Sc. 2*

What's past, and what's to come, is strew'd with husks and formless ruin of oblivion.
— *Troilus and Cressida, Act 4, Sc. 5*

The fortune of the day quite turned from him.
— *Henry IV, Part I, Act 5, Sc. 5*

. . . to see him so little of his great self.

— *Henry VIII, Act 3, Sc. 2*

Why, what is pomp, rule, reign, but earth and dust? And, live we how we can, yet die we must.

— *Henry VI, Part III, Act 5, Sc. 2*

For time is like a fashionable host that slightly shakes his parting guest by the hand, and with his arms outstretch'd, as he would fly, grasps in the comer; welcome ever smiles, and farewell goes out sighing.

— *Troilus and Cressida, Act 3, Sc. 3*

Like the lily, that once was mistress of the field and flourish'd, I'll hang my head and perish.

— *Henry VIII, Act 3, Sc. 1*

When that this body did contain a spirit, a kingdom for it was too small a bound, but now two paces of the vilest earth is room enough.

— *Henry IV, Part I, Act 5, Sc. 4*

. . . being but a private man again.

— *Henry VIII, Act 5, Sc. 3*

But yesterday the word of Caesar might have stood against the world; now lies he there, and none so poor to do him reverence.

— *Julius Caesar, Act 3, Sc. 2*

. . . the abject people . . . with envious looks laughing at thy shame, that erst did follow thy proud chariot-wheels, when thou didst ride in triumph through the streets.

— *Henry VI, Part II, Act 2, Sc. 4*

No sun shall ever usher forth mine honours, or gild again the noble troops that waited upon my smiles.

— *Henry VIII, Act 3, Sc. 2*

But now mischance hath trod my title down, and with dishonour laid me on the ground; where I must take like seat unto my fortune, and to my humble seat conform myself.

— *Henry VI, Part III, Act 3, Sc. 3*

You may my glories and my state depose. But not my griefs, still I am king of those.

— *Richard II, Act 4, Sc. 1*

Glory is like a circle in the water, which never ceaseth to enlarge itself, 'til by broad spreading it disperse to nought.

— *Henry VI, Part I, Act 1, Sc. 2*

My pride fell with my fortunes.

— *As You Like It, Act 1, Sc. 2*

Men shut their doors against a setting sun.

— *Timon of Athens, Act 1, Sc. 2*

What the declined is, he shall as soon read in the eyes of others as feel in his own fall.

— *Troilus and Cressida, Act 3, Sc. 3*

The great man down, you mark his favourite flies.

— *Hamlet, Act 3, Sc. 2*

Time's thievish progress to eternity . . .

— *Sonnet 77*

. . . and many strokes, though with a little axe, hew down and fell the hardest-timber'd oak.

— *Henry VI, Part III, Act 2, Sc. 1*

Fortune . . . it is still her use to let the wretched man outlive his wealth, to view with hollow eye and wrinkled brow an age of poverty.

— *Merchant of Venice, Act 4, Sc. 1*

Now our sands are almost run . . .

— *Pericles, Act 5, Sc. 2*

Would he not fall down, since pride must have a fall?

— *Richard II, Act 5, Sc. 5*

17

THIEVES

. . . pilfering borderers . . . coursing snatchers . . .
> — *Henry V, Act 1, Sc. 2*

A purse of gold most resolutely snatched on Monday night and most dissolutely spent on Tuesday morning.
> — *Henry IV, Part I, Act 1, Sc. 2*

The robb'd that smiles steals something from the thief . . .
> — *Othello, Act 1, Sc. 3*

The jury . . . may in the sworn twelve have a thief or two guiltier than him they try.
> — *Measure for Measure, Act 2, Sc. 1*

Where shall I find one that can steal well? O, for fine thief!
> — *Henry IV, Part I, Act 3, Sc. 3*

His filching was like an unskilful singer; he kept not time.
> — *Merry Wives of Windsor, Act 1, Sc. 3*

But for your conscience? — Ay, sir, where lies that?
> — *The Tempest, Act 2, Sc. 1*

The thief doth fear each bush an officer.
> — *Henry VI, Part III, Act 5, Sc. 6*

If my wind were but long enough to say my prayers, I would repent.
> — *Merry Wives of Windsor, Act 4, Sc. 5*

They do confound their skill in covetousness.
> — *King John, Act 4, Sc. 2*

We that take purses go by the moon and the seven stars.
> — *Henry IV, Part I, Act 1, Sc. 2*

. . . for thieves do foot by night.
> — *Merry Wives of Windsor, Act 2, Sc. 1*

. . . putting the hand in the pocket and extracting it clutched?
> — *Measure for Measure, Act 3, Sc. 2*

In thy weak hive a wandering wasp hath crept, and suck'd the honey . . .
> — *Rape of Lucrece*

Thieves and robbers range abroad unseen . . .
— Richard II, Act 3, Sc. 2

This place is famous for the creatures of prey that keep upon't.
— Winter's Tale, Act 3, Sc. 3

We have locks to safeguard necessaries, and pretty traps to catch the petty thieves.
— Henry V, Act 1, Sc. 2

Injurious wasps, to feed on such honey, and kill the bees that yield it with your stings!
— Two Gentlemen of Verona, Act 1, Sc. 2

I will first make bold with your money . . .
— Merry Wives of Windsor, Act 2, Sc. 2

. . . Thievish living on the common road.
— As You Like It, Act 2, Sc. 3

They say this town is full of . . . nimble jugglers that deceive the eye.
— Comedy of Errors, Act 1, Sc. 2

You wrangling pirates, that fall out in sharing that which you have pill'd from me.
— Richard III, Act 1, Sc. 3

(Enter certain outlaws.)
— Two Gentlemen of Verona, Act 4, Sc. 1

You have beaten my men, killed my deer and broke open my lodge. — But not kissed your keeper's daughter.
—Merry Wives of Windsor, Act 1, Sc. 1

Still you keep o' the windy side of the law.
— Twelfth Night, Act 3, Sc. 4

. . . pilferings and most common trespasses . . .
— King Lear, Act 2, Sc. 2

Let him show himself what he is and steal out of your company.
— Much Ado About Nothing, Act 3, Sc. 3

I see a good amendment of life in thee; from praying to purse-taking. — Why, 'tis my vocation . . . 'tis no sin for a man to labour in his vocation.
— Henry IV, Part I, Act 1, Sc. 2

A mere anatomy, a mountebank, a threadbare juggler . . .
— Comedy of Errors, Act 5, Sc. 1

Flat burglary as ever was committed.
> — *Much Ado about Nothing, Act 4, Sc. 2*

Rob me the exchequer the first thing thou doest, and do it with unwashed hands, too.
> — *Henry IV, Part I, Act 3, Sc. 3*

I have sat in the stocks for puddings he hath stolen.
> — *Two Gentlemen of Verona, Act 4, Sc. 4*

One that is like to be executed for robbing a church.
> — *Henry V, Act 3, Sc. 6*

. . . walk in thievish ways . . .
> — *Romeo and Juliet, Act 4, Sc. 1*

. . . gored the gentle bosom of peace with pillage and robbery.
> — *Henry V, Act 4, Sc. 1*

For the robbery, lad, how is that answered?
> — *Henry IV, Part I, Act 3, Sc. 3*

Where shall we take a purse tomorrow, Jack?
> — *Act 1, Sc. 2*

It's an honourable kind of thievery.
> — *Two Gentlemen of Verona, Act 4, Sc. 1*

Let no assembly of twenty be without a score of villains . . .
> — *Timon of Athens, Act 3, Sc. 6*

. . . an empty eagle were set to guard the chicken . . .
> — *Henry VI, Part II, Act 3, Sc. 1*

He hath offended the law, and, sir, we take him to be a thief, too . . .
> — *Measure for Measure, Act 3, Sc. 2*

Thou variest no more from picking of purses than giving direction doth from labouring; thou layest the plot how.
> — *Henry IV, Part I, Act 2, Sc. 1*

Like the sanctimonious pirate, that went to sea with the Ten Commandments, but scraped one out of the table.
> — *Measure for Measure, Act 1, Sc. 1*

. . . as familiar with men's pockets as with their gloves or their handkerchiefs.
> — *Henry V, Act 3, Sc. 2*

18
EASY LADIES

. . . to be naked with her friend in bed an hour or more, not meaning any harm.

— *Othello, Act 4, Sc. 1*

Jane Nightwork . . .

— *Henry IV, Part II, Act 3, Sc. 2*

She adulterates hourly . . .

— *King John, Act 3, Sc. 1*

. . . of their going to bed, and of other motions . . .

— *All's Well that Ends Well, Act 5, Sc. 3*

To win his heart, she touch'd him here and there . . .

— *Passionate Pilgrim*

Were beauty under twenty locks kept fast,
Yet love breaks through, and picks them all at last.

— *Venus and Adonis*

. . . no sooner met but they looked, no sooner looked but they loved, no sooner loved but they sighed, no sooner sighed but they asked one another the reason, no sooner knew the reason but they sought the remedy . . .

— *As You Like It, Act 5, Sc. 2*

For little England, you'ld venture an emballing . . .

— *Henry VIII, Act 2, Sc. 3*

Journeys end in lovers meeting, every wise man's son doth know.

— *Twelfth Night, Act 2, Sc. 3*

For there was never yet fair woman but she made mouths in a glass.

— *King Lear, Act 3, Sc. 2*

Well, if you were but an inch of fortune better than I, where would you choose it? — Not in my husband's nose.

— *Antony and Cleopatra, Act 1, Sc. 2*

The stealth of our most mutual entertainment.

— *Measure for Measure, Act 1, Sc. 2*

Have we some strange Indian with the great tool come to court, the women so besiege us?
— *Henry VIII, Act 5, Sc. 4*

O, mistress mine, where are you roaming?
— *Twelfth Night, Act 2, Sc. 3*

When it stands well with him, it stands well with her.
— *Two Gentlemen of Verona, Act 2, Sc. 5*

. . . the primrose path of dalliance . . .
— *Hamlet, Act 1, Sc. 3*

And was a common gamester to the camp.
— *All's Well that Ends Well, Act 5, Sc. 3*

Since you are dear bought, I will love you dear.
— *Merchant of Venice, Act 3, Sc. 2*

. . . so sweet a bedfellow.
— *Henry VIII, Act 2, Sc. 2*

A bawd of eleven years' continuance.
— *Measure for Measure, Act 3, Sc. 2*

That nature with a beauteous wall doth oft close in pollution.
— *Twelfth Night, Act 1, Sc. 2*

. . . make her go back even to the yielding.
— *Cymbeline, Act 1, Sc. 4*

And their daughters profit very greatly under you.
— *Love's Labour's Lost, Act 4, Sc. 2*

. . . she's a bed-swerver.
— *Winter's Tale, Act 2, Sc. 1*

Yet they do wink and yield . . .
— *Henry V, Act 5, Sc. 2*

(to a little girl) Dost thou fall upon thy face? Thou wilt fall backward when thou hast more wit.
— *Romeo and Juliet, Act 1, Sc. 3*

Now comes in the sweetest morsel of the night . . .
— *Henry IV, Part II, Act 2, Sc. 4*

When my love swears that she is made of truth,
I do believe her though I know she lies.
— *Sonnet 138*

. . . her sweet harmony and other chosen attractions . . .
— *Pericles, Act 5, Sc. 1*

For I can sing and speak to him in many sorts of music.
— *Twelfth Night, Act 1, Sc. 2*

I spy entertainment in her . . . She gives the leer of invitation.
— *Merry Wives of Windsor, Act 1, Sc. 3*

'Tis the strumpet's plague to beguile many and be beguiled by one.
— *Othello, Act 4, Sc. 1*

. . . an approved wanton.
— *Much Ado about Nothing, Act 4, Sc. 1*

I see the lady hath a thing to grant.
— *Henry VI, Part III, Act 3, Sc. 2*

For the bawdy hand of the dial is now upon the prick of noon.
— *Romeo and Juliet, Act 2, Sc. 4*

. . . a fond and desperate creature, whom sometime I have laughed with.
— *All's Well that Ends Well, Act 5, Sc. 3*

Item: She is too liberal. — . . . Of her purse she shall not . . . now, of another thing she may.
— *Two Gentlemen of Verona, Act 3, Sc. 1*

. . . your chaste treasure open to his unmaster'd importunity.
— *Hamlet, Act 1, Sc. 3*

Have you limbs to bear that load?
— *Henry VIII, Act 2, Sc. 3*

She is young and apt . . .
— *Timon of Athens, Act 1, Sc. 1*

I hope to see a housewife take thee between her legs . . .
— *Twelfth Night, Act 1, Sc. 3*

Go, girl, seek happy nights to happy days.
— *Romeo and Juliet, Act 1, Sc. 3*

Will you . . . bestow your love and your affections upon a stranger?
— *Pericles, Act 2, Sc. 5*

We have willing dames enough, . . . so many as will to greatness dedicate themselves . . .
— *Macbeth, Act 4, Sc. 3*

(She) What would you have me do? (He) A juggling trick, to be secretly open.

> — *Troilus and Cressida*, Act 5, Sc. 2

. . . ope her lap.

> — *Romeo and Juliet*, Act 1, Sc. 1

Your mistress bears well. — Me well; which is the prescript praise and perfection of a good and particular mistress.

> — *Henry V*, Act 3, Sc. 7

They do let heaven see the pranks they dare not show their husbands.

> — *Othello*, Act 3, Sc. 3

It is a wise father that knows his own child.

> — *Merchant of Venice*, Act 2, Sc. 2

Love sought is good, but given unsought is better.

> — *Twelfth Night*, Act 3, Sc. 1

There's language in her eye, her cheek, her lip; nay, her foot speaks; her wanton spirits look out at every joint and motive of her body.

> — *Troilus and Cressida*, Act 4, Sc. 5

. . . her fine foot, straight leg and quivering thigh, and the demesnes that there adjacent lie.

> — *Romeo and Juliet*, Act 2, Sc. 1

. . . a fit man to teach her that wherein she delights.

> — *Taming of the Shrew*, Act 1, Sc. 1

She does so take on with her men; they mistook their erection.

> — *Merry Wives of Windsor*, Act 3, Sc. 5

A housewife that by selling her desires buys herself bread and clothes.

> — *Othello*, Act 4, Sc. 1

. . . country copulatives . . .

> — *As You Like It*, Act 5, Sc. 4

She bids you on the wanton rushes lay you down . . .

> — *Henry IV, Part I*, Act 3, Sc. 1

A woman is a dish for the gods, if the devil dress her not.

> — *Antony and Cleopatra*, Act 5, Sc. 2

He on her belly falls, she on her back.

> — *Venus and Adonis*

A thousand honey secrets shalt thou know.
> — *Venus and Adonis*

After they closed in earnest, they parted very fairly in jest.
> — *Two Gentlemen of Verona*, Act 2, Sc. 5

This maid will serve my turn, sir.
> — *Love's Labour's Lost*, Act 1, Sc. 1

Ladies that . . . will have a bout with you.
> — *Romeo and Juliet*, Act 1, Sc. 5

She did so course o'er my exteriors with such a greedy intention . . .
> — *Merry Wives of Windsor*, Act 1, Sc. 3

You rise to play, and go to bed to work.
> — *Othello*, Act 2, Sc. 1

If she'ld do the deed of darkness . . .
> — *Pericles*, Act 4, Sc. 6

That thou art my son, I have partly thy mother's word, partly my own opinion . . .
> — *Henry IV, Part I*, Act 2, Sc. 4

. . . lends embracements to every stranger.
> — *Venus and Adonis*

And learn me how to lose a winning match, play'd for a pair of stainless maidenhoods.
> — *Romeo and Juliet*, Act 3, Sc. 2

How bravely thou becomest thy bed.
> — *Cymbeline*, Act 2, Sc. 2

"In night," quoth she, "desire sees best of all."
> — *Venus and Adonis*

When ladies crave to be encountered with.
> — *Henry VI, Part I*, Act 2, Sc. 2

The maid that stood in the way for my wish shall show me the way to my will.
> — *Henry V*, Act 5, Sc. 2

Have you not heard it said full oft,
A woman's nay doth stand for nought.
> — *Passionate Pilgrim*

For maids, well summered and warm kept, . . . and then they will endure handling.
> — *Henry V*, Act 5, Sc. 2

But if she be less than an honest woman, she is indeed more than I took her for.

> — *Merchant of Venice, Act 3, Sc. 5*

. . . encompass'd with thy lustful paramours!

> — *Henry VI, Part I, Act 3, Sc. 2*

Unhappy were you, madam, ere I came;
But by my coming I have made you happy.

> — *Two Gentlemen of Verona, Act 5, Sc. 4*

. . . she playeth on her back . . .

> — *Titus Andronicus, Act 4, Sc. 1*

At the first sight, they have changed eyes.

> — *The Tempest, Act 1, Sc. 2*

. . . the warm approach of sweet desire.

> — *Venus and and Adonis*

How her acquaintance grew with this lewd fellow.

> — *Much Ado about Nothing, Act 5, Sc. 1*

But there is never a fair woman has a true face.

> — *Antony and Cleopatra, Act 2, Sc. 6*

Pray you, without any more virginal fencing, will you use him kindly?
He will line your apron with gold.

> — *Pericles, Act 4, Sc. 6*

And when a woman woos, what woman's son
Will sourly leave her till she have prevailed?

> — *Sonnet 41*

If there sit twelve women at a table, let a dozen of them be — as they are.

> — *Timon of Athens, Act 3, Sc. 6*

O curse of marriage, that we can call these delicate creatures ours, and not their appetites.

> — *Othello, Act 3, Sc. 3*

. . . live in pleasure . . . and taste gentlemen of all fashions.

> — *Pericles, Act 4, Sc. 2*

Mistress Quickly.

> — *Henry IV, Parts I and II*

Doll Tearsheet.

> — *Part II*

19
LAWYERS

The first thing we do, let's kill all the lawyers.
— *Henry VI, Part II, Act 4, Sc. 2*

. . . lawyers' fingers, who straight dream on fees.
— *Romeo and Juliet, Act 1, Sc. 4*

There is boundless theft in limited professions.
— *Timon of Athens, Act 4, Sc. 3*

In law, what plea so tainted and corrupt, but, being season'd with a gracious voice, obscures the show of evil?
— *Merchant of Venice, Act 3, Sc. 2*

Comest thou with deep premeditated lines, with written pamphlets studiously devised?
— *Henry VI, Part I, Act 3, Sc. 1*

All scholars, lawyers, courtiers, gentlemen they call false caterpillars . . .
— *Part II, Act 4, Sc. 4*

And will have no attorney but myself.
— *Comedy of Errors, Act 5, Sc. 1*

Which is the justice, which is the thief?
— *King Lear, Act 4, Sc. 6*

In these nice sharp quillets of the law, good faith, I am no wiser than a daw.
— *Henry VI, Part I, Act 2, Sc. 4*

Since law itself is perfect wrong . . .
— *King John, Act 3, Sc. 1*

And liberty plucks justice by the nose.
— *Measure for Measure, Act 1, Sc. 3*

. . . the subtle-shining secrecies writ in the glassy margents of such books.
— *Rape of Lucrece.*

. . . wrangling pedant . . .
— *Taming of the Shrew, Act 3, Sc.1*

Those that understood him smiled at one another and shook their heads, but for mine own part it was Greek to me.
— *Julius Caesar, Act 1, Sc. 2*

. . . the law, which is past depth to those that without heed do plunge into it.
— *Timon of Athens, Act 3, Sc. 5*

I will try confusions with him.
— *Merchant of Venice, Act 2, Sc. 2*

But thou art too fine in thy evidence.
— *All's Well that Ends Well, Act 5, Sc. 3*

Where be his quiddities now, his quillets, his cases, his tenures and his tricks?
— *Hamlet, Act 5, Sc. 1*

. . . the rusty curb of old father antic the law.
— *Henry IV, Part I, Act 1, Sc. 2*

. . . clerkly couch'd . . .
— *Henry VI, Part II, Act 3, Sc. 1*

How fiery and forward our pedant is!
— *Taming of the Shrew, Act 3, Sc. 1*

Why, brother, wherefore stand you on nice points?
— *Henry VI, Part III, Act 4, Sc. 7*

And yet, methinks, I could be well content to be mine own attorney in this case.
— *Part I, Act 5, Sc. 3*

The sad-eyed justice, with his surly hum . . .
— *Henry V, Act 1, Sc. 2*

Crack the lawyer's voice, that he may never more false title plead, nor sound his quillets shrilly.
— *Timon of Athens, Act 4, Sc. 3*

Came to the bar, where to his accusations he pleaded still not guilty, and alleged many sharp reasons to defeat the law.
— *Henry VIII, Act 2, Sc. 1*

They that dally nicely with words may quickly make them wanton.
— *Twelfth Night, Act 3, Sc. 1*

Is all your strict preciseness come to this?
— *Henry VI, Part I, Act 5, Sc. 4*

Hath a mint of phrases in his brain.
— *Love's Labour's Lost, Act 1, Sc. 1*

Which is the wiser here? Justice or iniquity?
　　　　　　　　　　— *Measure for Measure, Act 2, Sc. 1*

On the winking of authority to understand a law . . .
　　　　　　　　　　— *King John, Act 4, Sc. 2*

Justices of the peace, to call poor men before them about matters they
were not able to answer.
　　　　　　　　　　— *Henry VI, Part II, Act 4, Sc. 7*

Windy attorneys . . .
　　　　　　　　　　— *Richard III, Act 4, Sc. 4*

How shall we then dispense with that contract?
　　　　　　　　　　— *Henry VI, Part I, Act 5, Sc. 5*

When law can do no right . . .
　　　　　　　　　　— *King John, Act 3, Sc. 1*

Your answer, sir, is enigmatical.
　　　　　　　　　　— *Much Ado about Nothing, Act 5, Sc. 4*

. . . relate in high-born words . . .
　　　　　　　　　　— *Love's Labour's Lost, Act 1, Sc. 1*

It is a judgement maim'd and most imperfect . . .
　　　　　　　　　　— *Othello, Act 1, Sc. 3*

. . . our indentures tripartite are drawn . . .
　　　　　　　　　　— *Henry IV, Part I, Act 3, Sc. 1*

Why tender'st thou that paper to me, with a look untender?
　　　　　　　　　　— *Cymbeline, Act 3, Sc. 4*

Then we may go pipe for justice . . .
　　　　　　　　　　— *Titus Andronicus, Act 4, Sc. 3*

. . . his statutes, his recognizances, his fines, his double vouchers.
　　　　　　　　　　— *Hamlet, Act 5, Sc. 1*

Some flattery for this evil. — Some authority how to proceed, some tricks,
some quillets . . .
　　　　　　　　　　— *Love's Labour's Lost, Act 4, Sc. 3*

Is not this a lamentable thing, . . . that parchment, being scribbled o'er,
should undo a man?
　　　　　　　　　　— *Henry VI, Part II, Act 4, Sc. 2*

'Twill be recorded for a precedent, and many an error, by the same example, will rush into the state.

— *Merchant of Venice, Act 4, Sc. 1*

You are full of pretty answers.

— *As You Like It, Act 3, Sc. 2*

. . . his opinion, which is rotten as ever oak or stone was sound.

— *Winter's Tale, Act 2, Sc. 3*

Thieves for their robbery have authority when judges steal themselves.

— *Measure for Measure, Act 2, Sc. 2*

. . . a matter of more worth than to be dealt in by attorneyship.

— *Henry VI, Part I, Act 5, Sc. 5*

We need more light to find your meaning out.

— *Love's Labour's Lost, Act 5, Sc. 2*

. . . disguised in sober robes . . .

— *Taming of the Shrew, Act 1, Sc. 2*

Be plain, good son, and homely in thy drift.

— *Romeo and Juliet, Act 2, Sc. 3*

. . . the golden fee for which I plead . . .

— *Richard III, Act 3, Sc. 5*

20

CONFUSION

All is uneven, and everything is left at six and seven.
— *Richard II, Act 2, Sc. 2*

My mother weeping, my father wailing, my sister crying, our maid howling, our cat wringing her hands and all our house in a great perplexity.
— *Two Gentlemen of Verona, Act 2, Sc. 3*

O Time! Thou must untangle this, not I. It is too hard a knot for me to untie.
— *Twelfth Night, Act 2, Sc. 2*

Unguided days and rotten times . . .
— *Henry IV, Part II, Act 4, Sc. 4*

. . . like a tangled chain, nothing impaired but all disordered.
— *Midsummer Night's Dream, Act 5, Sc. 1*

Dire combustion and confused events.
— *Macbeth, Act 2, Sc. 3*

'Tis the time's plague, when madmen lead the blind.
— *King Lear, Act 4, Sc. 1*

All form is formless, order orderless . . .
— *King John, Act 3, Sc. 1*

But then are we in order when we are most out of order.
— *Henry VI, Part II, Act 4, Sc. 2*

. . . progress, more or less . . .
— *All's Well that Ends Well, Act 5, Sc. 3*

Some one way, some another.
— *Othello, Act 1, Sc. 1*

It is a reeling world, indeed . . .
— *Richard III, Act 3, Sc. 2*

The shoemaker should meddle with his yard and the tailor with his last, the fisher with his pencil and the painter with his nets.
— *Romeo and Juliet, Act 1, Sc. 2*

Many things, having full reference to one consent, may work contrariously.
— *Henry V, Act 1, Sc. 2*

Unquiet meals make ill digestions . . .

— *Comedy of Errors, Act 5, Sc. 4*

Nothing but inexplicable dumb shows and noise.

— *Hamlet, Act 3, Sc. 2*

Commotions, uproars, with a general taint of the whole state.

— *Henry VIII, Act 5, Sc. 3*

Where every something, being blent together, turns to a wild of nothing.

— *Merchant of Venice, Act 3, Sc. 2*

These most brisk and giddy paced times.

— *Twelfth Night, Act 2, Sc. 4*

What storm is this that blows so contrary?

— *Romeo and Juliet, Act 3, Sc. 2*

What halloing and what stir is this today?

— *Two Gentlemen of Verona, Act 5, Sc. 4*

I am amazed, methinks, and lose my way among the thorns and dangers of this world.

— *King John, Act 4, Sc. 3*

Here's a maze trod, indeed, through forth-rights and meanders . . .

— *The Tempest, Act 3, Sc. 3*

. . . with most admired disorder.

— *Macbeth, Act 3, Sc. 4*

Blows dust in others' eyes . . .

— *Pericles, Act 1, Sc. 1*

When two authorities are up, neither supreme, how soon confusion may enter.

— *Coriolanus, Act 3, Sc. 1*

All torment, trouble, wonder and amazement inhabits here.

— *The Tempest, Act 5, Sc. 1*

What a caterwauling do you keep here!

— *Twelfth Night, Act 2, Sc. 3*

. . . have sent a dozen sequent messengers this very night at one another's heels.

— *Othello, Act 1, Sc. 2*

. . . swearing and stern looks, diffused attire and everything that seems unnatural.

— *Henry V, Act 5, Sc. 2*

Hounds and echo in conjuction . . .

— *Midsummer Night's Dream, Act 4, Sc. 1*

What means this scene of rude impatience?

— *Richard III, Act 2, Sc. 2*

What error drives our eyes and ears amiss?

— *Comedy of Errors, Act 2, Sc. 2*

. . . this distracted globe.

— *Hamlet, Act 1, Sc. 5*

His industry is upstairs and downstairs.

— *Henry IV, Part I, Act 2, Sc. 4*

. . . these affairs, thus thrust disorderly into my hands.

— *Richard II, Act 2, Sc. 2*

. . . machinations, hollowness, treachery and all ruinous disorders.

— *King Lear, Act 1, Sc. 2*

What mischiefs work the wicked ones, heaping confusion on their own heads thereby.

— *Henry VI, Part II, Act 2, Sc. 1*

Now powers from home and discontents at home meet in one line, and vast confusion waits.

— *King John, Act 4, Sc. 3*

O, what a scene of foolery have I seen.

— *Love's Labour's Lost, Act 4, Sc. 3*

. . . unquiet wrangling days.

— *Richard III, Act 2, Sc. 4*

. . . hence grew the general wreck and massacre.

— *Henry VI, Part I, Act 1, Sc. 1*

What relish is this? How runs the stream? Or I am mad, or else this is a dream.

— *Twelfth Night, Act 4, Sc. 1*

Hostility and civil tumult reigns.

— *King John, Act 4, Sc. 2*

The times and titles now are alter'd strangely.
> — *Henry VIII, Act 4, Sc. 2*

Mercy o' me, what a multitude are here! . . . There's a trim rabble let in, are all these your faithful friends o' the suburbs?
> — *Act 5, Sc. 4*

. . . the scambling and unquiet time.
> — *Henry V, Act 1, Sc. 1*

The time itself unsorted.
> — *Henry IV, Part I, Act 2, Sc. 3*

The seasons change their manners, as the year had found some months asleep and leap'd them over.
> — *Part II, Act 4, Sc. 4*

Let's follow, to see the end of this ado.
> — *Taming of the Shrew, Act 5, Sc. 1*

My thoughts are whirled like a potter's wheel; I know not where I am, nor what I do.
> — *Henry VI, Part I, Act 1, Sc. 5*

How got they in . . . ? — Alas, I know not, how gets the tide in?
> — *Henry VIII, Act 5, Sc. 4*

The frame and huge foundation of the earth shaked like a coward.
> — *Henry IV, Part I, Act 3, Sc. 1*

. . . such a sore of time should seek a plaster . . .
> — *King John, Act 5, Sc. 2*

How sour sweet music is, when time is broke and no proportion kept!
> — *Richard II, Act 5, Sc. 5*

21
FLATTERERS

God hath given you one face, and you make yourselves another.
— *Hamlet, Act 3, Sc. 1*

Every man will be thy friend,
Whilst thou hast wherewith to spend.

— *Passionate Pilgrim*

. . . The tongues of soothers . . .
— *Henry IV, Part I, Act 4, Sc. 1*

But when I tell him he hates flatterers, he says he does, being then most
flattered.
— *Julius Caesar, Act 2, Sc. 1*

What things in the world canst thou nearest compare to thy flatterers?
— Women nearest; but men, men are the things themselves.
— *Timon of Athens, Act 4, Sc. 3*

Think not I flatter, for I swear I do not.
— *Two Gentlemen of Verona, Act 4, Sc. 3*

A courtier, which could say, "God morrow, sweet lord! How dost thou,
sweet lord?"
— *Hamlet, Act 5, Sc. 1*

. . . false-faced soothing . . .
— *Coriolanus, Act 1, Sc. 9*

The learned pate ducks to the golden fool.
— *Timon of Athens, Act 4, Sc. 3*

I should fear those that dance before me now would one day stamp upon
me; 't has been done.
— *Timon of Athens, Act 1, Sc. 2*

Why, what a candy deal of courtesy this fawning greyhound then did
proffer me!
— *Henry IV, Part I, Act 1, Sc. 3*

. . . the petty traffickers, that curt'sy to them, do them reverence.
— *Merchant of Venice, Act 1, Sc. 1*

'Twas never merry world, since lowly feigning was called compliment.
— *Twelfth Night, Act 3, Sc. 1*

Nice customs curtsy to great kings.

— *Henry V, Act 5, Sc. 2*

When Signior Sooth here does proclaim a peace, he flatters you, makes war upon your life.

— *Pericles, Act 1, Sc. 2*

The glass-faced flatterer . . .

— *Timon of Athens, Act 1, Sc. 1*

I do profess that for your highness' good I ever labour'd more than mine own . . .

— *Henry VIII, Act 3, Sc. 2*

The painted flourish of your praise . . .

— *Love's Labour's Lost, Act 2, Sc. 1*

Flatter and praise, commend, extol their graces . . .

— *Two Gentlemen of Verona, Act 3, Sc. 1*

He that loves to be flattered is worthy of the flatterer.

— *Timon of Athens, Act 1, Sc. 1*

Yet for necessity of present life, I must show out a flag and sign of love, which is indeed but sign.

— *Othello, Act 1, Sc. 1*

I do fawn on men and hug them hard, and after scandal them . . .

— *Julius Caesar, Act 1, Sc. 2*

You were ever good at sudden commendations . . . But know, I come not to hear such flattery now, and in my presence; they are too thin and bare to hide offences.

— *Henry VIII, Act 5, Sc. 3*

Thy flatterers yet wear silk, drink wine, lie soft, hug their diseased perfumes . . .

— *Timon of Athens, Act 4, Sc. 3*

. . . flatter and speak fair, smile in men's faces, smooth, deceive and cog, duck with French nods and apish courtesy . . .

— *Richard III, Act 1, Sc. 3*

When the means are gone that buy this praise, the breath is gone whereof this praise is made.

— *Timon of Athens, Act 2, Sc. 2*

That which melteth fools, I mean, sweet words, low-crooked courtesies and base spaniel fawning.

— *Julius Caesar, Act 3, Sc. 1*

When he fawns, he bites . . .
                                    — *Richard III, Act 1, Sc. 3*

Smooth not thy tongue with filed talk.
                                    — *Passionate Pilgrim*

He water'd his new plants with dews of flattery . . .
                                    — *Coriolanus, Act 5, Sc. 6*

O place and greatness, millions of false eyes are stuck upon thee!
                                    — *Measure for Measure, Act 4, Sc. 1*

How many tales to please me hath she coined.
                                    — *Passionate Pilgrim*

No visor does become black villany so well as soft and tender flattery.
                                    — *Pericles, Act 4, Sc. 4*

He plies the Duke at morning and at night.
                                    — *Merchant of Venice, Act 3, Sc. 2*

You play the spaniel, and think with wagging of your tongue to win me.
                                    — *Henry VIII, Act 5, Sc. 3*

Sweet flattery! Then she loves but me alone.
                                    — *Sonnet 42*

My friends . . . praise me and make an ass of me; now, my foes tell me
    plainly I am an ass; so that by my foes, sir, I profit in the knowledge of
    myself, and by my friends I am abused.
                                    — *Twelfth Night, Act 5, Sc. 1*

They that fawn'd on him before, use his company no more.
                                    — *Passionate Pilgrim*

. . . flatter thee in thoughts unlikely.
                                    — *Venus and Adonis*

a sponge . . . that soaks up the king's countenance, his rewards, his
    authorities.
                                    — *Hamlet, Act 4, Sc. 2*

Their base throats tear with giving him glory.
                                    — *Coriolanus, Act 5, Sc. 6*

Poor wretches that depend on greatness' favour . . .
                                    — *Cymbeline, Act 5, Sc. 4*

Dismiss your vows, your feigned tears, your flattery . . .
                                    — *Venus and Adonis*

A back-friend, a shoulder-clapper . . .

— *Comedy of Errors, Act 4, Sc. 2*

But manhood is melted into courtesies, valour into compliment, and men are only turned into tongue, and trim ones, too.

— *Much Ado about Nothing, Act 4, Sc. 1*

. . . those soft parts of conversation that chamberers have . . .

— *Othello, Act 3, Sc. 3*

If I prove honey-mouth'd, let my tongue blister . . .

— *Winter's Tale, Act 2, Sc. 2*

There are certain signs to know,
Faithful friend from flattering foe.

— *Passionate Pilgrim*

. . . dialogue of compliment . . .

— *King John, Act 1, Sc. 1*

. . . ceremonious courtiers . . .

— *Troilus and Cressida, Act 1, Sc. 3*

22

INSULTS, THREATS AND MALEDICTIONS

I have now found thee; when I lose thee again, I care not.
— *All's Well that Ends Well, Act 2, Sc. 3*

Methink'st, thou art a general offence . . .
— *Act 2, Sc. 3*

Who's his tailor?
— *Act 2, Sc. 3*

You give me most egregious indignity. — Ay, with all my heart, and thou
art worthy of it.
— *Act 2, Sc. 3*

Thy casement I need not open, for I look through thee.
— *Act 2, Sc. 3*

If I were but two hours younger, I'ld beat thee.
— *Act 2, Sc. 3*

There can be no kernel in this light nut; the soul of this man is in his
clothes.
— *Act 2, Sc. 5*

The most infectious pestilence upon thee!
— *Antony and Cleopatra, Act 2, Sc. 5*

Thou shalt be whipp'd with wire, and stew'd in brine, smarting in lingering
pickle.
— *Act 2, Sc. 5*

Who might be your mother . . . ?
— *As You Like It, Act 3, Sc. 5*

I was seeking for a fool when I found you.
— *Act 3, Sc. 2*

'Tis such fools as you that makes the world full of ill-favoured children.
— *Act 3, Sc. 5*

I will kill thee a hundred and fifty ways; therefore tremble, and depart.
— *Act 5, Sc. 1*

Now I do frown on thee with all my heart.
— *Act 3, Sc. 5*

'Tis pity that thou livest to walk where any honest men resort.
— *Comedy of Errors*, Act 5, Sc. 1

All the contagion of the south lie on you . . . !
— *Coriolanus*, Act 1, Sc. 4

Your misery increase with your age!
— *Act 5, Sc. 2*

Your wit will not so soon out as another man's will; 'tis strongly wedged up in a blockhead.
— *Act 2, Sc. 3*

They lie deadly that tell you you have good faces.
— *Act 2, Sc. 1*

By the very truth of it, I care not for you.
— *Cymbeline*, Act 2, Sc. 3

War and confusion . . . pronounce I 'gainst thee.
— *Act 3, Sc. 1*

Your life . . . must shuffle for itself.
— *Act 5, Sc. 5*

. . . measured how long a fool you were upon the ground.
— *Act 1, Sc. 2*

. . . the hugeness of your unworthy thinking.
— *Act 1, Sc. 4*

I shall unfold equal discourtesy to your best kindness.
— *Act 2, Sc. 3*

Assume a virtue, if you have it not.
— *Hamlet*, Act 3, Sc. 4

Do thou amend thy face, and I'll amend my life.
— *Henry IV, Part I*, Act 3, Sc. 3

There's neither honesty, manhood, nor good fellowship in thee.
— *Act 1, Sc. 2*

There's no room for faith, truth, nor honesty in this bosom of thine; it is all filled up with guts and midriff.
— *Act 3, Sc. 3*

. . . or you shall hear in such a kind from me as will displease you.
— *Act 1, Sc. 3*

What wind blew you hither?
>
> — *Henry IV, Part II, Act 5, Sc. 3*

Whether I shall ever see thee again or no, there is nobody cares.
>
> — *Act 2, Sc. 4*

To punish you by the heels would amend the attention of your ears.
>
> — *Act 1, Sc. 2*

I'll tickle your catastrophe.
>
> — *Act 2, Sc. 1*

You speak . . . now you know not what.
>
> — *Act 4, Sc. 1*

I will not excuse you; you shall not be excused; excuses shall not be admitted; there is no excuse shall serve.
>
> — *Act 5, Sc. 1*

I should be angry with you, if the time were convenient.
>
> — *Henry V, Act 4, Sc. 1*

I have an humour to knock you indifferently well.
>
> — *Act 2, Sc. 1*

I will cut thy throat, one time or another, in fair terms.
>
> — *Act 2, Sc. 1*

Guard thy head, for I intend to have it ere long.
>
> — *Henry VI, Part I, Act 1, Sc. 3*

May never glorious sun reflex his beams
Upon the country where you make abode,
But darkness and the gloomy shade of death
Environ you, till mischief and despair
Drive you to break your necks or hang yourselves.
>
> — *Act 5, Sc. 4*

I'll note you in my book of memory . . .
>
> — *Act 2, Sc. 4*

Were mine eye-balls into bullets turn'd,
That I in rage might shoot them at your faces!
>
> — *Act 4, Sc. 7*

We will meet; to thy cost, be sure.
>
> — *Act 1, Sc. 3*

There's two of you; the devil make a third!
>
> — *Part II, Act 3, Sc. 2*

Thy mother took into her blameful bed some stern untutor'd churl, . . .
whose fruit thou art . . .
— *Henry VI, Part II, Act 3, Sc. 2*

I'll make thee eat iron like an ostrich, and swallow my sword like a great
pin . . .
— *Act 4, Sc. 10*

Could I come near your beauty with my nails, I'ld set my ten commandments in your face.
— *Act 1, Sc. 3*

Thou art as opposite to every good as the Antipodes are unto us.
— *Part III, Act 1, Sc. 4*

But that I hate thee deadly, I should lament thy miserable state.
— *Act 1, Sc. 4*

I will not do thee so much ease.
— *Act 5, Sc. 5*

His curses and his blessings touch me alike; they're breath I not believe in.
— *Henry VIII, Act 2, Sc. 2*

. . . I'll make your head ache.
— *Act 5, Sc. 4*

All goodness is poison to thy stomach.
— *Act 3, Sc. 2*

This good man — few of you deserve that title.
— *Act 5, Sc. 3*

Will you dine with me tomorrow? — Ay, if I be alive, and your mind hold,
and your dinner worth the eating.
— *Julius Caesar, Act 1, Sc. 2*

Tear him to pieces, he's a conspirator. — I am Cinna, the poet . . . — Tear
him for his bad verses.
— *Act 3, Sc. 3*

O, fair affliction, peace!
— *King John, Act 3, Sc. 4*

Thou shalt rue this hour within the hour.
— *Act 3, Sc. 1*

Thou dost shame thy mother and wound her honour . . .
— *Act 1, Sc. 1*

There is not yet so ugly a fiend of hell as thou shalt be . . .
— *King John, Act 4, Sc. 3*

He means to recompense the pains you take by cutting off your heads.
— *Act 5, Sc. 4*

A plague upon your epileptic visage!
— *King Lear, Act 2, Sc. 2*

. . . son and heir of a mongrel bitch . . .
— *Act 2, Sc. 2*

I have seen better faces in my time than stands on any shoulder that I see before me at this instant.
— *Act 2, Sc. 2*

Who's there, besides foul weather?
— *Act 3, Sc. 1*

You are not worth the dust which the rude wind blows in your face.
— *Act 4, Sc. 2*

What are you? your name, your quality?
— *Act 5, Sc. 3*

Prescribe not to us our duties.
— *Act 1, Sc. 1*

By the north pole, I do challenge thee.
— *Love's Labour's Lost, Act 5, Sc. 2*

Go, whip thy gig.
— *Act 5, Sc. 1*

Since you are strangers . . . we'll not be nice.
— *Act 5, Sc. 2*

O Lord, sir, it were pity you should get your living by reckoning, sir.
— *Act 5, Sc. 2*

Thou halfpenny purse of wit . . .
— *Act 5, Sc. 1*

In the catalogue ye go for men . . .
— *Macbeth, Act 3, Sc. 1*

. . . thou cream-faced loon. Where got'st that goose look?
— *Act 5, Sc. 3*

I'll teach you how you shall arraign your conscience . . .
> — *Measure for Measure*, Act 2, Sc. 3

All the accommodations that thou bear'st are nursed by baseness.
> — *Act 3, Sc. 1*

Thou art good velvet; thou'rt a three-piled piece, I warrant thee.
> — *Act 1, Sc. 2*

. . . thou mayst have leave to hang thyself.
> — *Merchant of Venice*, Act 4, Sc. 1

Be assured thou shalt have justice, more than thou desirest.
> — *Act 4, Sc. 1*

I hope, upon familiarity will grow more contempt.
> — *Merry Wives of Windsor*, Act 1, Sc. 1

I have matter in my head against you.
> — *Act 1, Sc. 1*

I am   for swearing to gentlemen my friends, you were good
    soldiers all fellows . . .
> — *Act 2, Sc. 2*

I do begin to perceive that I am made an ass. — Ay, and an ox too; both
the proofs are extant.
> — *Act 5, Sc. 5*

Neighbours, you are tedious.
> — *Much Ado about Nothing*, Act 3, Sc. 5

Is my lord well, that he doth speak so wide?
> — *Act 4, Sc. 1*

. . . you be a cursing hypocrite once, you must be looked to.
> — *Act 5, Sc. 1*

Are you yet living?
> — *Act 1, Sc. 1*

Scratching could not make it worse . . . such a face as yours . . .
> — *Act 1, Sc. 1*

Heaven truly knows that thou art false as hell.
> — *Othello*, Act 4, Sc. 2

O, you are well tuned now, but I'll set down the pegs that make this
music.
> — *Act 2, Sc. 1*

Let's all go visit him; Pray God we may make haste, and come too late!
— *Richard II*, Act 1, Sc. 4

Have done thy charm . . .
— *Richard III*, Act 1, Sc. 3

I do love thee so, that I will shortly send thy soul to heaven.
— *Act 1, Sc. 1*

Out of my sight! Thou dost infect my eyes.
— *Act 1, Sc. 2*

What comfortable hour canst thou name, that ever graced me in thy company?
— *Act 4, Sc. 4*

A plague o' both your houses . . .
— *Romeo and Juliet*, Act 3, Sc. 1

Wife, we scarce thought us blest that God had lent us but this only child; but now I see this one is one too much.
— *Act 3, Sc. 5*

When nature calls thee to be gone, what acceptable audit canst thou leave?
— *Sonnet 4*

. . . that thou none lovest is most evident.
— *Sonnet 10*

. . . thou among the wastes of time must go.
— *Sonnet 12*

For what care I who calls me well or ill . . . ?
— *Sonnet 112*

In so profound abysm I throw all care of others' voices.
— *Sonnet 112*

Well have you heard, but something hard of hearing.
— *Taming of the Shrew*, Act 2, Sc. 1

Look what I speak, or do, or think to do, you are still crossing it.
— *Act 4, Sc. 3*

For I am he am born to tame you.
— *Act 2, Sc. 1*

Are not the streets as free for me as for you?
— *Act 1, Sc. 2*

. . . thou dost give me pains . . .
— *The Tempest, Act 1, Sc. 2*

By this hand, I will supplant some of your teeth.
— *Act 3, Sc. 2*

For this, be sure, tonight thou shalt have cramps . . .
— *Act 1, Sc. 2*

A southwest blow on ye and blister you all o'er!
— *Act 1, Sc. 2*

Lingering perdition . . . shall step by step attend you . . .
— *Act 3, Sc. 3*

You're a dog. — Thy mother's of my generation . . .
— *Timon of Athens, Act 1, Sc. 1*

If thou wilt curse, thy father, that poor rag, must be thy subject, who in spite put stuff to some she beggar and compounded thee poor rogue hereditary.
— *Act 4, Sc. 3*

I'll beat thee, but I should infect my hands.
— *Act 4, Sc. 3*

How does your mistress? — She's e'en now setting on water to scald such chickens as you are.
— *Act 2, Sc. 2*

I am gone — . . . Thou outrun'st grace.
— *Act 2, Sc. 2*

Most smiling, smooth, detested parasites, courteous destroyers, affable wolves, meek bears . . .
— *Act 3, Sc. 6*

Excellent workman! Thou canst not paint a man so bad as is thyself.
— *Act 5, Sc. 1*

I know thee too, and more than that I know thee I not desire to know.
— *Act 4, Sc. 3*

What folly I commit, I dedicate to you.
— *Troilus and Cressida, Act 3, Sc. 5*

That that likes not you pleases me best.
— *Act 5, Sc. 2*

I shall be plagued. — Farewell till then.
                    — Troilus and Cressida, Act 5, Sc. 2

Thy horse will sooner con an oration than thou learn a prayer without book.
                    — Act 2, Sc. 1

Though you bite so sharp at reasons, you are so empty of them.
                    — Act 2, Sc. 2

What, blushing still? Have you not done talking yet?
                    — Act 3, Sc. 2

Thou art bought and sold among those of any wit.
                    — Act 2, Sc. 1

Thou hast no more brain than I have in mine elbows.
                    — Act 2, Sc. 1

In my conscience, sir, I do not care for you.
                    — Twelfth Night, Act 3, Sc. 1

Go shake your ears.
                    — Act 2, Sc. 3

Infirmity, that decays the wise, doth ever make the better fool. — God send you, sir, a speedy infirmity, for the better increasing your folly.
                    — Act 1, Sc. 5

. . . such impossible passages of grossness.
                    — Act 3, Sc. 2

You are well derived. — True; from a gentleman to a fool.
                    — Two Gentlemen of Verona, Act 5, Sc. 2

O exceeding puppet!
                    — Act 2, Sc. 1

23

MADNESS

. . . there is such disorder in my wit.
— *King John, Act 3, Sc. 4*

Thou art essentially mad, without seeming so.
— *Henry IV, Part I, Act 2, Sc. 4*

. . . as if some planet had unwitted men.
— *Othello, Act 2, Sc. 3*

. . . these boiled brains.
— *Winter's Tale, Act 3, Sc. 3*

Unbonneted he runs.
— *King Lear, Act 3, Sc. 1*

Madmen have no ears. — How should they, when wise men have no eyes?
— *Romeo and Juliet, Act 3, Sc. 3*

Infected minds . . .
— *Macbeth, Act 5, Sc. 1*

. . . from his reason fall'n . . .
— *Hamlet, Act 2, Sc. 2*

In most uneven and distracted manner.
— *Measure for Measure, Act 4, Sc. 4*

He takes false shadows for true substances.
— *Titus Andronicus, Act 3, Sc. 2*

A lunatic lean-witted fool.
— *Richard II, Act 2, Sc. 1*

Now see that noble and most sovereign reason, like sweet bells jangled, out
of tune and harsh.
— *Hamlet, Act 3, Sc. 1*

How comes it that thou art then estranged from thyself?
— *Comedy of Errors, Act 2, Sc. 2*

They say, poor gentleman, he's much distract . . .
— *Twelfth Night, Act 5, Sc. 1*

. . . deprive your sovereignty of reason . . .
— *Hamlet, Act 1, Sc. 4*

Some strange commotion is in his brain . . .
— *Henry VIII, Act 3, Sc. 2*

109

He raves in saying nothing.

— *Troilus and Cressida, Act 3, Sc. 3*

. . . grown incapable of reasonable affairs?

— *Winter's Tale, Act 4, Sc. 4*

Such stuff as madmen tongue, and brain not.

— *Cymbeline, Act 5, Sc. 4*

You only speak from your distracted soul.

— *Timon of Athens, Act 3, Sc. 4*

A grievous sickness . . . that makes him gasp and stare and catch the air.

— *Henry VI, Part II, Act 3, Sc. 2*

The lunatic, the lover and the poet . . .

— *Midsummer Night's Dream, Act 5, Sc. 1*

Your looks are pale and wild.

— *Romeo and Juliet, Act 5, Sc. 1*

. . . turbulent and dangerous lunacy.

— *Hamlet, Act 3, Sc. 1*

There is a mutiny in 's mind.

— *Henry VIII, Act 3, Sc. 2*

When the age is in, the wit is out.

— *Much Ado about Nothing, Act 3, Sc. 5*

Mine hair be fixed on end, as one distract . . .

— *Henry VI, Part II, Act 3, Sc. 2*

. . . with wrinkled brows, with nods, with rolling eyes.

— *King John, Act 4, Sc. 2*

He talks at random . . .

— *Henry VI, Part I, Act 5, Sc. 3*

To be wise and love exceeds man's might; that dwells with gods above.

— *Troilus and Cressida, Act 3, Sc. 2*

He that is giddy thinks the world turns round.

— *Taming of the Shrew, Act 5, Sc. 2*

Sense is apoplex'd . ..

— *Hamlet, Act 3, Sc. 4*

I think his understanding is bereft.

— *Henry VI, Part III, Act 2, Sc. 6*

They devour their reason . . .

— *The Tempest, Act 5, Sc. 1*

You flow to great distraction.

— *Troilus and Cressida, Act 5, Sc. 2*

The o'ergrowth of some complexion, oft breaking down the pales and forts of reason.

— *Hamlet, Act 1, Sc. 4*

His wits begin to unsettle.

— *King Lear, Act 3, Sc. 4*

I never heard a passion so confused, so strange, outrageous and so variable . . .

— *Merchant of Venice, Act 2, Sc. 8*

Methinks his words do from such passion fly, that he believes himself; so do not I.

— *Twelfth Night, Act 3, Sc. 4*

. . . not in his perfect wits . . .

— *Comedy of Errors, Act 5, Sc. 1*

. . . all knit up in their distractions.

— *The Tempest, Act 3, Sc. 3*

Untuned and jarring senses . . .

— *King Lear, Act 4, Sc. 7*

. . . the ignorant fumes that mantle their clearer reason.

— *The Tempest, Act 5, Sc. 1*

Have we eaten on the insane root that takes reason prisoner?

— *Macbeth, Act 1, Sc. 3*

Many legions of strange fantasies.

— *King John, Act 5, Sc. 7*

. . . with some diffused song.

— *Merry Wives of Windsor, Act 4, Sc. 4*

It is the very error of the moon; she comes more nearer earth than she was wont and makes men mad.

— *Othello, Act 5, Sc. 2*

. . . a false creation, proceeding from the heat-oppressed brain.

— *Macbeth, Act 2, Sc. 1*

These are but wild and whirling words.

— *Hamlet, Act 1, Sc. 5*

24
INGRATITUDE

The little number of your doubtful friends.

— *King John, Act 5, Sc. 1*

Blow, blow, thou winter wind, thou art not so unkind as man's ingratitude.

— *As You Like It, Act 2, Sc. 7*

Christ . . . in twelve found truth in all but one; I, in twelve thousand, none.

— *Richard II, Act 4, Sc. 1*

For these my present friends, as they are to me nothing, so in nothing bless them, and to nothing are they welcome.

— *Timon of Athens, Act 3, Sc. 6*

What might'st thou do . . . were all thy children kind and natural!

— *Henry V, Act 2, Prologue*

Now I dare not say I have one friend alive . . .

— *Two Gentlemen of Verona, Act 5, Sc. 4*

Thou art so leaky that we must leave thee to thy sinking.

— *Antony and Cleopatra, Act 3, Sc. 13*

There's never a one of you but trusts a knave that mightily deceives you.

— *Timon of Athens, Act 5, Sc. 1*

Rebellion lay in his way, and he found it.

— *Henry IV, Part I, Act 5, Sc. 1*

Good deeds past, which are devour'd as fast as they are made, forgot as soon as done.

— *Troilus and Cressida, Act 3, Sc. 3*

Grant I may never prove so fond.
To trust man on his oath or bond,
Or a harlot for her weeping,
Or a dog that seems a-sleeping,
Or a keeper with my freedom,
Or my friends if I should need 'em.

— *Timon of Athens, Act 1, Sc. 2*

Chosen out of the gross band of the unfaithful.

— *As You Like It, Act 4, Sc. 1*

How sharper than a serpent's tooth it is to have a thankless child.
— *King Lear, Act 1, Sc. 4*

Walk aside the true folk, and let the traitors stay.
— *Love's Labour's Lost, Act 4, Sc. 3*

Left and abandon'd of his velvet friends.
— *As You Like It, Act 2, Sc. 1*

Et tu, Brute?
— *Julius Caesar, Act 3, Sc. 1*

Those you make friends and give your hearts to, when they once perceive the least rub in your fortunes, fall away like water from ye, never found again but where they mean to sink ye.
— *Henry VIII, Act 2, Sc. 1*

They confess toward thee forgetfulness too general, gross . . .
— *Timon of Athens, Act 5, Sc. 1*

Oft good turns are shuffled off with such uncurrent pay.
— *Twelfth Night, Act 3, Sc. 3*

Mud not the fountain that gave drink to thee.
— *Rape of Lucrece*

It pleased your majesty to turn your looks of favour from myself and all our house; and yet I must remember you, my lord, we were the first and dearest of your friends.
— *Henry IV, Part I, Act 5, Sc. 1*

. . . cannot cover the monstrous bulk of this ingratitude with any size of words.
— *Timon of Athens, Act 5, Sc. 1*

Being fed by us you used us.
— *Henry IV, Part I, Act 5, Sc. 1*

. . . inconstant and damnable ingrateful.
— *Winter's Tale, Act 3, Sc. 2*

We come to do you service and you think we are ruffians.
— *Othello, Act 1, Sc. 1*

His dishonesty appears in leaving his friend here in necessity and denying him.
— *Twelfth Night, Act 3, Sc. 4*

Like the bee, culling from every flower the virtuous sweets, our thighs pack'd with wax, our mouths with honey, we bring it to the hive; and, like bees, are murder'd for our pains.

— *Henry IV, Part II, Act 4, Sc. 5*

They have all been touch'd and found base metal, for they have all denied him.

— *Timon of Athens, Act 3, Sc. 3*

This was the most unkindest cut of all.

— *Julius Caesar, Act 3, Sc. 2*

When Fortune in her shift and change of mood spurns down her late beloved, all of his dependents which labour'd after him to the mountain's top, even on their knees and hands, let him slip down, not one accompanying his declining foot.

— *Timon of Athens, Act 1, Sc. 1*

Art thou so hasty? I have stay'd for thee, God knows, in anguish, pain and agony.

— *Richard III, Act 4, Sc. 4*

. . . a nest of hollow bosoms . . .

— *Henry V, Act 2, Prologue*

Words are easy, like the wind,
Faithful friends are hard to find.

— *Passionate Pilgrim*

Many a duteous and knee-crooking knave . . . wears out his time, much like his master's ass, for nought but provender, and when he's old, cashier'd.

— *Othello, Act 1, Sc. 1*

. . . like favourites, made proud by princes, that advance their pride against that power that bred it.

— *Much Ado about Nothing, Act 3, Sc. 1*

Hath he so long held out with me untired, and stops he now for breath?

— *Richard III, Act 4, Sc. 2*

For their tongues to be silent . . . were a kind of ingrateful injury.

— *Coriolanus, Act 2, Sc. 2*

You are fool'd, discarded and shook off by him for whom these shames ye underwent?

— *Henry IV, Part I, Act 1, Sc. 3*

A friend should bear his friend's infirmities . . . — I do not like your faults.
— A friendly eye could never see such faults.

> — *Julius Caesar, Act 4, Sc. 3*

That sir which serves and seeks for gain,
And follows but for form,
Will pack when it begins to rain,
And leave thee in the storm.

> — *King Lear, Act 2, Sc. 4*

. . . coming too short of thanks . . .

> — *Love's Labour's Lost, Act 5, Sc. 2*

Rewards he my true service with such deep contempt?

> — *Richard III, Act 4, Sc. 2*

I am sure . . . this kindness merits thanks. What, not a word?

> — *Taming of the Shrew, Act 4, Sc. 3*

Men in rage strike those that wish them best.

> — *Othello, Act 2, Sc. 3*

What man didst thou ever know unthrift that was beloved after his means?

> — *Timon of Athens, Act 4, Sc. 3*

A word, Lucilius, how he received you. —
With courtesy and with respect enough, but not . . . with such free and
   friendly conference, as he hath used of old. —
Thou hast described a hot friend cooling; ever note, Lucilius, when love
   begins to sicken and decay, it useth an enforced ceremony.

> — *Julius Caesar, Act 4, Sc. 2*

. . . rich left heirs that let their fathers lie without a monument.

> — *Cymbeline, Act 4, Sc. 2*

. . . mouth-friends!

> — *Timon of Athens, Act 3, Sc. 6*

25

RECKLESSNESS

. . . like an angry hive of bees . . . , scatter up and down and care not who
they sting . . .
— *Henry VI, Part II, Act 3, Sc. 2*

Come, where is this young gallant that is so desirous to lie with his mother
earth?
— *As You Like It, Act 1, Sc. 2*

Our coffers, with too great a court and liberal largess, are grown somewhat
light.
— *Richard II, Act 1, Sc. 4*

That's a valiant flea that dare eat his breakfast on the lip of a lion.
— *Henry V, Act 3, Sc. 7*

I am sorry one so learned and so wise . . . should slip
heat of blood, and lack of temper'd judgement after
— *Measure for Measure, Sc. 1*

I would there were no age between ten and three-and-twenty, or that youth
would sleep out the rest, for there is nothing in the between but getting
wenches with child, wronging the ancientry, stealing, fighting . . .
— *Winter's Tale, Act 3, Sc. 3*

Thus honest fools lay out their wealth on court'sies.
— *Timon of Athens, Act 1, Sc. 2*

. . . whose large style agrees not with the leanness of his purse.
— *Henry VI, Part II, Act 1, Sc. 1*

I can get no remedy against this consumption of the purse; borrowing only
lingers and lingers it out, but the disease is incurable.
— *Henry IV, Part II, Act 1, Sc. 2*

. . . wild dedication of yourselves to unpath'd waters, undream'd shores.
— *Winter's Tale, Act 4, Sc. 4*

These fellows ran about the streets, crying confusion.
— *Coriolanus, Act 4, Sc. 6*

And whither fly the gnats but to the sun?
— *Henry VI, Part III, Act 2, Sc. 6*

We have kiss'd away kingdoms and provinces.
— *Antony and Cleopatra, Act 3, Sc. 10*

Mend your speech a little, lest it may mar your fortunes.

— *King Lear, Act 1, Sc. 1*

You must confine yourself within the modest limits of order.

— *Twelfth Night, Act 1, Sc. 3*

It is too rash, too unadvised, too sudden . . .

— *Romeo and Juliet, Act 2, Sc. 2*

Hot and hasty, like a Scotch jig, and full as fantastical . . .

— *Much Ado about Nothing, Act 2, Sc. 1*

Why, what a madcap hath heaven lent us here!

— *King John, Act 1, Sc. 1*

Since of your lives you set so slight a valuation . . .

— *Cymbeline, Act 4, Sc. 4*

As thriftless sons (spend) their scraping fathers' gold.

— *Richard II, Act 5, Sc. 3*

. . . felt a fever of the mad, and play'd some tricks of desperation.

— *The Tempest, Act 1, Sc. 2*

My thoughts were like unbridled children, grown too headstrong for their mother.

— *Troilus and Cressida, Act 3, Sc. 2*

Your means are very slender, and your waste is great.

— *Henry IV, Part II, Act 1, Sc. 2*

You should be ruled and led by some discretion that discerns your state better than you yourself.

— *King Lear, Act 2, Sc. 4*

. . . all too confident to give admittance to a thought of fear.

— *Henry IV, Part II, Act 4, Sc. 1*

. . . negligence, not weighing well the end . . .

— *Winter's Tale, Act 1, Sc. 2*

. . . to set so rich a main on the nice hazard of one doubtful hour?

— *Henry IV, Part I, Act 4, Sc. 1*

. . . to waste his borrow'd purse.

— *Merchant of Venice, Act 2, Sc. 5*

Beggars mounted run their horse to death.

— *Henry VI, Part III, Act 1, Sc. 4*

Our rash faults make trivial price of serious things we have.
— *All's Well that Ends Well, Act 5, Sc. 3*

The days are wax'd shorter with him; you must consider that a prodigal course is like the sun's; but not, like his, recoverable.
— *Timon of Athens, Act 3, Sc. 4*

We hear this fearful tempest sing, yet seek no shelter to avoid the storm.
— *Richard II, Act 2, Sc. 1*

. . . a gentleman that have spent much . . .
— *Merry Wives of Windsor, Act 2, Sc. 2*

I find my tongue is too foolhardy . . .
— *All's Well that Ends Well, Act 4, Sc. 1*

. . . upstart unthrifts . . .
— *Richard II, Act 2, Sc. 3*

So far as my coin would stretch; and where it would not, I have used my credit.
— *Henry IV, Part I, Act 1, Sc. 2*

Lives like a drunken sailor on a mast, ready, with every nod, to tumble down . . .
— *Richard III, Act 3, Sc. 4*

26
BEAUTIFUL PEOPLE

The wealthy curled darlings of our nation . . .

— *Othello, Act 1, Sc. 2*

Golden lads and girls all must,
As chimney sweepers, come to dust.

— *Cymbeline, Act 4, Sc. 2*

The rich stream of lords and ladies . . .

— *Henry VIII, Act 4, Sc. 1*

But only painted, like his varnish'd friends . . .

— *Timon of Athens, Act 4, Sc. 2*

. . . whose apprehensive senses all but new things disdain.

— *All's Well that Ends Well, Act 1, Sc. 2*

In the world I fill up a place, which may be better supplied when I have
made it empty.

— *As You Like It, Act 1, Sc. 2*

. . . gilded butterflies . . .

— *King Lear, Act 5, Sc. 3*

With silken coats and caps and golden rings, with ruffs and cuffs and
fardingales and things . . .

— *Taming of the Shrew, Act 4, Sc. 3*

Our bodies are gardens, to the which our wills are gardeners; . . . either to
have it sterile with idleness or manured with industry . . .

— *Othello, Act 1, Sc. 3*

I have thought some of nature's journeymen had made men, and not made
them well, they imitated humanity so abominably.

— *Hamlet, Act 3, Sc. 2*

And never suffers matter of the world enter his thoughts, save such as do
revolve and ruminate himself . . .

— *Troilus and Cressida, Act 2, Sc. 3*

. . . the infinite flatteries that follow youth and opulency.

— *Timon of Athens, Act 5, Sc. 1*

. . . fleet the time carelessly, as they did in the golden world.

— *As You Like It, Act 1, Sc. 1*

Do not dull thy palm with entertainment . . .

— *Hamlet, Act 1, Sc. 3*

. . . the excellent foppery of the world.
— *King Lear, Act 1, Sc. 2*

What dost thou with thy best apparel on?
— *Julius Caesar, Act 1, Sc. 1*

An extravagant and wheeling stranger of here and everywhere.
— *Othello, Act 1, Sc. 1*

. . . in the perfumed chambers of the great, under the canopies of costly state, and lull'd with sound of sweetest melody.
— *Henry IV, Part II, Act 3, Sc. 1*

. . . an unperfect actor on the stage.
— *Sonnet 23*

Neither deserve, and yet are steeped in favours.
— *Cymbeline, Act 5, Sc. 4*

So quick bright things come to confusion.
— *Midsummer Night's Dream, Act 1, Sc. 1*

. . . the idle pleasures of these days.
— *Richard III, Act 1, Sc. 1*

Our graver business frowns at this levity.
— *Antony and Cleopatra, Act 2, Sc. 7*

. . . that choose by show, not learning more than the fond eye doth teach, which pries not to the interior.
— *Merchant of Venice, Act 2, Sc. 9*

A whole tribe of fops . . .
— *King Lear, Act 1, Sc. 2*

I'll be at charges for a looking-glass, and entertain some score or two of tailors, to study fashions to adorn my body; since I am crept in favour of myself . . .
— *Richard III, Act 1, Sc. 5*

Their tables were stored full, to glad the sight, and not so much to feed on as delight.
— *Pericles, Act 1, Sc. 4*

Through tatter'd clothes small vices do appear; robes and furr'd gowns hide all.
— *King Lear, Act 4, Sc. 6*

Is the jay more precious than the lark, because his feathers are more beautiful?
— *Taming of the Shrew, Act 4, Sc. 3*

Why, is not this a lamentable thing, grandsire, that we should be thus afflicted with these strange flies, these fashion-mongers, these per-donami's, who stand so much on the new form that they cannot sit at ease on the old bench?
— *Romeo and Juliet, Act 2, Sc. 4*

What needs these feasts, pomps and vain-glories?
— *Timon of Athens, Act 1, Sc. 2*

. . . men and dames so jetted and adorn'd . . .
— *Pericles, Act 1, Sc. 4*

That great baby you see there . . .
— *Hamlet, Act 2, Sc. 2*

What a sweep of vanity comes this way!
— *Timon of Athens, Act 1, Sc. 2*

For mine own part, I shall be glad to learn of noble men.
— *Julius Caesar, Act 4, Sc. 3*

How sleek and wanton ye appear . . .
— *Henry VIII, Act 3, Sc. 2*

O heaven, the vanity of wretched fools.
— *Measure for Measure, Act 5, Sc. 1*

A habitation giddy and unsure hath he that buildeth on the vulgar heart.
— *Henry IV, Part II, Act 1, Sc. 3*

If all the years were playing holidays, to sport would be as tedious as to work.
— *Henry IV, Part I, Act 1, Sc. 2*

A brittle glory shineth in this face: As brittle as the glory is the face.
— *Richard II, Act 4, Sc. 1*

Great is his comfort in this earthly vale . . .
— *Henry VI, Part II, Act 2, Sc. 1*

What a loss our ladies will have of these trim vanities!
— *Henry VIII, Act 1, Sc. 3*

Hast thou not worldly pleasure at command . . .
— *Henry VI, Part II, Act 1, Sc. 2*

Brighter than glass, and yet, as glass is, brittle.
— *Passionate Pilgrim*

. . . our travell'd gallants, that fill the court with quarrels, talk and tailors.
— *Henry VIII, Act 1, Sc. 3*

27
GREED

Bell, book and candle shall not drive me back, when gold and silver becks me to come on.

— *King John*, Act 3, Sc. 3

Master, I marvel how the fishes live in the sea. — Why, as men do a-land, the great ones eat up the little ones.

— *Pericles*, Act 2, Sc. 1

Happy always was it for that son whose father for his hoarding went to hell.

— *Henry VI, Part III*, Act 2, Sc. 2

Why, man, there be good fellows in the world . . . would take her with all her faults, and money enough.

— *Taming of the Shrew*, Act 1, Sc. 1

When thou art old and rich, thou hast neither heat, affection, limb nor beauty to make thy riches pleasant.

— *Measure for Measure*, Act 3, Sc. 1

He hath much land, and fertile . . . as I say, spacious in the possession of dirt.

— *Hamlet*, Act 5, Sc. 2

Great men have reaching hands . . .

— *Henry VI, Part II*, Act 4, Sc. 7

Put in her tender heart the aspiring flame of golden sovereignty . . .

— *Richard III*, Act 4, Sc. 4

Nothing comes amiss so money comes withal.

— *Taming of the Shrew*, Act 1, Sc. 2

Thou bear'st thy heavy riches but a journey, and death unloads thee.

— *Measure for Measure*, Act 3, Sc. 1

When men come to borrow . . . they approach sadly and go away merry.

— *Timon of Athens*, Act 2, Sc. 2

. . . so full of fear as one with treasure laden, hemm'd with thieves . . .

— *Venus and Adonis*

But in the way of bargain . . . I'll cavil on the ninth part of a hair.

— *Henry IV, Part I*, Act 3, Sc. 1

I hope you do not mean to cheat me so.

— *Comedy of Errors*, Act 4, Sc. 3

. . . thrust thy hand . . . deep into the purse of rich prosperity . . .
— *King John, Act 5, Sc. 2*

For they say, if money go before, all ways do lie open.
— *Merry Wives of Windsor, Act 2, Sc. 2*

It hath pleased the gods to remember my father's age, and call him to long peace. He is gone happy, and has left me rich.
— *Timon of Athens, Act 1, Sc. 2*

. . . a dowager of great revenue . . .
— *Midsummer Night's Dream, Act 1, Sc. 1*

Malice and lucre in them have laid this woe here.
— *Cymbeline, Act 4, Sc. 2*

Take this purse of gold, and let me buy your friendly help . . .
— *All's Well that Ends Well, Act 3, Sc. 7*

. . . as vigilant as a cat to steal cream.
— *Henry IV, Part I, Act 4, Sc. 2*

. . . stanchless avarice . . .
— *Macbeth, Act 4, Sc. 3*

. . . such strife as 'twixt a miser and his wealth is found.
— *Sonnet 75*

This life is . . . richer than doing nothing for a bauble.
— *Cymbeline, Act 3, Sc. 3*

(To soothsayer) Good sir, give me good fortune. — I make not, but foresee. — Pray then, foresee me one.
— *Antony and Cleopatra, Act 1, Sc. 2*

The instances that second marriage move are base respects of thrift, but none of love.
— *Hamlet, Act 3, Sc. 2*

. . . their love lies in their purses . . .
— *Richard II, Act 2, Sc. 2*

Out of that I'll work myself a former fortune.
— *Coriolanus, Act 5, Sc. 3*

. . . this action for the wide world's revenue.
— *Troilus and Cressida, Act 2, Sc. 2*

Who would not wish to be from wealth exempt, since riches point to misery and contempt?
— *Timon of Athens, Act 4, Sc. 2*

She hath more hair than wit, and more faults than hairs, and more wealth than faults . . . — Why, that word makes the faults gracious. Well, I'll have her . . .

— *Two Gentlemen of Verona, Act 3, Sc. 1*

Touch them with several fortunes, the greater scorns the lesser.

— *Timon of Athens, Act 4, Sc. 3*

. . . his possessions are so huge . . .

— *Two Gentlemen of Verona, Act 2, Sc. 4*

. . . dispraise the thing that you desire to buy . . .

— *Troilus and Cressida, Act 4, Sc. 1*

Rich preys make true men thieves . . .

— *Venus and Adonis*

'Tis gold which buys admittance . . .

— *Cymbeline, Act 2, Sc. 3*

Gold were as good as twenty orators, and will, no doubt, tempt him to any thing.

— *Richard III, Act 4, Sc. 2*

All that glisters is not gold; often have you heard that told.

— *Merchant of Venice, Act 2, Sc. 7*

A merchant of great traffic through the world.

— *Taming of the Shrew, Act 1, Sc. 1*

When we for recompense have praised the vile . . .

— *Timon of Athens, Act 1, Sc. 1*

Is your gold and silver ewes and rams? — I cannot tell, I make it breed as fast.

— *Merchant of Venice, Act 1, Sc. 3*

The sheep for fodder follow the sheperd.

— *Two Gentlemen of Verona, Act 1, Sc. 1*

I am a man that from my first have been inclined to thrift.

— *Timon of Athens, Act 1, Sc. 1*

I have been dear to him, lad, some two thousand strong, or so.

— *Twelfth Night, Act 3, Sc. 2*

. . . as rich men deal gifts, expecting in return twenty to one . . .

— *Timon of Athens, Act 4, Sc. 3*

. . . whom corrupting gold would tempt unto a close exploit . . .

— *Richard III, Act 4, Sc. 2*

O, what a world of vile ill-favour'd faults looks handsome in three hundred pounds a year!
— *Merry Wives of Windsor, Act 3, Sc. 4*

Error i' the bill, sir, error i' the bill.
— *Taming of the Shrew, Act 4, Sc. 3*

I'll say thou hast gold; thou wilt be throng'd to shortly.
— *Timon of Athens, Act 4, Sc. 3*

We that sell by gross, the Lord doth know, have not the grace to grace it with such show.
— *Love's Labour's Lost, Act 5, Sc. 2*

. . . gold . . . what can it not do and undo?
— *Cymbeline, Act 2, Sc. 3*

Your presence makes us rich, most noble lord . . . — Evermore thanks, the exchequer of the poor.
— *Richard II, Act 2, Sc. 3*

For I did dream of moneybags tonight.
— *Merchant of Venice, Act 2, Sc. 5*

You have a quick wit. — And yet it cannot overtake your slow purse.
— *Two Gentlemen of Verona, Act 1, Sc. 1*

I pray for no man but myself.
— *Timon of Athens, Act 1, Sc. 2*

Dumb jewels often in their silent kind more than quick words do move a woman's mind.
— *Two Gentlemen of Verona, Act 3, Sc. 1*

What piles of wealth hath he accumulated to his own portion! . . . How, i' the name of thrift, does he rake this together?
— *Henry VIII, Act 3, Sc. 2*

Shall we now contaminate our fingers with base bribes, and sell the mighty space of our large honours for so much trash as may be grasped thus? I had rather be a dog, and bay the moon . . .
— *Julius Caesar, Act 4, Sc. 3*

Plate sin with gold, and the strong lance of justice hurtless breaks; arm it in rags, a pigmy's straw does pierce it.
— *King Lear, Act 4, Sc. 6*

. . . 'tis the account of all that world of wealth I have drawn together for mine own ends.
— *Henry VIII, Act 3, Sc. 2*

Think'st thou I'll endanger my soul gratis?
— *Merry Wives of Windsor, Act 2, Sc. 2*

In converting Jews to Christians, you raise the price of pork.
— *Merchant of Venice, Act 3, Sc. 5*

. . . those quondam carpet-mongers . . .
— *Much Ado about Nothing, Act 5, Sc. 2*

. . . innumerable substance, by what means got, I leave to your own conscience.
— *Henry VIII, Act 3, Sc. 2*

What a god's gold, that he is worshipp'd in a baser temple than where swine feed.
— *Timon of Athens, Act 5, Sc. 1*

. . . a power of high resolved men, bent to the spoil.
— *Titus Andronicus, Act 4, Sc. 4*

. . . to repay that money will be a biting affliction.
— *Merry Wives of Windsor, Act 5, Sc. 5*

Our purses shall be proud, our garments poor.
— *Taming of the Shrew, Act 4, Sc. 3*

Tell me, didst thou never hear that things ill-got had ever bad success?
— *Henry VI, Part III, Act 2, Sc. 2*

Remuneration! Why, it is a fairer name than French crown . . .
— *Love's Labour's Lost, Act 3, Sc. 1*

Gold? Yellow, glittering, precious gold? . . . will make foul fair, wrong right, base noble, old young, coward valiant.
— *Timon of Athens, Act 4, Sc. 3*

I'll follow, as they say, for reward. He that rewards me, God reward him!
— *Henry IV, Part I, Act 5, Sc. 4*

We wait for certain money here, sir.
— *Timon of Athens, Act 3, Sc. 4*

I did send to you for certain sums of gold, which you denied me.
— *Julius Caesar, Act 4, Sc. 3*

Now I play a merchant's part, and venture madly on a desperate mart.
— *Taming of the Shrew, Act 2, Sc. 1*

. . . that goodness of gleaning all the land's wealth into one, into your own hands . . .
— *Henry VIII, Act 3, Sc. 2*

126

You owe me money, Sir John, and now you pick a quarrel to beguile me of it.
— *Henry IV, Part I, Act 3, Sc. 3*

It's an honourable kind of thievery.
— *Two Gentlemen of Verona, Act 4, Sc. 1*

. . . unsatisfied in getting . . .
— *Henry VIII, Act 4, Sc. 2*

They have e'en put my breath from me . . . Creditors? Devils!
— *Timon of Athens, Act 3, Sc. 4*

This juggling witchcraft with revenue cherish . . .
— *King John, Act 3, Sc. 1*

How quickly nature falls into revolt when gold becomes her object! For this the foolish over-careful fathers have broke their sleep with thoughts, their brains with care, their bones with industry.
— *Henry IV, Part II, Act 3, Sc. 2*

A man can no more separate age and covetousness than a' can part young limbs and lechery.
— *Act 1, Sc. 2*

Our well-dealing countrymen, who, wanting guilders to redeem their lives . . .
— *Comedy of Errors, Act 1, Sc. 1*

The man that once did sell the lion's skin while the beast lived, was killed with hunting him.
— *Henry V, Act 4, Sc. 3*

O, then, I see you will part but with light gifts; in weightier things you'll say a beggar nay.
— *Richard III, Act 3, Sc. 1*

I do it for some piece of money.
— *Measure for Measure, Act 2, Sc. 1*

Since this fortune falls to you, be content and seek no new . . .
— *Merchant of Venice, Act 3, Sc. 2*

Large-handed robbers your grave masters are and pill by law.
— *Timon of Athens, Act 4, Sc. 1*

A thousand pounds a year for pure respect! No other obligation!
— *Henry VIII, Act 2, Sc. 3*

. . . the vulgar sort of market men that come to gather money for their corn.
— *Henry VI, Part I, Act 3, Sc. 2*

28
COWARDS

You go so much backward when you fight.
> — *All's Well that Ends Well, Act 1, Sc. 1*

. . . but for these vile guns, he would himself have been a soldier.
> — *Henry IV, Part I, Act 1, Sc. 3*

A most devout coward, religious in it.
> — *Twelfth Night, Act 3, Sc. 4*

Lead your battle softly on . . .
> — *Julius Caesar, Act 5, Sc. 1*

What is the trust or strength of foolish man? They that of late were daring with their scoffs are glad and fain by flight to save themselves.
> — *Henry VI, Part I, Act 3, Sc. 2*

Our doctors say this is no month to bleed.
> — *Richard II, Act 1, Sc. 1*

He excels his brother for a coward, yet his brother is reputed one of the best that is.
> — *All's Well that Ends Well, Act 4, Sc. 3*

Can honour set to a leg? no; or an arm? no; or take away the grief of a wound? no. Honour hath no skill in surgery, then? no. What is honour? a word . . . Who hath it? he that died o' Wednesday. Doth he feel it? no; Doth he hear it? no. . . Therefore I'll none of it.
> — *Henry IV, Part I, Act 5, Sc. 1*

When you and I met at Saint Alban's last, your legs did better service than your hands.
> — *Henry VI, Part III, Act 2, Sc. 2*

. . . would have given their honours to have saved their carcasses.
> — *Cymbeline, Act 5, Sc. 3*

. . . they have only stomachs to eat and none to fight.
> — *Henry V, Act 3, Sc. 7*

And in the managing of quarrels you may say he is wise; for either he avoids them with great discretion, or undertakes them with a most Christian-like fear.
> — *Much Ado about Nothing, Act 2, Sc. 3*

Why, thou owest God a death. — 'Tis not due yet; I would be loath to pay
him before his day. What need I be so forward with him that calls not
on me?
— *Henry IV, Part I, Act 5, Sc. 1*

Your hands than mine are quicker for a fray,
My legs are longer, though, to run away.
— *Midsummer Night's Dream, Act 3, Sc. 2*

Thou thing of no bowels . . .
— *Troilus and Cressida, Act 2, Sc. 1*

Lions make leopards tame . . .
— *Richard II, Act 1, Sc. 1*

Of all the wonders that I yet have heard, it seems to me most strange that
men should fear; seeing that death, a necessary end, will come when it
will come.
— *Julius Caesar, Act 2, Sc. 2*

I have fled myself and have instructed cowards to run and show their
shoulders.
— *Antony and Cleopatra, Act 3, Sc. 2*

. . . show outward hideousness, and speak off half a dozen dangerous
words, how they might hurt their enemies . . . and this is all.
— *Much Ado about Nothing, Act 5, Sc. 1*

We'll have a swashing and martial outside, as many other mannish cowards
have . . .
— *As You Like It, Act 1, Sc. 3*

Some certain of your brethren roar'd, and ran from the noise of our own
drums.
— *Coriolanus, Act 2, Sc. 3*

Show it a fair pair of heels and run from it.
— *Henry IV, Part I, Act 2, Sc. 4*

They that have the voice of lions and the act of hares . . .
— *Troilus and Cressida, Act 3, Sc. 2*

Great lords and gentlemen, what means this silence? Dare no man answer
in a case of truth?
— *Henry VI, Part I, Act 2, Sc. 4*

. . . our grace is only in our heels, and that we are most lofty runaways.
— *Henry V, Act 3, Sc. 5*

. . . but one part wisdom and ever three parts coward.
— *Hamlet, Act 4, Sc. 4*

Thunder'st with thy tongue, and with thy weapon nothing darest perform.
— *Titus Andronicus, Act 2, Sc. 1*

. . . this soft courage makes your followers faint.
— *Henry VI, Part III, Act 2, Sc. 2*

The better part of valour is discretion . . .
— *Henry IV, Part I, Act 5, Sc. 4*

So cowards fight when they can fly no further . . .
— *Henry VI, Part III, Act 1, Sc. 4*

By flight I'll shun the danger which I fear.
— *Pericles, Act 1, Sc. 1*

If we live thus tamely . . . farewell nobility.
— *Henry VIII, Act 3, Sc. 2*

I am sick and capable of fears . . . full of fears . . . subject to fears . . .
naturally born to fears . . .
— *King John, Act 3, Sc. 1*

I have seen them shiver and look pale, make periods in the midst of
sentences.
— *Midsummer Night's Dream, Act 5, Sc. 1*

And men are flesh and blood, and apprehensive . . .
— *Julius Caesar, Act 3, Sc. 1*

. . . pants and looks pale, as if a bear were at his heels.
— *Twelfth Night, Act 3, Sc. 4*

Have at you with a proverb.
— *Comedy of Errors, Act 3, Sc. 1*

. . . quake and tremble all this day.
— *King John, Act 3, Sc. 1*

His guts are made of puddings.
— *Merry Wives of Windsor, Act 2, Sc. 1*

Small curs are not regarded when they grin, but great men tremble when
the lion roars.
— *Henry VI, Part II, Act 3, Sc. 1*

It fits us then to be as provident as fear may teach us . . .
— *Henry V, Act 2, Sc. 4*

You scarcely have the hearts to tell me so, and therefore cannot have the
hearts to do it.

— Richard III, Act 1, Sc. 4

God keep lead out of me! I need no more weight than my own bowels.

— Henry IV, Part I, Act 5, Sc. 3

Each shadow makes him stop, each murmur stay . . .

— Venus and Adonis

What would you have me do? go to the wars, would you? where a man
may serve seven years for the loss of a leg, and have not money enough
in the end to buy him a wooden one?

— Pericles, Act 4, Sc. 6

29
HURRY UP!

It is no time to discourse . . . 'tis shame to stand still . . . there is throats to
be cut, and works to be done . . .
— Henry V, Act 3, Sc. 2

Each man to his stool, with that spur as he would to the lip of his mistress.
— Timon of Athens, Act 3, Sc. 6

You are looked for and called for, asked for and sought for . . .
— Romeo and Juliet, Act 1, Sc. 5

Wilt thou go along? — Better do so than tarry and be hang'd.
— Henry VI, Part III, Act 4, Sc. 5

In delay there lies no plenty, then come kiss me, sweet and twenty, youth's
a stuff will not endure.
— Twelfth Night, Act 2, Sc. 3

He requires your haste-post-haste appearance, even on the instant.
— Othello, Act 1, Sc. 2

Come, we burn daylight . . .
— Romeo and Juliet, Act 1, Sc. 4

I stand on fire; come to the matter.
— Cymbeline, Act 5, Sc. 5

Patience is stale, and I am weary of it.
— Richard II, Act 5, Sc. 5

Make use of thy salt hours . . .
— Timon of Athens, Act 4, Sc. 3

He doth me wrong to feed me with delays.
— Titus Andronicus, Act 4, Sc. 3

I must hear from thee every day in the hour, for in a minute there are many
days.
— Romeo and Juliet, Act 3, Sc. 5

Whose hand . . . thou shalt soon feel, to thy cold comfort, for being slow in
thy hot office.
— Taming of the Shrew, Act 4, Sc. 1

Come, lords, we trifle time away.
— Henry VIII, Act 5, Sc. 3

'Tis not sleepy business, but must be look'd to speedily and strongly.
— *Cymbeline, Act 3, Sc. 5*

Make use of time, let not advantage slip.
— *Venus and Adonis*

Defer no time, delays have dangerous ends.
— *Henry VI, Part I, Act 3, Sc. 2*

. . . wishing clocks more swift . . .
— *Winter's Tale, Act 1, Sc. 2*

The current that with gentle murmur glides, thou know'st, being stopp'd, impatiently doth rage.
— *Two Gentlemen of Verona, Act 2, Sc. 7*

. . . hath sent about three several quests to search you out.
— *Othello, Act 1, Sc. 2*

The hour steals on; I pray you, sir, dispatch.
— *Comedy of Errors, Act 4, Sc. 1*

My business cannot brook this dalliance.
— *Act 4, Sc. 1*

Strike now, or else the iron cools.
— *Henry VI, Part III, Act 5, Sc. 1*

Be Mercury, set feathers to thy heels and fly like thought . . .
— *King John, Act 4, Sc. 2*

. . . on serious business, craving quick dispatch, importunes personal conference with his Grace . . .   ·
— *Love's Labour's Lost, Act 2, Sc. 1*

The sun shines hot, and if we use delay, cold biting winter mars our hoped-for hay.
— *Henry VI, Part III, Act 4, Sc. 8*

Impatience hath his privilege. — 'Tis true, to hurt his master, no man else.
— *King John, Act 4, Sc. 3*

Let's kiss and part, for we have much to do.
— *Titus Andronicus, Act 3, Sc. 1*

I desire no more delight than to be under sail and gone tonight.
— *Merchant of Venice, Act 2, Sc. 6*

Do it without invention, suddenly.
— *Henry VI, Part I, Act 3, Sc. 1*

It is a business of some heat.

— *Othello, Act 1, Sc. 2*

O slow-wing'd turtle! shall a buzzard take thee?

— *Taming of the Shrew, Act 2, Sc. 1*

. . . ere the glass, that now begins to run, finish the process of his sandy hour.

— *Henry VI, Part I, Act 4, Sc. 2*

My relief must not be toss'd and turn'd to me in words, but must find supply immediate.

— *Timon of Athens, Act 2, Sc. 1*

Like a brace of greyhounds having the fearful flying hare in sight.

— *Henry VI, Part III, Act 2, Sc. 5*

Standing on slippers, which his nimble haste had falsely thrust upon contrary feet.

— *King John, Act 4, Sc. 2*

Swift as a shadow, short as any dream; brief as the lightning . . .

— *Midsummer Night's Dream, Act 1, Sc. 1*

Come, sir, leave me your snatches and yield me a direct answer.

— *Measure for Measure, Act 4, Sc. 2*

Injurious time now with a robber's haste crams his rich thievery up.

— *Troilus and Cressida, Act 4, Sc. 4*

Come, come, away! The sun is high, and we outwear the day.

— *Henry V, Act 4, Sc. 2*

. . . softly and swiftly, sir . . .

— *Taming of the Shrew, Act 5, Sc. 1*

30
ARGUMENT

Besides that he's a fool, he's a great quarreler; and but that he hath the gift of a coward to allay the gust he hath in quarreling, 'tis thought among the prudent he would quickly have the gift of a grave.
— *Twelfth Night, Act 1, Sc. 3*

. . . too disputable for my company.
— *As You Like It, Act 2, Sc. 5*

But we shall meet, and break our minds at large.
— *Henry VI, Part I, Act 1, Sc. 3*

There has been much throwing about of brains.
— *Hamlet, Act 2, Sc. 2*

To bandy word for word and frown for frown.
— *Taming of the Shrew, Act 5, Sc. 2*

. . . meets in mere oppugnancy . . .
— *Troilus and Cressida, Act 1, Sc. 3*

No malice, sir, no more than becomes so good a quarrel and so bad a peer.
— *Henry VI, Part II, Act 2, Sc. 1*

Good wits will be jangling . . . this civil war of wits . . .
— *Love's Labour's Lost, Act 2, Sc. 1*

A man may break a word with you, sir; and words are but wind; Ay, and break it in your face, so he break it not behind.
— *Comedy of Errors, Act 3, Sc. 1*

Will you voutsafe me, look you, a few disputations . . . in the way of argument, look you, and friendly communication . . .
— *Henry V, Act 3, Sc. 2*

You shall have time to wrangle in when you have nothing else to do.
— *Antony and Cleopatra, Act 2, Sc. 2*

. . . this petty brabble . . .
— *Titus Andronicus, Act 2, Sc. 1*

They never meet but there's a skirmish of wit between them.
— *Much Ado about Nothing, Act 1, Sc. 1*

135

I have not sought the day of this dislike. — You have not sought it! How comes it then?

— *Henry IV, Part I, Act 5, Sc. 1*

The bitter clamour of two eager tongues . . .

— *Richard II, Act 1, Sc. 1*

Leave this peevish broil . . .

— *Henry VI, Part I, Act 3, Sc. 1*

. . . do hourly carp and quarrel . . .

— *King Lear, Act 1, Sc. 4*

What a war of looks was then between them!

— *Venus and Adonis*

. . . angry parle . . .

— *Hamlet, Act 1, Sc. 1*

Keep you out of prawls, and prabbles, and quarrels, and dissensions, and, I warrant you, it is the better for you.

— *Henry V, Act 4, Sc. 8*

Better a little chiding than a great deal of heart-break.

— *Merry Wives of Windsor, Act 5, Sc. 3*

What, will you tear impatient answers from my gentle tongue?

— *Midsummer Night's Dream, Act 3, Sc. 2*

Beware of entrance to a quarrel; but being in, bear't that the opposed may beware of thee.

— *Hamlet, Act 1, Sc. 3*

You two never meet but you fall to some discord.

— *Henry IV Part II, Act 2, Sc. 4*

. . . this divided friendship . . .

— *Richard III, Act 1, Sc. 4*

I do say thou art quick in answers; thou heatest my blood.

— *Love's Labour's Lost, Act 1, Sc. 2*

For what is wedlock forced but a hell, an age of discord and continual strife?

— *Henry VI, Part I, Act 5, Sc. 5*

. . . face to face, and frowning brow to brow . . .

— *Richard II, Act 1, Sc. 1*

I had rather hear them scold than fight.
                    — *Merry Wives of Windsor, Act 2, Sc. 1*

. . . the gentlemen do not agree with the gentlewomen, which was never
seen before in such an assembly.
                    — *Henry IV, Part II, Epilogue*

. . . these domestic and particular broils . . .
                    — *King Lear, Act 5, Sc. 1*

I have heard of some kind of men that put quarrels purposely on others . . .
                    — *Twelfth Night, Act 3, Sc. 4*

Words before blows; is it so, countrymen?
                    — *Julius Caesar, Act 5, Sc. 1*

If I longer stay, we shall begin our ancient bickerings . . .
                    — *Henry VI, Part II, Act 1, Sc. 1*

And do as adversaries do in law, strive mightily, but eat and drink as
friends.
                    — *Taming of the Shrew, Act 1, Sc. 2*

. . . mortal and intestine jars . . .
                    — *Comedy of Errors, Act 1, Sc. 1*

I will not undergo this sneap without reply.
                    — *Henry IV, Part II, Act 2, Sc. 1*

Envenom him with words . . .
                    — *King John, Act 3, Sc. 1*

Why, thou wilt quarrel with a man that hath a hair more, or a hair less, in
his beard than thou hast; thou wilt quarrel with a man for cracking
nuts, having no other reason but because thou hast hazel eyes . . .
                    — *Romeo and Juliet, Act 3, Sc. 1*

. . . voluble and sharp discourse . . .
                    — *Comedy of Errors, Act 2, Sc. 1*

Divided in their dire division . . .
                    — *Richard III, Act 5, Sc. 5*

. . . scold and raise up such a storm that mortal ears might hardly endure
the din.
                    — *Taming of the Shrew, Act 1, Sc. 1*

How irksome is this music to my heart! When such strings jar, what hope
of harmony?
                    — *Henry VI, Part II, Act 2, Sc. 1*

137

Be not so hasty to confound my meaning.
                                    — *Richard III, Act 4, Sc. 4*

More rancorous spite, more furious raging broils, than yet can be imagined
  or supposed.
                              — *Henry VI, Part I, Act 4, Sc. 1*

Thus cavils she with every thing she sees.
                                          — *Rape of Lucrece*

These are very bitter words . . . this will grow to a brawl anon.
                              — *Henry IV, Part II, Act 2, Sc. 4*

Fools on both sides!
                        — *Troilus and Cressida, Act 1, Sc. 1*

. . . this keen encounter of our wits.
                                  — *Richard III, Act 1, Sc. 2*

. . . a theme for disputation . . .
                                          — *Rape of Lucrece*

Believe me, sir, they butt together well.
                          — *Taming of the Shrew, Act 5, Sc. 2*

. . . ill-disposed in brawl ridiculous.
                                — *Henry V, Act 4, Prologue*

When contention and occasion meet.
                        — *Troilus and Cressida, Act 4, Sc. 1*

The envious barking of your saucy tongue . . .
                              — *Henry VI, Part I, Act 3, Sc. 4*

Well bandied both; a set of wit well play'd.
                            — *Love's Labour's Lost, Act 5, Sc. 2*

. . . the murmuring lips of discontent . . .
                                    — *King John, Act 4, Sc. 2*

31

CEREMONY

I am for the house with the narrow gate, which I take to be too little for pomp to enter.
> — *All's Well that Ends Well*, Act 4, Sc. 5

Ceremony was but devised at first to set a gloss on faint deeds, hollow welcomes, recanting goodness . . .
> — *Timon of Athens*, Act 1, Sc. 2

When beggars die there are no comets seen; the heavens themselves blaze forth the death of princes.
> — *Julius Caesar*, Act 2, Sc. 2

. . . pomp and circumstance . . .
> — *Othello*, Act 3, Sc. 3

And what have kings that privates have not too, save ceremony, save general ceremony?
> — *Henry V*, Act 4, Sc. 1

Should I don this robe, and trouble you?
> — *Titus Andronicus*, Act 1, Sc. 1

All sanctimonious ceremonies . . .
> — *The Tempest*, Act 4, Sc. 1

This is the ape of form, monsieur the nice . . .
> — *Love's Labour's Lost*, Act 5, Sc. 2

A sad face, a reverend carriage, a slow tongue, in the habit of some sir of note, and so forth.
> — *Twelfth Night*, Act 3, Sc. 4

. . . all the accoutrement, complement and ceremony of it.
> — *Merry Wives of Windsor*, Act 4, Sc. 2

. . . my cloud of dignity . . .
> — *Henry IV, Part II*, Act 4, Sc. 5

O be sick, great greatness, and bid thy ceremony give thee cure! Think'st thou the fiery fever will go out with titles blown from adulation?
> — *Henry V*, Act 4, Sc. 1

. . . all nicety and prolixious blushes.
> — *Measure for Measure*, Act 2, Sc. 4

Hiding the grossness with fair ornament.
— *Merchant of Venice, Act 3, Sc. 2*

O ceremony, show me but thy worth! . . . Art thou aught else but place, degree and form, creating awe and fear in other men?
— *Henry V, Act 4, Sc. 1*

Gives not the hawthorn-bush a sweeter shade to shepherds looking on their silly sheep, than doth a rich embroidered canopy to kings that fear their subjects' treachery?
— *Henry VI, Part III, Act 2, Sc. 5*

. . . gilded honour shamefully misplaced.
— *Sonnet 66*

In all his dressings, characts, titles, forms . . .
— *Measure for Measure, Act 5, Sc. 1*

How ceremonious, solemn and unearthly it was . . .
— *Winter's Tale, Act 3, Sc. 1*

To be possess'd with double pomp, to guard a title that was rich before, to gild refined gold, to paint the lily . . . is wasteful and ridiculous excess.
— *King John, Act 4, Sc. 2*

Are you so formal, sir?
— *Taming of the Shrew, Act 3, Sc. 1*

A garment nobler than that it covers.
— *Cymbeline, Act 5, Sc. 4*

. . . habit and device, exterior form, outward accoutrement . . .
— *King John, Act 1, Sc. 1*

The appurtenance of welcome is fashion and ceremony.
— *Hamlet, Act 2, Sc. 2*

. . . all true rites and lawful ceremonies.
— *Julius Caesar, Act 3, Sc. 1*

Some delightful ostentation, or show, or pageant, or antique, or firework.
— *Love's Labour's Lost, Act 5, Sc. 1*

And what art thou, thou idol ceremony? What kind of god art thou . . . ?
— *Henry V, Act 4, Sc. 1*

. . . rich in titles, honours and promotions . . .
— *King John, Act 2, Sc. 1*

Power, pre-eminence and all the large effects that troop with majesty.
— *King Lear, Act 1, Sc. 1*

The property by what it is should go, not by the title.
— *All's Well that Ends Well, Act 2, Sc. 3*

What pageantry, what feats, what shows . . .
— *Pericles, Act 5, Sc. 2*

The glass of fashion and the mould of form.
— *Hamlet, Act 3, Sc. 1*

The sword, the mace, the crown imperial, the intertissued robe of gold and pearl, . . . the throne he sits on, . . . No, not all these, thrice-gorgeous ceremony, not all these, laid in bed majestical, can sleep so soundly as the wretched slave . . .
— *Henry V, Act 4, Sc. 1*

. . . this insubstantial pageant . . .
— *The Tempest, Act 4, Sc. 1*

They'll be for the flowery way . . .
— *All's Well that Ends Well, Act 4, Sc. 5*

. . . the antique and well noted face of plain old form . . .
— *King John, Act 4, Sc. 2*

. . . to appertainings and to ornament.
— *Lover's Complaint*

Here is a silly stately style indeed!
— *Henry VI, Part I, Act 4, Sc. 7*

The world is still deceived with ornament.
— *Merchant of Venice, Act 3, Sc. 2*

Knighthoods and honours . . . are titles but of scorn.
— *Cymbeline, Act 5, Sc. 2*

. . . gilded loam or painted clay.
— *Richard II, Act 1, Sc. 1*

The tide of pomp that beats upon the high shore of this world.
— *Henry V, Act 4, Sc. 1*

. . . our superfluous lackeys . . . who in unnecessary action swarm about . . .
— *Henry V, Act 4, Sc. 2*

Neither will they bate one jot of ceremony.
— *Coriolanus, Act 2, Sc. 2*

Betwixt their titles and low names, there's nothing differs but the outward fame.
— *Richard III, Act 1, Sc. 4*

. . . tricks and ceremonies, which I have seen thee careful to observe.
— *Titus Andronicus, Act 5, Sc. 1*

Tradition, form and ceremonious duty.
— *Richard II, Act 3, Sc. 2*

That monster, custom, who all sense doth eat . . .
— *Hamlet, Act 3, Sc. 4*

But shall we wear these honours for a day, or shall they last?
— *Richard III, Act 4, Sc. 2*

Hath not old custom made this life more sweet than that of painted pomp?
— *As You Like It, Act 2, Sc. 1*

32

DULLARDS

No better than a fellow, look you now, of no merits . . .
> — *Henry V, Act 5, Sc. 1*

To say nothing, to do nothing, to know nothing, and to have nothing is to be a great part of your title.
> — *All's Well that Ends Well, Act 2, Sc. 4*

What modicums of wit he utters!
> — *Troilus and Cressida, Act 2, Sc. 1*

. . . looked on him without the help of admiration . . .
> — *Cymbeline, Act 1, Sc. 4*

In his sleep he does little harm, save to his bedclothes about him . . .
> — *All's Well that Ends Well, Act 4, Sc. 3*

Ah, how the poor world is pestered with such waterflies . . .
> — *Troilus and Cressida, Act 5, Sc. 1*

. . . the picture of nobody.
> — *The Tempest, Act 3, Sc. 2*

A poor player that struts and frets his hour upon the stage and then is heard no more . . .
> — *Macbeth, Act 5, Sc. 5*

He is a marvellous good neighbour, faith, and a very good bowler . . .
> — *Love's Labour's Lost, Act 5, Sc. 2*

For we have a number of shadows to fill up the musterbook.
> — *Henry IV, Part II, Act 3, Sc. 2*

. . . great clerks . . .
> — *Midsummer Night's Dream, Act 5, Sc. 1*

. . . shall be of as little memory when he is earth'd . . .
> — *The Tempest, Act 2, Sc. 1*

. . . diminutives of nature . . .
> — *Troilus and Cressida, Act 5, Sc. 1*

God made him, and therefore let him pass for a man.
> — *Merchant of Venice, Act 1, Sc. 2*

. . . a fellow of this temper, whose face is not worth sun-burning, that never looks in the glass for love of anything he sees there . . .
— *Henry V, Act 5, Sc. 2*

Nay, let them go, a couple of quiet ones.
— *Taming of the Shrew, Act 3, Sc. 2*

This is a slight unmeritable man, meet to be sent on errands . . .
— *Julius Caesar, Act 4, Sc. 1*

That which ordinary men are fit for, I am qualified in . . .
— *King Lear, Act 1, Sc. 4*

. . . such creatures as we count not worth the hanging.
— *Cymbeline, Act 1, Sc. 5*

A good shallow young fellow.
— *Henry IV, Part II, Act 2, Sc. 4*

. . . neither wit, nor words, nor worth, action, nor utterance, nor the power of speech to stir men's blood . . .
— *Julius Caesar, Act 3, Sc. 2*

For though they cannot greatly sting to hurt, yet look to have them buzz to offend thine ears.
— *Henry VI, Part III, Act 2, Sc. 6*

Other men, of slender reputation.
— *Two Gentlemen of Verona, Act 1, Sc. 3*

This same half-faced fellow . . .
— *Henry IV, Part II, Act 3, Sc. 2*

You are idle shallow things.
— *Twelfth Night, Act 3, Sc. 4*

Come, thou shalt bear a letter to him straight. — Let me bear another to his horse, for that's the more capable creature.
— *Troilus and Cressida, Act 3, Sc. 3*

. . . these honours . . . he shall but bear them as the ass bears gold, to groan and sweat under the business, either led or driven, as we point the way. And having brought our treasure where we will, then take we down his load and turn him off, like to the empty ass, to shake his ears and graze in commons.
— *Julius Caesar, Act 4, Sc. 1*

Thou seek'st the greatness that will overwhelm thee.
— *Henry IV, Part II, Act 4, Sc. 5*

. . . hath more qualities than a water-spaniel . . .
— *Two Gentlemen of Verona*, Act 3, Sc. 1

Small have continual plodders ever won, save base authority from others' books.
— *Love's Labour's Lost*, Act 1, Sc. 1

Dear Kate, take a fellow of plain and uncoined constancy; for he perforce must do thee right, because he hath not the gift to woo in other places.
— *Henry V*, Act 5, Sc. 2

. . . inferior eyes, that borrow their behaviours from the great . . .
— *King John*, Act 5, Sc. 1

. . . hath no music in himself, nor is not moved with concord of sweet sounds . . .
— *Merchant of Venice*, Act 5, Sc. 1

So much is my poverty of spirit, so mighty and so many my defects . . .
— *Richard III*, Act 3, Sc. 7

A fellow of no mark nor likelihood.
— *Henry IV, Part I*, Act 3, Sc. 2

I found him under a tree, like a dropped acorn.
— *As You Like It*, Act 3, Sc. 2

I will description the matter to you, if you be capacity of it.
— *Merry Wives of Windsor*, Act 1, Sc. 1

Even such a man, so faint, so spiritless, so dull, so dead in look, so woe-begone . . .
— *Henry IV, Part II*, Act 1, Sc. 1

. . . a steward still, the fellow of servants, and not worthy to touch Fortune's fingers.
— *Twelfth Night*, Act 2, Sc. 5

A man of no estimation in the world.
— *Henry V*, Act 3, Sc. 6

We are but shrubs, no cedars we . . .
— *Titus Andronicus*, Act 4, Sc. 3

The motions of his spirit are dull as night.
— *Merchant of Venice*, Act 5, Sc. 1

. . . that low-spirited swain, that base minnow . . .
— *Love's Labour's Lost*, Act 1, Sc. 1

He must be taught, and train'd, and bid go forth; a barren-spirited fellow . . .
— *Julius Caesar, Act 4, Sc. 1*

'Tis but a base ignoble mind that mounts no higher than a bird can soar.
— *Henry VI, Part II, Act 2, Sc. 1*

A creature that I teach to fight, to stop, to run directly on, his corporal motion govern'd by my spirit.
— *Julius Caesar, Act 4, Sc. 1*

. . . through his lips do throng weak words . . .
— *Rape of Lucrece*

Men at some time are masters of their fates. The fault, dear Brutus, is not in our stars, but in ourselves, that we are underlings.
— *Julius Caesar, Act 1, Sc. 2*

You are the fount that makes small brooks to flow.
— *Henry VI, Part III, Act 4, Sc. 8*

I am slow of study.
— *Midsummer Night's Dream, Act 1, Sc. 2*

. . . that unlettered small-knowing soul, . . . that shallow vassal . . .
— *Love's Labour's Lost, Act 1, Sc. 1*

The odds is that we scarce are men . . .
— *Cymbeline, Act 5, Sc. 2*

Francis Feeble.
— *Henry IV, Part II, Act 3, Sc. 2*

Sell when you can; you are not for all markets.
— *As You Like It, Act 3, Sc. 5*

Learn this, brother, we live not to be griped by meaner persons.
— *Henry VIII, Act 2, Sc. 2*

. . . errs in ignorance and not in cunning.
— *Othello, Act 3, Sc. 3*

A very superficial, ignorant, unweighing fellow.
— *Measure for Measure, Act 3, Sc. 2*

Like a dull actor now I have forgot my part . . .
— *Coriolanus, Act 5, Sc. 3*

He is not quantity enough . . .
— *Love's Labour's Lost, Act 5, Sc. 1*

A paltry fellow . . . one that never in his life felt so much cold as overshoes in snow.

— *Richard III, Act 5, Sc. 3*

Hear you this Triton of the minnows?

— *Coriolanus, Act 3, Sc. 1*

Why, man, he doth bestride the narrow world like a Colossus, and we petty men walk under his huge legs and peep about to find ourselves dishonourable graves.

— *Julius Caesar, Act 1, Sc. 2*

Universal plodding prisons up the nimble spirits in the arteries . . .

— *Love's Labour's Lost, Act 4, Sc. 3*

Thou art clerkly, thou art clerkly . . .

— *Merry Wives of Windsor, Act 4, Sc. 5*

. . . some quantity of barren spectators . . .

— *Hamlet, Act 3, Sc. 2*

Will as tenderly be led by the nose as asses are.

— *Othello, Act 1, Sc. 3*

. . . vital commoners and inland petty spirits . . .

— *Henry IV, Part I, Act 4, Sc. 3*

33
HYPOCRISY

Hath given countenance to his speech with almost all the holy vows of heaven.

— *Hamlet, Act 1, Sc. 3*

He is gracious, if he be observed.

— *Henry IV, Part II, Act 4, Sc. 4*

Who preferreth peace more than I do? — except I be provoked.

— *Henry VI, Part I, Act 3, Sc. 1*

I will pray, if ever I remember to be holy.

— *King John, Act 3, Sc. 3*

You have a double tongue within your mask . . .

— *Love's Labour's Lost, Act 5, Sc. 2*

But all hoods make not monks.

— *Henry VIII, Act 3, Sc. 1*

Tut, I can counterfeit the deep tragedian, . . . tremble and start . . . ghastly looks are at my service, like enforced smiles, and both are ready in their offices, at any time, to grace my stratagems.

— *Richard III, Act 3, Sc. 5*

And if the boy have not a woman's gift to rain a shower of commanded tears, an onion will do . . .

— *Taming of the Shrew, Induction, Sc. 1*

Thou hast entertained a fox to be the sheperd of thy lambs.

— *Two Gentlemen of Verona, Act 4, Sc. 4*

False face must hide what the false heart doth know.

— *Macbeth, Act 1, Sc. 7*

All men's faces are true, whatsoe'er their hands are.

— *Antony and Cleopatra, Act 2, Sc. 6*

Are you like the painting of a sorrow, a face without a heart?

— *Hamlet, Act 4, Sc. 7*

. . . a most princely hypocrite . . .

— *Henry IV, Part II, Act 2, Sc. 2*

Who makes the fairest show means most deceit.

— *Pericles, Act 1, Sc. 4*

That is the way to make an offence gracious, though few have the grace to do it.

— *Love's Labour's Lost*, Act 5, Sc. 1

Canst thou quake, and change thy colour, murder thy breath in the middle of a word, and then begin again, and stop again, as if thou wert distraught?

— *Richard III*, Act 3, Sc. 5

Look like the innocent flower, but be the serpent under't.

— *Macbeth*, Act 1, Sc. 5

The path is smooth that leadeth on to danger.

— *Venus and Adonis*

Hide not thy poison with such sugar'd words.

— *Henry VI, Part II*, Act 3, Sc. 2

Bear a fair presence, though your heart be tainted.

— *Comedy of Errors*, Act 3, Sc. 2

The devil hath power to assume a pleasing shape.

— *Hamlet*, Act 2, Sc. 2

How smooth and even they do bear themselves!

— *Henry V*, Act 2, Sc. 2

I am not what I am.

— *Twelfth Night*, Act 3, Sc. 1

Where we are there's daggers in men's smiles . . .

— *Macbeth*, Act 2, Sc. 3

His givings-out were of an infinite distance from his true-meant design.

— *Measure for Measure*, Act 1, Sc. 4

Nor more can you distinguish of a man than of his outward show; which, God he knows, seldom or never jumpeth with the heart.

— *Richard III*, Act 3, Sc. 1

Ye have angels' faces, but heaven knows your hearts.

— *Henry VIII*, Act 3, Sc. 1

Play one scene of excellent dissembling, and let it look like perfect honour.

— *Antony and Cleopatra*, Act 1, Sc. 3

I speak of peace, while covert enmity under the smile of safety wounds the world.

— *Henry IV, Part II*, Induction

It cannot be, I find, but such a face should bear a wicked mind.

— Rape of Lucrece

Another lean unwash'd artificer . . .

— King John, Act 4, Sc. 2

. . . the borrowed veil of modesty . . .

— Merry Wives of Windsor, Act 3, Sc. 2

Having God, her conscience, and these bars against me, and I no friends to back my suit at all, but the plain devil and dissembling looks, and yet to win . . . !

— Richard III, Act 1, Sc. 2

. . . under covert and convenient seeming . . .

— King Lear, Act 3, Sc. 2

. . . silken, sly insinuating jacks.

— Richard III, Act 1, Sc. 3

How angerly I taught my brow to frown, when inward joy enforced my heart to smile!

— Two Gentlemen of Verona, Act 1, Sc. 2

Here comes the trout that must be caught with tickling.

— Twelfth Night, Act 2, Sc. 5

Why, I can smile, and murder whiles I smile, . . . and wet my cheeks with artificial tears, and frame my face to all occasions.

— Henry VI, Part III, Act 3, Sc. 2

How canst thou urge God's dreadful law to us, when thou hast broke it in so dear degree?

— Richard III, Act 1, Sc. 4

. . . dost, with thine angel's face, seize with thine eagle's talons.

— Pericles, Act 4, Sc. 3

. . . seeming to be most which we indeed least are.

— Taming of the Shrew, Act 5, Sc. 2

Be secret-false . . . what simple thief brags of his own attaint?

— Comedy of Errors, Act 3, Sc. 2

You're meek and humble-mouth'd . . . in full seeming with meekness and humility, but . . .

— Henry VIII, Act 2, Sc. 4

The harlot's cheek, beautied with plastering art, is not more ugly . . . than is my deed to my most painted word.
— *Hamlet, Act 3, Sc. 1*

When the lion fawns upon the lamb, the lamb will never cease to follow him.
— *Henry VI, Part III, Act 4, Sc. 8*

What an equivocal companion is this!
— *All's Well that Ends Well, Act 5, Sc. 3*

There is a kind of confession in your looks, which your modesties have not craft enough to colour.
— *Hamlet, Act 2, Sc. 2*

Seems he a dove? His feathers are but borrow'd, for he's disposed as the hateful raven. Is he a lamb? His skin is surely lent him, for he's inclined as is the ravenous wolf.
— *Henry VI, Part II, Act 3, Sc. 1*

. . . practised how to cloak offences with a cunning brow.
— *Rape of Lucrece*

Fairing the foul with art's false borrow'd face.
— *Sonnet 127*

That word "grace" in an ungracious mouth is but profane.
— *Richard II, Act 2, Sc. 3*

Being done unknown, I should have found it afterwards well done, but must condemn it now.
— *Antony and Cleopatra, Act 2, Sc. 7*

. . . fain to shuffle, to hedge and to lurch.
— *Merry Wives of Windsor, Act 2, Sc. 2*

I can set down a story of faults concealed . . .
— *Sonnet 88*

A huge translation of hypocrisy . . .
— *Love's Labour's Lost, Act 5, Sc. 2*

O, what may man within him hide, though angel on the outward side!
— *Measure for Measure, Act 3, Sc. 2*

Supposed sincere and holy in his thoughts . . . derives from heaven his quarrel and his cause.
— *Henry IV, Part II, Act 1, Sc. 1*

There is no vice so simple, but assumes some mark of virtue on his outward parts.
— *Merchant of Venice, Act 3, Sc. 2*

This sober form of yours hides wrongs.
— *Julius Caesar, Act 4, Sc. 2*

. . . most unrighteous tears . . .
— *Hamlet, Act 1, Sc. 2*

. . . give him another hope, to betray him to another punishment.
— *Merry Wives of Windsor, Act 3, Sc. 3*

That there should be small love 'mongst these sweet knaves, and all this courtesy!
— *Timon of Athens, Act 1, Sc. 1*

. . . how quaint an orator you are.
— *Henry VI, Part II, Act 3, Sc. 2*

Some that smile have in their hearts, I fear, millions of mischiefs.
— *Julius Caesar, Act 4, Sc. 1*

We will fool him black and blue.
— *Twelfth Night, Act 2, Sc. 5*

The fellow that sits next him now, parts bread with him, . . . is the readiest man to kill him, 't has been proved.
— *Timon of Athens, Act 1, Sc. 2*

. . . we cite our faults, that they may hold excused our lawless lives.
— *Two Gentlemen of Verona, Act 4, Sc. 1*

. . . as the snake roll'd in a flowering bank, . . . doth sting a child that for the beauty thinks it excellent.
— *Henry VI, Part II, Act 3, Sc. 1*

How he did seem to dive into their hearts with humble and familiar courtesy.
— *Richard II, Act 1, Sc. 4*

Can this be so, that in alliance, amity and oaths there should be found such false dissembling guile?
— *Henry VI, Part I, Act 4, Sc. 1*

And then I stole all courtesy from heaven, and dress'd myself in such humility that I did pluck allegiance from men's hearts . . .
— *Henry IV, Part I, Act 3, Sc. 2*

To show an unfelt sorrow is an office which the false man does easy.
— *Macbeth, Act 2, Sc. 3*

Smooth runs the water where the brook is deep; and in his simple show he harbours treason.
— *Henry VI, Part II, Act 3, Sc. 1*

. . . putting on the mere form of civil and humane seeming.
— *Othello, Act 2, Sc. 1*

. . . so dear a show of zeal . . .
— *Henry IV, Part I, Act 5, Sc. 4*

Some of you with Pilate wash your hands, showing an outward pity.
— *Richard II, Act 4, Sc. 1*

Mine eyes smell onions; I shall weep anon.
— *All's Well that Ends Well, Act 5, Sc. 3*

. . . lies well steel'd with weighty arguments . . .
— *Richard III, Act 1, Sc. 1*

. . . to dispraise my lord with that same tongue which she hath praised him with above compare so many thousand times?
— *Romeo and Juliet, Act 3, Sc. 5*

So Judas kiss'd his master, and cried "all hail" when as he meant all harm.
— *Henry VI, Part III, Act 5, Sc. 7*

. . . sung, with feigning voice, verses of feigning love . . .
— *Midsummer Night's Dream, Act 1, Sc. 1*

.I have sounded the very base-string of humility.
— *Henry IV, Part I, Act 2, Sc. 4*

You must seem to do that fearfully which you commit willingly, despise profit where you have most gain.
— *Pericles, Act 4, Sc. 2*

I am angling now, though you perceive me not how I give line.
— *Winter's Tale, Act 1, Sc. 2*

This outward-sainted deputy.
— *Measure for Measure, Act 3, Sc. 1*

34
ENEMIES

I had as lief thou didst break his neck as his finger.
> — *As You Like It, Act 1, Sc. 1*

He that escapes me without some broken limb shall acquit him well.
> — *Act 1, Sc. 1*

If thou dost him any slight disgrace, . . . he will practise against thee by poison, entrap thee by some treacherous device, and never leave thee till he hath ta'en thy life by some indirect means or other.
> — *Act 1, Sc. 1*

Time is the old justice that examines all such offenders . . .
> — *Act 4, Sc. 1*

They say poor suitors have strong breaths; they shall know we have strong arms, too.
> — *Coriolanus, Act 1, Sc. 1*

They have had inkling, this fortnight, what we intend to do, which now we'll show 'em in deeds.
> — *Act 1, Sc. 1*

. . . he shall feel mine edge . . .
> — *Act 1, Sc. 4*

When he shall come to his account, he knows not what I can urge against him.
> — *Act 4, Sc. 7*

. . . give him death by inches.
> — *Act 5, Sc. 4*

The south-fog rot him!
> — *Cymbeline, Act 2, Sc. 3*

Take him hence; The whole world shall not save him.
> — *Act 5, Sc. 5*

Send out for torturers ingenious . . .
> — *Act 5, Sc. 5*

. . . put the strong law on him . . .
> — *Hamlet, Act 4, Sc. 3*

Let come what comes; only I'll be revenged most thoroughly . . .
> — *Act 4, Sc. 5*

And where the offence is let the great axe fall.
                                        — *Hamlet, Act 4, Sc. 5*

I will embrace him with a soldier's arm, that he shall shrink under my
    courtesy.
                                        — *Henry IV, Part I, Act 5, Sc. 2*

. . . there is many a soul shall pay full dearly for this encounter.
                                        — *Act 5, Sc. 1*

. . . malevolent to you in all aspects.
                                        — *Act 1, Sc. 1*

. . . would be glad he met with some mischance.
                                        — *Act 1, Sc. 3*

. . . push against a kingdom . . . we shall o'erturn it topsy-turvy down.
                                        — *Act 4, Sc. 1*

The hour is come to end the one of us.
                                        — *Act 5, Sc. 4*

I can no longer brook thy vanities.
                                        — *Act 5, Sc. 4*

That shall be the day, whene'er it lights . . .
                                        — *Act 3, Sc. 2*

The time will come that I shall make this northern youth exchange his
    glorious deeds for my indignities.
                                        — *Act 3, Sc. 2*

And I will call him to so strict account . . .
                                        — *Act 3, Sc. 2*

. . . on the barren mountains let him starve.
                                        — *Act 1, Sc. 3*

The tongue offends not that reports his death.
                                        — *Part II, Act 1, Sc. 1*

. . . hath sent out a speedy power to encounter you.
                                        — *Act 1, Sc. 1*

. . . are brought to the correction of your law.
                                        — *Act 4, Sc. 4*

Men may sleep, and they may have their throats about them at that time,
    and some say knives have edges.
                                        — *Henry V, Act 2, Sc. 1*

This was a merry message. — We hope to make the sender blush at it.
— *Henry V, Act 1, Sc. 2*

They shall be apprehended by and by.
— *Act 2, Sc. 2*

Let him be punish'd . . . lest example breed, by his sufferance, more of such
a kind.
— *Act 2, Sc. 2*

He'll call you to so hot an answer of it . . .
— *Act 2, Sc. 4*

I have sworn to take him a box o' the ear.
— *Act 4, Sc. 7*

. . . till I see him once again, and then I will tell him a little piece of my
desires.
— *Act 5, Sc. 1*

If I owe you any thing, I will pay you in cudgels.
— *Act 5, Sc. 1*

All hell shall stir for this.
— *Act 5, Sc. 1*

Let frantic Talbot triumph for a while, and like a peacock sweep along his
tail; we'll pull his plumes and take away his train . . .
— *Henry VI, Part I, Act 3, Sc. 3*

Your hearts I'll stamp out with my horse's heels, and make a quagmire of
your mingled brains.
— *Act 1, Sc. 4*

. . . give him chastisement for this abuse.
— *Act 4, Sc. 1*

. . . those bitter injuries . . . I doubt not but with honour to redress.
— *Act 2, Sc. 5*

After that things are set in order here, we'll follow them with all the power
we have.
— *Act 2, Sc. 2*

. . . means no goodness by his looks.
— *Act 3, Sc. 2*

Well, seeing gentle words will not prevail, assail them . . .
— *Part II, Act 4, Sc. 2*

So, one by one, we'll weed them all at last.
                                    — *Henry VI, Part II, Act 1, Sc. 3*

Let him have all the rigour of the law.
                                    — *Act 1, Sc. 3*

. . . I will deal with him, that henceforth he shall trouble us no more.
                                    — *Act 3, Sc. 1*

The welfare of us all hangs on the cutting short that fraudful man.
                                    — *Act 3, Sc. 1*

Now 'tis the spring, and weeds are shallow-rooted; suffer them now, and
they'll o'ergrow the garden . . .
                                    — *Act 3, Sc. 1*

Shall we after them? — Nay, before them, if we can.
                                    — *Act 5, Sc. 3*

The wound that bred this meeting here cannot be cured by words.
                                    — *Part III, Act 2, Sc. 2*

Tears then for babes; blows and revenge for me!
                                    — *Act 2, Sc. 1*

Take time to do him dead.
                                    — *Act 1, Sc. 4*

I was the chief that raised him . . . , and I'll be chief to bring him down
again.
                                    — *Act 3, Sc. 3*

What satisfaction canst thou make for . . . all the trouble thou hast turned
me to?
                                    — *Act 5, Sc. 5*

You have many enemies that know not why they are so, but, like to village
curs, bark when their fellows do.
                                    — *Henry VIII, Act 2, Sc. 4*

He's a rank weed . . . and we must root him out.
                                    — *Act 5, Sc. 1*

I'll venture one have-at-him.
                                    — *Act 2, Sc. 2*

Call him to present trial; if he may find mercy in the law, 'tis his; if none, let
him not seek it of us.
                                    — *Act 1, Sc. 2*

How much, methinks, I could despise this man, but that I am bound in charity against it.
— *Henry VIII, Act 3, Sc. 2*

Be near me, that I may remember you. — . . . (Aside) And so near will I be, that your best friends shall wish I had been further.
— *Julius Caesar, Act 2, Sc. 2*

For we will shake him, or worse days endure.
— *Act 1, Sc. 2*

. . . adverse foreigners affright my towns with dreadful pomp of stout invasion.
— *King John, Act 4, Sc. 2*

He is a very serpent in my way; and wheresoe'er this foot of mine doth tread, he lies before me.
— *Act 3, Sc. 3*

Well, ruffian, I must pocket up these wrongs . . .
— *Act 3, Sc. 1*

Leave him to my displeasure.
— *King Lear, Act 3, Sc. 7*

To know our enemies' minds, we'ld rip their hearts; their papers, is more lawful.
— *Act 4, Sc. 6*

No contraries hold more antipathy than I and such a knave.
— *Act 2, Sc. 2*

Pell-mell, down with them!
— *Love's Labour's Lost, Act 4, Sc. 3*

. . . suffer him to take no delight . . .
— *Act 1, Sc. 2*

He shall endure such public shame as the rest of the court can possibly devise.
— *Act 1, Sc. 1*

And follows close the rigour of the statute to make him an example.
— *Measure for Measure, Act 1, Sc. 4*

He hath a neighbourly charity in him; for he borrowed a box of the ear of the Englishman, and swore he would pay him again when he was able.
— *Merchant of Venice, Act 1, Sc. 2*

. . . a lodged hate and a certain loathing . . .
— *Merchant of Venice, Act 4, Sc. 1*

He cannot choose but break. — I am very glad of it.
— *Act 3, Sc. 1*

Thou call'dst me dog before thou hadst a cause; but since I am a dog, beware my fangs.
— *Act 3, Sc. 3*

Tarry . . . the law hath yet another hold on you.
— *Act 4, Sc. 1*

Beg that thou mayst have leave to hang thyself; and yet, thy wealth being forfeit to the state, thou hast not left the value of a cord; therefore thou must be hang'd at the state's charge.
— *Act 4, Sc. 1*

But if there be no great love in the beginning, yet heaven may decrease it on better acquaintance . . .
— *Merry Wives of Windsor, Act 1, Sc. 1*

I will cut all his two stones.
— *Act 1, Sc. 4*

He will clapper-claw thee tightly.
— *Act 2, Sc. 3*

If I can cross him any way, I bless myself every way.
— *Much Ado About Nothing, Act 1, Sc. 3*

The proudest of them shall well hear of it.
— *Act 4, Sc. 1*

May his pernicious soul rot half a grain a day!
— *Othello, Act 5, Sc. 2*

I endure him not . . .
— *Act 2, Sc. 1*

Nothing can or shall content my soul till I am even'd with him.
— *Act 2, Sc. 1*

So will I . . . make the net that shall enmesh them all.
— *Act 2, Sc. 3*

I follow him to serve my turn upon him . . .
— *Act 1, Sc. 1*

Poison his delight . . . and, though he in a fertile climate dwell, plague him with flies.

— *Othello, Act 1, Sc. 1*

And put in every honest hand a whip to lash the rascals naked through the world even from the east to the west!

— *Act 4, Sc. 2*

But yet she is a goodly creature. — The fitter then the gods should have her.

— *Pericles, Act 4, Sc. 1*

I'll tame you, I'll bring you in subjection.

— *Act 2, Sc. 5*

Now put it, God, in the physician's mind to help him to his grave immediately!

— *Richard II, Act 1, Sc. 4*

Shall I be plain? I wish the bastards dead.

— *Richard III, Act 4, Sc. 2*

It stands me much upon, to stop all hopes whose growth may damage me.

— *Act 4, Sc. 2*

Foes to my rest and sweet sleep's disturbers are they that I would have thee deal upon . . .

— *Act 4, Sc. 2*

. . . that bottled spider, whose deadly web ensnareth thee about.

— *Act 1, Sc. 3*

I shall live . . . to give them thanks that were the cause of my imprisonment.

— *Act 1, Sc. 1*

. . . ancient knot of dangerous adversaries.

— *Act 3, Sc. 1*

I'll bring mine action on the proudest he that stops my way . . .

— *Taming of the Shrew, Act 3, Sc. 2*

I will go sit and weep till I can find occasion of revenge.

— *Act 2, Sc. 1*

And I am mean, indeed, respecting you.

— *Act 5, Sc. 2*

The rarer action is in virtue than in vengeance.

— *The Tempest, Act 5, Sc. 1*

Not all the whips of heaven are large enough . . .
                              — *Timon of Athens, Act 5, Sc. 1*

The law shall bruise him.
                              — *Act 3, Sc. 5*

I thank them, and would send them back the plague, could I but catch it for them.
                              — *Act 5, Sc. 1*

And let confusion live! Plagues incident to men,
Your potent and infectious fevers heap
On Athens, ripe for stroke! Thou cold sciatica,
Cripple our senators, that their limbs may halt
As lamely as their manners! Lust and liberty
Creep in the minds and marrows of our youth,
That 'gainst the stream of virtue they may strive,
And drown themselves in riot! Itches, blains,
Sow all the Athenian bosoms, and their crop
Be general leprosy! Breath infect breath,
That their society, as their friendship, may
Be merely poison!
                              — *Act 4, Sc. 1*

Let not this wasp outlive us both to sting.
                              — *Titus Andronicus, Act 2, Sc. 3*

I shall never come to bliss till all these mischiefs be return'd again even in their throats that have committed them.
                              — *Act 3, Sc. 1*

. . . a stratagem, which, cunningly effected, will beget a very excellent piece of villany . . . for their unrest . . .
                              — *Act 2, Sc. 3*

But if I live, his feigned ecstasies shall be no shelter to these outrages.
                              — *Act 4, Sc. 4*

Let her rest in her unrest awhile . . .
                              — *Act 4, Sc. 2*

. . . let them bide until we have devised some never-heard-of torturing pain for them.
                              — *Act 4, Sc. 2*

After this, the vengeance on the whole camp! or, rather, the Neapolitan bone-ache!
                              — *Troilus and Cressida, Act 2, Sc. 3*

He would pun thee into shivers with his fist, as a sailor breaks a biscuit.
— *Troilus and Cressida, Act 2, Sc. 1*

Their fraction is more our wish than their faction.
— *Act 2, Sc. 3*

By Jove, I'll play the hunter for thy life with all my force, pursuit and policy.
— *Act 4, Sc. 1*

Hurt him in eleven places.
— *Twelfth Night, Act 3, Sc. 2*

. . . highly hold in hate.
— *Two Gentlemen of Verona, Act 3, Sc. 2*

He nought esteems that face of thine . . .
— *Venus and Adonis*

35

CAROUSING

I am glad I was up so late; for that's the reason I was up so early.
— *Cymbeline, Act 2, Sc. 3*

For he's in the third degree of drink . . .
— *Twelfth Night, Act 1, Sc. 5*

We have heard the chimes at midnight.
— *Henry IV, Part II, Act 3, Sc. 2*

Drink, sir, is a great provoker of three things . . . nose-painting, sleep, and
urine. Lechery, sir, it provokes and unprovokes; it provokes the desire
but it takes away the performance.
— *Macbeth, Act 2, Sc. 3*

To be up late is to be up late.
— *Twelfth Night, Act 2, Sc. 3*

One that converses more with the buttock of the night than with the
forehead of the morning.
— *Coriolanus, Act 2, Sc. 1*

Thou art so fat-witted, with drinking of old sack and unbuttoning thee
after supper and sleeping upon benches after noon . . .
— *Henry IV, Part I, Act 1, Sc. 2*

Live a little . . .
— *As You Like It, Act 2, Sc. 6*

I am that merry wanderer of the night.
— *Midsummer Night's Dream, Act 2, Sc. 1*

You must come in earlier o' nights . . .
— *Twelfth Night, Act 1, Sc. 3*

. . . wantons light of heart . . .
— *Romeo and Juliet, Act 1, Sc. 4*

I do not only marvel where thou spendest thy time, but also how thou art
accompanied . . .
— *Henry IV, Part I, Act 2, Sc. 4*

'Tis ever common that men are merriest when they are from home.
— *Henry V, Act 1, Sc. 2*

. . . a fellow of much license.
— *Measure for Measure, Act 3, Sc. 2*

I will see what physic the tavern affords.
— *Henry VI, Part I, Act 3, Sc. 1*

. . . lust and late-walking through the realm.
— *Merry Wives of Windsor, Act 5, Sc. 5*

O God, that men should put an enemy in their mouths to steal away their brains!
— *Othello, Act 2, Sc. 3*

Pleasure will be paid, one time or another.
— *Twelfth Night, Act 2, Sc. 4*

All delights are vain.
— *Love's Labour's Lost, Act 1, Sc. 1*

He is given to sports, to wildness and much company.
— *Julius Caesar, Act 2, Sc. 1*

When wilt thou leave fighting o' days and foining o' nights, and begin to patch up thine old body for heaven?
— *Henry IV, Part II, Act 2, Sc. 4*

Let's have one other gaudy night.
— *Antony and Cleopatra, Act 3, Sc. 13*

. . . a puff'd and reckless libertine.
— *Hamlet, Act 1, Sc. 3*

Hath learn'd to sport and dance, to toy, to wanton, dally, smile and jest.
— *Venus and Adonis*

His addiction was to courses vain, . . . his hours fill'd up with riots, banquets, sports, and never noted in him any study, any retirement, any sequestration from open haunts and popularity.
Henry V, Act 1, Sc. 1

Jesu, Jesu, the mad days that I have spent!
— *Henry IV, Part II, Act 3, Sc. 2*

. . . holiday fool . . .
— *The Tempest, Act 2, Sc. 2*

Let's mock the midnight bell.
— *Antony and Cleopatra, Act 3, Sc. 13*

. . . revels long o'nights . . .

— *Julius Caesar, Act 2, Sc. 2*

These clothes are good enough to drink in . . .

— *Twelfth Night, Act 1, Sc. 3*

Let us devise some entertainment.

— *Love's Labour's Lost, Act 2, Sc. 2*

Thy violent vanities can never last.

— *Rape of Lucrece*

This heavy-handed revel east and west.

— *Hamlet, Act 1, Sc. 4*

A good sherris-sack hath a two-fold operation in it. It ascends me into the brain; dries me there all the foolish and dull and crudy vapours which environ it; makes it apprehensive, quick, forgetive, full of nimble, fiery and delectable shapes; which, delivered o'er to the voice, the tongue, which is the birth, becomes excellent wit . . . The second property of your excellent sherris is, the warming of the blood . . . the sherris warms it and makes it course from the inwards to the parts extreme . . . If I had a thousand sons, the first humane principle I would teach them should be, to forswear thin potations, and to addict themselves to sack.

— *Henry IV, Part II, Act 4, Sc. 3*

The grosser manner of these world's delights . . .

— *Love's Labour's Lost, Act 1, Sc. 1*

How ill white hairs become a fool and a jester! . . . So surfeit-swell'd, so old and so profane.

— *Henry IV, Part II, Act 5, Sc. 5*

The proud day, attended with the pleasures of the world, is all too wanton . . .

— *King John, Act 3, Sc. 3*

For even to vice they are not constant, but are changing still one vice, but of a minute old, for one not half so old as that.

— *Cymbeline, Act 2, Sc. 5*

. . . profane hours here . . .

— *Richard II, Act 5, Sc. 1*

I'll drink no more than will do me good.

— *Henry IV, Part II, Act 2, Sc. 4*

Though you can guess what temperance should be, you know not what it is.

— *Antony and Cleopatra, Act 3, Sc. 13*

. . . admirable pleasures and very honest knaveries . . .
— *Merry Wives of Windsor*, Act 4, Sc. 4

I'll not be tied to hours nor 'pointed times . . .
— *Taming of the Shrew*, Act 3, Sc. 1

. . . with unrestrained loose companions . . .
— *Richard II*, Act 5, Sc. 3

I would entreat you rather to put on your boldest suit of mirth, for we have friends that purpose merriment.
— *Merchant of Venice*, Act 2, Sc. 2

. . . lascivious wassails.
— *Antony and Cleopatra*, Act 1, Sc. 4

I drink to the general joy of the whole table.
— *Macbeth*, Act 3, Sc. 4

His rash fierce blaze of riot cannot last.
— *Richard II*, Act 2, Sc. 1

His days are foul and his drink dangerous.
— *Timon of Athens*, Act 3, Sc. 5

Gripe not at earthly joys.
— *Pericles*, Act 1, Sc. 1

. . . fat-kidneyed rascal . . .
— *Henry IV, Part I*, Act 2, Sc. 2

Let not the sound of shallow foppery enter my sober house.
— *Merchant of Venice*, Act 2, Sc. 5

What's a drunken man like, fool? — Like a drowned man, a fool, and a mad man. One draught above heat makes him a fool; the second mads him, and a third drowns him.
— *Twelfth Night*, Act 1, Sc. 5

. . . honest water, which ne'er left man i' the mire.
— *Timon of Athens*, Act 1, Sc. 2

Each man to what sport and revels his addiction leads him.
— *Othello*, Act 2, Sc. 2

Where all the treasure of thy lusty days . . .
— *Sonnet 2*

It was excess of wine that set him on.
— *Henry V*, Act 2, Sc. 2

. . . your sleeve unbuttoned, your shoe untied, and every thing about you demonstrating a careless desolation.
— *As You Like It, Act 3, Sc. 2*

. . . to taste the pleasures of the world, . . . to be infected with delight.
— *King John, Act 4, Sc. 3*

These should be hours for necessities, not for delights.
— *Henry VIII, Act 5, Sc. 1*

Go, suck the subtle blood of the grape, till the high fever seethe your blood to froth.
— *Timon of Athens, Act 4, Sc. 3*

. . . and afterward consort you till bedtime.
— *Comedy of Errors, Act 1, Sc. 2*

I can drink with any tinker in his own language . . .
— *Henry IV, Part I, Act 2, Sc. 4*

. . . quicken his embraced heaviness with some delight or other.
— *Merchant of Venice, Act 2, Sc. 8*

Youth, the more it is wasted, the sooner it wears.
— *Henry IV, Part I, Act 2, Sc. 4*

That quaffing and drinking will undo you.
— *Twelfth Night, Act 1, Sc. 3*

. . . not in ashes and sackcloth, but in new silk and old sack.
— *Henry IV, Part II, Act 1, Sc. 2*

Be the jacks fair within, the jills fair without, the carpets laid, and everything in order?
— *Taming of the Shrew, Act 4, Sc. 1*

Why, thou globe of sinful continents, what a life dost thou lead!
— *Henry IV, Part II, Act 2, Sc. 4*

I warrant thou art a merry fellow and carest for nothing.
— *Twelfth Night, Act 3, Sc. 1*

. . . frame your mind to mirth and merriment, which bars a thousand harms and lengthens life.
— *Taming of the Shrew, Induction, Sc. 2*

He is given to sports, to wildness and much company.
— *Julius Caesar, Act 2, Sc. 1*

A cup of wine that's brisk and fine.
>   — *Henry IV, Part II, Act 5, Sc. 3*

What abridgement have you for this evening? How shall we beguile the
lazy time, if not with some delight?
>   — *Midsummer Night's Dream, Act 5, Sc. 1*

No profit grows where is no pleasure ta'en . . .
>   — *Taming of the Shrew, Act 1, Sc. 1*

Where is the life that late I led . . . ?
>   — *Henry IV, Part II, Act 5, Sc. 3*

When all our offices have been oppress'd with riotous feeders, when our
vaults have wept with drunken spilth of wine, when every room hath
blazed with lights and bray'd with minstrelsy . . .
>   — *Timon of Athens, Act 2, Sc. 2*

It is so very very late, that we may call it early by and by . . .
>   — *Romeo and Juliet, Act 3, Sc. 4*

Where is our usual manager of mirth? What revels are in hand?
>   — *Midsummer Night's Dream, Act 5, Sc. 1*

36

WHAT FOOLS THESE MORTALS BE
— Midsummer Night's Dream, Act 3, Sc. 2

What a piece of work is a man!
— Hamlet, Act 2, Sc. 2

I did never see such pitiful rascals. — . . . Tush, man, mortal men, mortal men.
— Henry IV, Part I, Act 4, Sc. 2

We make guilty of our disasters the sun, the moon and the stars, as if we were villains by necessity, fools by heavenly compulsion.
— King Lear, Act 1, Sc. 2

If to do were as easy as to know what were good to do, chapels had been churches, and poor men's cottages princes' palaces. It is a good divine that follows his own instructions; I can easier teach twenty what were good to be done, than be one of the twenty to follow mine own teaching.
— Merchant of Venice, Act 1, Sc. 2

Lord, Lord, to see what folly reigns in us!
— Two Gentlemen of Verona, Act 1, Sc. 2

You, gods, will give us some faults to make us men.
— Antony and Cleopatra, Act 5, Sc. 1

For such as we are made of, such we be.
— Twelfth Night, Act 2, Sc. 2

Thus we play the fools with the time; and the spirits of the wise sit in the clouds and mock us.
— Henry IV, Part II, Act 2, Sc. 2

. . . this earthly world, where to do harm is often laudable, to do good sometime accounted dangerous folly.
— Macbeth, Act 4, Sc. 2

We are all men, in our own natures frail and capable of our flesh; few are angels.
— Henry VIII, Act 5, Sc. 3

Nature hath framed strange fellows in her time.
— Merchant of Venice, Act 1, Sc. 1

There was never yet philosopher that could endure the toothache patiently.
— Much Ado about Nothing, Act 5, Sc. 1

Bad is the world, and all will come to nought.
— *Richard III, Act 3, Sc. 6*

The web of our life is of a mingled yarn, good and ill together; our virtues would be proud, if our faults whipped them not, and our crimes would despair, if they were not cherished by our virtues.
— *All's Well that Ends Well, Act 4, Sc. 3*

Will fortune never come with both hands full, but write her fair words still in foulest letters? She either gives a stomach and no food; such are the poor, in health; or else a feast and takes away the stomach, such are the rich, that have abundance and enjoy it not.
— *Henry IV, Part II, Act 4, Sc. 4*

Well, whiles I am a beggar, I will rail and say there is no sin but to be rich, And being rich, my virtue then shall be to say there is no vice but beggary.
— *King John, Act 2, Sc. 1*

We, ignorant of ourselves, beg often our own harms, which the wise powers deny us for our good; so find we profit by losing our prayers.
— *Antony and Cleopatra, Act 2, Sc. 1*

The clamorous owl, that nightly hoots and wonders at our quaint spirits.
— *Midsummer Night's Dream, Act 2, Sc. 2*

The whole race of mankind, high and low . . .
— *Timon of Athens, Act 4, Sc. 1*

As we are ourselves, what things we are . . .
— *All's Well that Ends Well, Act 4, Sc. 3*

Roses have thorns and silver fountains mud; clouds and eclipses stain both moon and sun; and loathsome canker lives in sweetest bud; all men make faults.
— *Sonnet 35*

Thought's the slave of life, and life time's fool . . .
— *Henry IV, Part I, Act 5, Sc. 4*

. . . many for many virtues, excellent, none but for some, and yet all different.
— *Romeo and Juliet, Act 2, Sc. 3*

What's the news? — None, my lord, but that the world's grown honest. — Then is doomsday near, but your news is not true.
— *Hamlet, Act 2, Sc. 2*

Sweet are the uses of adversity; which, like the toad, ugly and venomous, wears yet a precious jewel in his head.
— *As You Like It, Act 2, Sc. 1*

They say, best men are moulded out of faults, and . . . become much more the better for being a little bad.

— *Measure for Measure, Act 5, Sc. 1*

Farewell! A long farewell to all my greatness!
This is the state of man; today he puts forth
The tender leaves of hopes; tomorrow blossoms,
And bears his blushing honours thick upon him;
The third day comes a frost, a killing frost,
And, when he thinks, good easy man, full surely
His greatness is a-ripening, nips his root,
And then he falls as I do. I have ventured,
Like little wanton boys that swim on bladders,
This many summers in a sea of glory,
But far beyond my depth; my high-blown pride
At length broke under me, and now has left me,
Weary and old with service, to the mercy
Of a rude stream that must for ever hide me.

— *Henry VIII, Act 3, Sc. 2*

Why rail'st thou on thy birth, the heaven and earth, since birth and heaven and earth, all three, do meet in thee at once.

— *Romeo and Juliet, Act 3, Sc. 3*

More water glideth by the mill than wots the miller of . . .

— *Titus Andronicus, Act 2, Sc. 1*

And must they all be hanged that swear and lie? — Every one. — Who must hang them? — Why, the honest men. — Then the liars and swearers are fools, for there are liars and swearers enow to beat the honest men and hang up them.

— *Macbeth, Act 4, Sc. 2*

There is occasions and causes, why and wherefore, in all things.

— *Henry V, Act 5, Sc. 1*

But 'tis a common proof, that lowliness is young ambition's ladder, whereto the climber-upward turns his face. But when he once attains the upmost round, he then unto the ladder turns his back, looks in the clouds, scorning the base degrees by which he did ascend.

— *Julius Caesar, Act 2, Sc. 1*

Is't possible the world should so much differ, and we alive that lived?

— *Timon of Athens, Act 3, Sc. 1*

Such harmony is in immortal souls, but whilst this muddy vesture of decay doth grossly close it in, we cannot hear it.

— *Merchant of Venice, Act 5, Sc. 1*

Peace . . . — It makes men hate one another. — Reason, because they then less need one another. The wars for my money . . .
— Coriolanus, Act 4, Sc. 5

. . . experience be a jewel that I have purchased at an infinite rate.
— Merry Wives of Windsor, Act 2, Sc. 2

Men can counsel and speak comfort to that grief which they themselves not feel; but, tasting it, their counsel turns to passion . . . 'Tis all men's office to speak patience to those that wring under the load of sorrow, but no man's virtue nor sufficiency, to be so moral when he shall endure the like himself. Therefore give me no counsel . . .
— Much Ado about Nothing, Act 5, Sc. 1

. . . in all shapes that man goes up and down in from fourscore to thirteen.
— Timon of Athens, Act 2, Sc. 2

I'll leave my son my virtuous deeds behind; and would my father had left me no more! For all the rest is held at such a rate as brings a thousand-fold more care to keep than in possession any jot of pleasure.
— Henry VI, Part III, Act 2, Sc. 2

All things that are, are with more spirit chased than enjoy'd.
— Merchant of Venice, Act 2, Sc. 6

Place, riches and favour, prizes of accident as oft as merit.
— Troilus and Cressida, Act 3, Sc. 3

Our virtues lie in the interpretation of the time.
— Coriolanus, Act 4, Sc. 7

Our remedies oft in ourselves do lie which we ascribe to heaven . . .
— All's Well that Ends Well, Act 1, Sc. 1

37

HESITATION

His fault was thought . . .
— *Richard III, Act 2, Sc. 1*

A fustian riddle! . . . Nay, but first, let me see, let me see, let me see.
— *Twelfth Night, Act 2, Sc. 5*

. . . doth come and go between his purpose and his conscience.
— *King John, Act 4, Sc. 2*

O, these flaws and starts . . .
— *Macbeth, Act 3, Sc. 4*

The mutual conference that my mind hath had, by day, by night, waking
and in my dreams . . .
— *Henry VI, Part II, Act 1, Sc. 1*

. . . a hovering temporizer . . .
— *Winter's Tale, Act 1, Sc. 2*

For many men that stumble at the threshold are well foretold that danger
lurks within.
— *Henry VI, Part III, Act 4, Sc. 7*

. . . in perplexity and doubtful dilemma.
— *Merry Wives of Windsor, Act 4, Sc. 5*

Drew . . . musings into my mind, with thousand doubts . . .
— *Pericles, Act 1, Sc. 2*

Fain would I go . . . but many thousand reasons hold me back.
— *Henry IV, Part II, Act 2, Sc. 3*

Who seeks, and will not take when once 'tis offer'd, shall never find it more.
— *Antony and Cleopatra, Act 2, Sc. 7*

A time, methinks, too short to make a world-without-end bargain in.
— *Love's Labour's Lost, Act 5, Sc. 2*

Fears and scruples shake us . . .
— *Macbeth, Act 2, Sc. 3*

To be or not to be; that is the question;
Whether 'tis nobler in the mind to suffer
The slings and arrows of outrageous fortune,
Or to take arms against a sea of troubles,
And by opposing end them . . .
Thus conscience does make cowards of us all,
And thus the native hue of resolution
Is sicklied o'er with the pale cast of thought,
And enterprises of great pitch and moment
With this regard their currents turn awry
And lose the name of action.

— Hamlet, Act 3, Sc. 1

. . . doubts, wringing of the conscience, fears and despairs . . .

— Henry VIII, Act 2, Sc. 2

'Tis with my mind as with the tide swell'd up unto his height, that makes a still-stand, running neither way.

— Henry IV, Part II, Act 2, Sc. 3

Our doubts are traitors, and make us lose the good we oft might win by fearing to attempt.

— Measure for Measure, Act 1, Sc. 4

Faster than spring-time showers comes thought on thought.

— Henry VI, Part II, Act 3, Sc. 1

Perplex'd in the extreme . . .

— Othello, Act 5, Sc. 2

To do't, or no, is certain to me a break-neck.

— Winter's Tale, Act 1, Sc. 2

Modest doubt is call'd the beacon of the wise, the tent that searches to the bottom of the worst.

— Troilus and Cressida, Act 2, Sc. 2

. . . some craven scruple of thinking too precisely on the event.

— Hamlet, Act 4, Sc. 4

I feel such sharp dissension in my breast, such fierce alarums both of hope and fear, as I am sick with working of my thoughts.

— Henry VI, Part I, Act 5, Sc. 5

Incertainties now crown themselves assured . . .

— Sonnet 107

Then we must rate the cost . . . , which if we find outweighs ability, what do we then . . . ?
— *Henry IV, Part II, Act 1, Sc. 3*

Infirm of purpose!
— *Macbeth, Act 2, Sc. 2*

He's full of alteration and self-reproving.
— *King Lear, Act 5, Sc. 1*

I had a thing to say, but I will fit it with some better time.
— *King John, Act 3, Sc. 3*

Nice affections wavering stood in doubt.
— *Lover's Complaint*

I have considered with myself . . .
— *Henry VI, Part II, Act 5, Sc. 1*

If I know how or which way to order these affairs . . . never believe me.
— *Richard II, Act 2, Sc. 2*

I hear, yet say not much, but think the more.
— *Henry VI, Part III, Act 4, Sc. 1*

I and my bosom must debate a while . . .
— *Henry V, Act 4, Sc. 1*

There is a tide in the affairs of men which taken at the flood leads on to fortune; omitted, all the voyage of their life is bound in shallows and in miseries. On such a full sea are we now afloat, and we must take the current when it serves, or lose our ventures.
— *Julius Caesar, Act 4, Sc. 3*

38
BOORS

Is there no manners left . . .?

— *Winter's Tale, Act 4, Sc. 4*

. . . after his undressed, unpolished, uneducated, unpruned, untrained, or rather, unlettered, or ratherest, unconfirmed fashion.

— *Love's Labour's Lost, Act 4, Sc. 2*

The elephant hath joints, but none for courtesy.

— *Troilus and Cressida, Act 2, Sc. 3*

. . . wears a garment shapeless and unfinish'd.

— *Venus and Adonis*

. . . usually talk of a noun and a verb, and such abominable words as no Christian ear can endure to hear.

— *Henry VI, Part II, Act 4, Sc. 7*

. . . proud Italy, whose manners still our tardy apish nation limps after in base imitation.

— *Richard II, Act 2, Sc. 1*

It is common for the younger sort to lack discretion.

— *Hamlet, Act 2, Sc. 1*

. . . had a tongue with a tang.

— *The Tempest, Act 2, Sc. 2*

For grace thou wilt have none . . . not so much as will serve to be prologue to an egg and butter.

— *Henry IV, Part I, Act 1, Sc. 2*

Rude, in sooth, in good sooth, very rude.

— *Troilus and Cressida, Act 3, Sc. 1*

You might have spoken a thousand things that would have done the time more benefit and graced your kindness better.

— *Winter's Tale, Act 5, Sc. 1*

If you were civil and knew courtesy . . .

— *Midsummer Night's Dream, Act 3, Sc. 2*

What hempen home-spuns have we swaggering here?

— *Act 3, Sc. 1*

You are too blunt; go to it orderly.

— *Taming of the Shrew, Act 2, Sc. 1*

Blunt-witted lord, ignoble in demeanour!

— *Henry VI, Part II, Act 3, Sc. 2*

Too rough, too rude, too boisterous . . .

— *Romeo and Juliet, Act 1, Sc. 4*

Melodious discord, heavenly tune harsh-sounding.

— *Venus and Adonis*

Is there no respect of place, persons nor time in you?

— *Twelfth Night, Act 2, Sc. 3*

It were a fault to snatch words from my tongue.

— *Love's Labour's Lost, Act 5, Sc. 2*

His garments are rich, but he wears them not handsomely.

— *Winter's Tale, Act 4, Sc. 4*

There's a great abatement of kindness . . .

— *King Lear, Act 1, Sc. 4*

Have you no wit, manners, nor honesty but to gabble like tinkers at this time of night?

— *Twelfth Night, Act 3, Sc. 2*

. . . you were saucy at my gates.

— *Act 1, Sc. 5*

. . . language unmannerly . . .

— *Henry VIII, Act 1, Sc. 2*

And you will come into court and swear that I have a poor pennyworth in the English.

— *Merchant of Venice, Act 1, Sc. 2*

. . . cleave the general ear with horrid speech . . .

— *Hamlet, Act 2, Sc. 2*

Throw away respect, tradition, form and ceremonious duty . . .

— *Richard II, Act 3, Sc. 2*

Thou hast the most unsavoury similes . . .

— *Henry IV, Part I, Act 1, Sc. 2*

I will not jump with the common spirits and rank me with the barbarous multitudes.

— *Merchant of Venice, Act 2, Sc. 9*

A hollow burst of bellowing.

— The Tempest, Act 2, Sc. 1

Knock the door hard. — Let him knock till it ache . . .

— Comedy of Errors, Act 3, Sc. 1

It were a very gross kind of behaviour, as they say.

— Romeo and Juliet, Act 2, Sc. 4

This apish and unmannerly approach.

— King John, Act 5, Sc. 2

. . . have not well the gift of tongue.

— Henry IV, Part I, Act 5, Sc. 2

Rude am I in my speech, and little blest with the soft phrase of peace.

— Othello, Act 1, Sc. 3

My tongue could never learn sweet smoothing words.

— Richard III, Act 1, Sc. 2

And more he spoke, which sounded like clamour in a vault . . .

— Henry VI, Part III, Act 5, Sc. 2

This rudeness is a sauce to his good wit, which gives men stomach to digest his words with better appetite.

— Julius Caesar, Act 1, Sc. 2

Thou art too wild, too rude and bold of voice . . .

— Merchant of Venice, Act 2, Sc. 2

. . . defect of manners, want.of government . . .

— Henry IV, Part I, Act 3, Sc. 1

Why, 'tis a boisterous and cruel style . . .

— As You Like It, Act 4, Sc. 3

Thy wit wants edge and manners.

— Titus Andronicus, Act 2, Sc. 1

I advise you use your manners discreetly in all kinds of companies.

— Taming of the Shrew, Act 1, Sc. 1

If I blush, it is to see a nobleman want manners . . .

— Henry VIII, Act 3, Sc. 2

. . . quite athwart goes all decorum.

— Measure for Measure, Act 1, Sc. 3

I have no cunning in protestation, only downright oaths.
— *Henry V, Act 5, Sc. 2*

Harsh, featureless and rude . . .
— *Sonnet 11*

Our tongue is rough, coz, and my condition is not smooth . . .
— *Henry V, Act 5, Sc. 2*

. . . one half lunatic, a mad-cap ruffian and a swearing Jack, that thinks with oaths to face the matter out.
— *Taming of the Shrew, Act 2, Sc. 1*

. . . as blunt as the fencer's foils, which hit, but hurt not.
— *Much Ado about Nothing, Act 5, Sc. 2*

The truth you speak doth lack some gentleness, and time to speak it in; you rub the sore, when you should bring the plaster.
— *The Tempest, Act 2, Sc. 1*

. . . of what coarse metal ye are moulded.
— *Henry VIII, Act 3, Sc. 2*

. . . the breath that from my mistress reeks.
— *Sonnet 130*

To be received plain, I'll speak more gross . . .
— *Measure for Measure, Act 2, Sc. 4*

Unbidden guests are often welcomest when they are gone.
— *Henry VI, Part I, Act 2, Sc. 2*

Alas, what need you be so boisterous-rough?
— *King John, Act 4, Sc. 1*

It was always yet the trick of our English nation, if they have a good thing, to make it too common . . .
— *Henry IV, Part II, Act 1, Sc. 2*

He knows me as the blind man knows the cuckoo, by the bad voice.
— *Merchant of Venice, Act 5, Sc. 1*

Speak what terrible language you will; though you understand it not yourselves, no matter . . .
— *All's Well that Ends Well, Act 4, Sc. 1*

It is not well done, mark you now, to take the tales out of my mouth, ere it is made and finished.
— *Henry V, Act 4, Sc. 7*

. . . country manners . . .
— *King John, Act 1, Sc. 1*

. . . country matters . . .
— *Hamlet, Act 3, Sc. 2*

. . . rough and envious disposition . . .
— *As You Like It, Act 1, Sc. 2*

My lord would speak . . . — If it be aught to the old tune, my lord, it is as fat and fulsome to mine ear as howling after music.
— *Twelfth Night, Act 5, Sc. 1*

If you have any pity, grace or manners, you would not make me such an argument.
— *Midsummer Night's Dream, Act 3, Sc. 2*

39

VANITY

Ego et Rex meus.

— *Henry VIII, Act 3, Sc. 2*

I know him to be valiant. — . . . He told me so himself, and he said he cared not who knew it.

— *Henry V, Act 3, Sc. 7*

If ladies be but young and fair, they have the gift to know it.

— *As You Like It, Act 2, Sc. 7*

So much for praising myself, who, I myself will bear witness, is praiseworthy.

— *Much Ado about Nothing, Act 5, Sc. 2*

For it will come to pass, that every braggart shall be found an ass.

— *All's Well that Ends Well, Act 4, Sc. 3*

Yet, forgive me, God, that I do brag thus!

— *Henry V, Act 3, Sc. 6*

Setting the attraction of my good parts aside, I have no other charms.

— *Merry Wives of Windsor, Act 2, Sc. 2*

How but well? It were impossible I should speed amiss.

— *Taming of the Shrew, Act 2, Sc. 1*

That were to enlard his fat already pride . . .

— *Troilus and Cressida, Act 2, Sc. 3*

I think of as many matters as he, but I give heaven thanks and make no boast of them.

— *As You Like It, Act 2, Sc. 5*

We wound our modesty and make foul the clearness of our deservings, when of ourselves we publish them.

— *All's Well that Ends Well, Act 1, Sc. 3*

For when no friends are by, men praise themselves.

— *Titus Andronicus, Act 5, Sc. 3*

Why, here he comes, swelling like a turkey-cock.

— *Henry V, Act 5, Sc. 1*

Men's faults do seldom to themselves appear.

— *Rape of Lucrece*

The worthiness of praise distains his worth, if that the praised himself bring
the praise forth.
                              — *Troilus and Cressida, Act 1, Sc. 3*

Further to boast were neither true nor modest, unless I add we are honest.
                              — *Cymbeline, Act 5, Sc. 5*

You are sick of self-love . . .
                              — *Twelfth Night, Act 1, Sc. 5*

This breast of mine hath buried thoughts of great value, worthy cogitations.
                              — *Julius Caesar, Act 1, Sc. 2*

I might in virtues, beauties, livings, friends exceed account . . .
                              — *Merchant of Venice, Act 3, Sc. 2*

I can see his pride peep through each part of him.
                              — *Henry VIII, Act 1, Sc. 1*

Art thou so confident?
                              — *All's Well that Ends Well, Act 2, Sc. 1*

    Some glory in their birth, some in their skill,
    Some in their wealth, some in their body's force,
    Some in their garments . . .
                              — *Sonnet 91*

I do hate a proud man, as I hate the engendering of toads.
                              — *Troilus and Cressida, Act 2, Sc. 3*

He'll remember with advantages what feats he did that day.
                              — *Henry V, Act 4, Sc. 3*

I am constant as the northern star, of whose true-fix'd and resting quality
there is no fellow in the firmament.
                              — *Julius Caesar, Act 3, Sc. 1*

I am to discourse wonders . . .
                              — *Midsummer Night's Dream, Act 4, Sc. 2*

I will rise there with so full a glory that I will dazzle all the eyes . . .
                              — *Henry V, Act 1, Sc. 2*

To brag unto them, thus I did, and thus.
                              — *Coriolanus, Act 2, Sc. 2*

. . . stalks up and down like a peacock . . .
                              — *Troilus and Cressida, Act 3, Sc. 3*

As good a man as yourself, both in the disciplines of war, and in the deriva-
tion of my birth, and in other particularities.
                              — *Henry V, Act 3, Sc. 2*

O, that men's ears should be to counsel deaf, but not to flattery.
— *Timon of Athens, Act 1, Sc. 2*

I thank my beauty, I am fair . . .
— *Love's Labour's Lost, Act 4, Sc. 1*

In our faults by lies we flatter'd be.
— *Sonnet 138*

There are a sort of men, whose visages do cream and mantle like a standing pond, and do a wilful stillness entertain, with purpose to be dress'd in an opinion of wisdom, gravity, profound conceit, as who should say, "I am Sir Oracle, and when I ope my lips, let no dog bark!"
— *Merchant of Venice, Act 1, Sc. 1*

Pride is his own glass, his own trumpet, his own chronicle, and whatever praises itself but in the deed, devours the deed in the praise.
— *Troilus and Cressida, Act 2, Sc. 3*

Sin of self-love possesseth all mine eye
And all my soul and all my every part,
And for this sin there is no remedy,
It is so grounded inward in my heart.
Methinks no face so gracious is as mine,
No shape so true, no truth of such account,
And for myself mine own worth do define,
As I all other in all worths surmount . . .

— *Sonnet 62*

I have done the state some service, and they know 't.
— *Othello, Act 5, Sc. 2*

The best persuaded of himself, so crammed, as he thinks, with excellencies, that it is his grounds of faith that all that look on him love him.
— *Twelfth Night, Act 2, Sc. 3*

. . . an admirable conceited fellow.
— *Winter's Tale, Act 4, Sc. 4*

One whom the music of his own vain tongue doth ravish like enchanting harmony.
— *Love's Labour's Lost, Act 1, Sc. 1*

Shine out, fair sun, till I have bought a glass, that I may see my shadow as I pass.
— *Richard III, Act 1, Sc. 2*

He has been yonder i' the sun practising behaviour to his own shadow this half hour.
— *Twelfth Night, Act 2, Sc. 5*

40

UNDEPENDABLE

Where have you been all this while? When every thing is ended, then you
come.
— *Henry IV, Part II, Act 4, Sc. 3*

Cousin, how have you come so early by this lethargy?
— *Twelfth Night, Act 1, Sc. 5*

How has he the leisure to be sick in such a justling time?
— *Henry IV, Part I, Act 4, Sc. 1*

The excuse that thou dost make in this delay is longer than the tale thou
dost excuse.
— *Romeo and Juliet, Act 2, Sc. 5*

Hereditary sloth instructs me.
— *The Tempest, Act 2, Sc. 1*

. . . many hands and no use . . .
— *Troilus and Cressida, Act 1, Sc. 2*

. . . velvet-guards and Sunday-citizens.
— *Henry IV, Part I, Act 3, Sc. 1*

Briefly die their joys that place them on the truth of girls and boys.
— *Cymbeline, Act 5, Sc. 5*

Indeed, a sheep doth very often stray, an if the shepherd be awhile away.
— *Two Gentlemen of Verona, Act 1, Sc. 1*

For man is a giddy thing, and this is my conclusion.
— *Much Ado about Nothing, Act 5, Sc. 4*

. . . a fickle wavering nation . . .
— *Henry VI, Part I, Act 4, Sc. 1*

He that trusts to you, where he should find you lions, finds you hares . . .
— *Coriolanus, Act 1, Sc. 1*

Living dully sluggardized at home, wear out thy youth with shapeless
idleness.
— *Two Gentlemen of Verona, Act 1, Sc. 1*

That we would do we should do when we would . . .
— *Hamlet, Act 4, Sc. 7*

Have you forgot all sense of place and duty?

— *Othello, Act 2, Sc. 3*

He hath every month a new sworn brother.

— *Much Ado about Nothing, Act 1, Sc. 1*

. . . inconstancy of man's disposition . . .

— *Merry Wives of Windsor, Act 4, Sc. 5*

Look, as I blow this feather from my face, and as the air blows it to me again, obeying with my wind when I do blow, and yielding to another when it blows, commanded always by the greater gust; such is the lightness of you common men.

— *Henry VI, Part III, Act 3, Sc. 1*

. . . whose constancies expire before their fashions.

— *All's Well that Ends Well, Act 1, Sc. 2*

Improvident soldiers! had your watch been good, this sudden mischief never could have fall'n.

— *Henry VI, Part I, Act 2, Sc. 1*

Not much unlike young men, whom Aristotle thought unfit to hear moral philosophy.

— *Troilus and Cressida, Act 2, Sc. 2*

The undeserver may sleep, when the man of action is called on.

— *Henry IV, Part II, Act 2, Sc. 4*

He wears his faith but as the fashion of his hat; it ever changes . . .

— *Much Ado about Nothing, Act 1, Sc. 1*

I am a feather for each wind that blows . . .

— *Winter's Tale, Act 2, Sc. 3*

Such summer-birds are men.

— *Timon of Athens, Act 3, Sc. 6*

. . . everlastingly. — But how long shall that title "ever" last?

— *Richard III, Act 4, Sc. 4*

Good sentences and well pronounced. — They would be better, if well followed.

— *Merchant of Venice, Act 1, Sc. 2*

He's mad that trusts in the tameness of a wolf, a horse's health, a boy's love, or a whore's oath.

— *King Lear, Act 3, Sc. 6*

One foot in sea and one on shore, to one thing constant never.
— *Much Ado about Nothing, Act 2, Sc. 3*

His pettish lunes, his ebbs, his flows . . .
— *Troilus and Cressida, Act 2, Sc. 3*

'Tis no trusting to yond foolish lout . . .
— *Two Gentlemen of Verona, Act 4, Sc. 4*

. . . those men in England that do no work today.
— *Henry V, Act 4, Sc. 3*

I am betray'd by keeping company with men like you, men of inconstancy.
— *Love's Labour's Lost, Act 4, Sc. 3*

With every minute you do change a mind . . .
— *Coriolanus, Act 1, Sc. 1*

. . . these drones, that rob the bee of her honey.
— *Pericles, Act 2, Sc. 1*

What service is here! I think our fellows are asleep.
— *Coriolanus, Act 4, Sc. 5*

You patch'd up your excuses.
— *Antony and Cleopatra, Act 2, Sc. 2*

If there be one . . . that holds his honour higher than his ease . . .
— *Troilus and Cressida, Act 1, Sc. 3*

. . . behind-hand slackness.
— *Winter's Tale, Act 5, Sc. 1*

Who else but I . . . sweat in this business?
— *King John, Act 5, Sc. 2*

What is a man, if his chief good and market of his time be but to sleep and feed?
— *Hamlet, Act 4, Sc. 4*

. . . a vane blown with all winds.
— *Much Ado about Nothing, Act 3, Sc. 1*

You wear out a good wholesome forenoon . . .
— *Coriolanus, Act 2, Sc. 1*

The ship splits on the rock, which industry and courage might have saved.
— *Henry VI, Part III, Act 5, Sc. 4*

Of no more trust than love that's hired!

— Antony and Cleopatra, Act 5, Sc. 2

What! a young knave, and begging! Is there not wars? Is there not employment?

— Henry IV, Part II, Act 1, Sc. 2

The dust on antique time would lie unswept . . .

— Coriolanus, Act 2, Sc. 3

Was ever feather so lightly blown to and fro as this multitude?

— Henry VI, Part II, Act 4, Sc. 8

By this light, he changes more and more.

— Much Ado about Nothing, Act 5, Sc. 1

Were man but constant, he were perfect. That one error fills him with faults.

— Two Gentlemen of Verona, Act 5, Sc. 4

You have said well . . . and 'tis a kind of good deed to say well; and yet words are no deeds.

— Henry VIII, Act 3, Sc. 2

A fellow that never had the ache in his shoulders.

— Henry IV, Part II, Act 5, Sc. 1

What a strange drowsiness possesses them!

— The Tempest, Act 2, Sc. 1

A very little little let us do.

— Henry V, Act 4, Sc. 2

Upon the earth's increase why shouldst thou feed, unless the earth with thy increase be fed?

— Venus and Adonis

You are no surer, no, than is the coal of fire upon the ice, or hailstone in the sun.

— Coriolanus, Act 1, Sc. 1

Weariness can snore upon the flint, when resty sloth finds the down pillow hard.

— Cymbeline, Act 3, Sc. 6

. . . the unyoked humour of your idleness.

— Henry IV, Part I, Act 1, Sc. 2

Drones hive not with me . . .

— Merchant of Venice, Act 2, Sc. 5

. . . a tardy sluggard here.
                              — *Richard III, Act 5, Sc. 3*

A kind of lethargy, . . . a kind of sleeping in the blood.
                              — *Henry IV, Part II, Act 1, Sc. 2*

. . . all the idle weeds that grow in our sustaining corn.
                              — *King Lear, Act 4, Sc. 4*

. . . slug-a-bed!
                              — *Romeo and Juliet, Act 4, Sc. 5*

At all times alike men are not still the same . . .
                              — *Timon of Athens, Act 5, Sc. 1*

41

EVIL DEEDS

. . . did . . . offence of mighty note . . .
> — *All's Well that Ends Well, Act 5, Sc. 3*

. . . hath been tutor'd in the rudiments of many desperate studies.
> — *As You Like It, Act 5, Sc. 4*

You have done me much ungentleness . . .
> — *Act 5, Sc. 2*

Time is the old justice that examines all such offenders.
> — *Act 4, Sc. 1*

I wonder much that you would put me to this shame and trouble.
> — *Comedy of Errors, Act 5, Sc. 1*

. . . doing displeasure to the citizens . . .
> — *Act 5, Sc. 1*

One whose hard heart is buttoned up with steel . . . pitiless and rough . . .
> — *Act 4, Sc. 2*

. . . the wrongs . . . that here and there his fury had committed . . .
> — *Act 5, Sc. 1*

Hath abused and dishonour'd me even in the strength and height of injury.
> — *Act 5, Sc. 1*

What ruins are in me that can be found by him not ruin'd? then is he the ground of my defeatures.
> — *Act 2, Sc. 1*

Ill deeds are doubled with an evil word.
> — *Act 3, Sc. 2*

. . . tearing his country's bowels out.
> — *Coriolanus, Act 5, Sc. 3*

You are never without your tricks.
> — *Act 2, Sc. 3*

Thou hast done a deed whereat valour will weep.
> — *Act 5, Sc. 6*

Where go you with bats and clubs?
> — *Act 1, Sc. 1*

Come, come, you have been too rough, something too rough, you must
return and mend it.
— *Coriolanus, Act 3, Sc. 2*

Thou hast beat me out twelve several times . . .
— *Act 4, Sc. 5*

The gods look down, and this unnatural scene they laugh at.
— *Act 5, Sc. 3*

The wrongs he did me were nothing prince-like . . .
— *Cymbeline, Act 5, Sc. 5*

They have proclaim'd their malefactions.
— *Hamlet, Act 2, Sc. 2*

Remorseless, treacherous, lecherous, kindless villain!
— *Act 2, Sc. 2*

Eyes without feeling, feeling without sight . . .
— *Act 3, Sc. 4*

. . . these feats, so crimeful and so capital in nature . . .
— *Act 4, Sc. 7*

. . . some act that has no relish of salvation in 't.
— *Act 3, Sc. 3*

My offence is rank, it smells to heaven . . .
— *Act 3, Sc. 3*

Tell him his pranks have been too broad to bear with.
— *Act 3, Sc. 4*

God help the while! A bad world, I say.
— *Henry IV, Part I, Act 2, Sc. 4*

Wherein villanous, but in all things? wherein worthy, but in nothing?
— *Act 2, Sc. 4*

Moody beggars, starving for a time of pellmell havoc and confusion.
— *Act 5, Sc. 1*

. . . such misuse, such beastly shameless transformation, . . . as may not be
without much shame retold or spoken of.
— *Act 1, Sc. 1*

. . . out of limit and true rule you stand . . .
— *Act 4, Sc. 3*

Broke oath on oath, committed wrong on wrong.
                    — *Henry IV, Part I, Act 4, Sc. 3*

Must you be blushing? Wherefore blush you now?
                    — *Part II, Act 2, Sc. 2*

The acts commenced on this ball of earth . . .
                    — *Induction*

There is no honesty in such dealing.
                    — *Act 2, Sc. 1*

And good from bad find no partition.
                    — *Act 4, Sc. 1*

How I came by the crown, O God forgive.
                    — *Act 4, Sc. 5*

What I have done that misbecame my place.
                    — *Act 5, Sc. 2*

Capital crimes, chew'd, swallow'd and digested . . .
                    — *Henry V, Act 2, Sc. 2*

. . . many irreconciled iniquities . . .
                    — *Act 4, Sc. 1*

Which pillage they with merry march bring home . . .
                    — *Act 1, Sc. 2*

Some are yet ungotten and unborn that shall have cause to curse . . .
                    — *Act 1, Sc. 2*

Mangle the work of nature and deface the patterns that . . . had twenty
years been made.
                    — *Act 2, Sc. 4*

Their villany goes against my weak stomach, and therefore I must cast it up.
                    — *Act 3, Sc. 2*

You do not use me with that affability as in discretion you ought to use
me . . .
                    — *Act 3, Sc. 2*

Break out into a second course of mischief.
                    — *Act 4, Sc. 3*

I have been a truant in the law, and never yet could frame my will to it, and
therefore frame the law unto my will.
                    — *Henry VI, Part I, Act 2, Sc. 4*

Thou dost then wrong me, as that slaughterer doth which giveth many wounds when one will kill.
— *Henry VI, Part I, Act 2, Sc. 5*

Such is thy audacious wickedness, thy lewd, pestiferous and dissentious pranks, as very infants prattle of thy pride.
— *Act 3, Sc. 1*

Thou hast by tyranny these many years wasted our country . . .
— *Act 2, Sc. 3*

. . . hath wrought this hellish mischief . . .
— *Act 3, Sc. 2*

Look on thy country . . . Behold the wounds, the most unnatural wounds, which thou thyself hast given . . .
— *Act 3, Sc. 3*

Which now they hold by force and not by right.
— *Part II, Act 2, Sc. 2*

This is close dealing.
— *Act 2, Sc. 4*

. . . whose filth and dirt troubles the silver spring where England drinks.
— *Act 4, Sc. 1*

. . . shame enough to shame thee, wert thou not shameless.
— *Part III, Act 1, Sc. 4*

. . . ruthful deeds . . .
— *Act 2, Sc. 5*

. . . a fault too too unpardonable . . .
— *Act 1, Sc. 4*

A persecutor, I am sure, thou art.
— *Act 5, Sc. 6*

Teeth hadst thou in thy head when thou wast born, to signify thou camest to bite the world.
— *Act 5, Sc. 6*

Now, if you can blush and cry "guilty", . . . you'll show a little honesty.
— *Henry VIII, Act 3, Sc. 2*

He was never, but where he meant to ruin, pitiful . . .
— *Act 4, Sc. 2*

. . . the grand sum of his sins, the articles collected from his life.
— *Henry VIII, Act 3, Sc. 2*

Your great goodness, out of holy pity, absolved him with an axe.
— *Act 3, Sc. 2*

Who did guide, I mean, who set the body and the limbs of this great sport
together, as you guess?
— *Act 1, Sc. 1*

Your purpled hands do reek and smoke . . .
— *Julius Caesar, Act 3, Sc. 1*

They that have done this deed are honourable; what private griefs they
have, alas, I know not, that made them do it; they are wise and honourable, and will, no doubt, with reasons answer you.
— *Act 3, Sc. 2*

The evil that men do lives after them . . .
— *Act 3, Sc. 2*

Blood and destruction . . . so in use, and dreadful objects so familiar.
— *Act 3, Sc. 1*

All pity choked with custom of fell deeds.
— *Act 3, Sc. 1*

. . . this foul deed shall smell above the earth . . .
— *Act 3, Sc. 1*

The work we have in hand, most bloody, fiery and most terrible.
— *Act 1, Sc. 3*

We know his handiwork.
— *King John, Act 1, Sc. 1*

. . . that indigest which he hath left so shapeless and so rude.
— *Act 5, Sc. 7*

In this the antique and well noted face of plain old form is much disfigured.
— *Act 4, Sc. 2*

The earth had not a hole to hide this deed.
— *Act 4, Sc. 3*

The graceless action of a heavy hand . . .
— *Act 4, Sc. 3*

Your breath first kindled the dead coal of wars . . . and brought in matter that should feed this fire; and now 'tis far too huge to be blown out with that same weak wind which enkindled it.

— *King John, Act 5, Sc. 2*

And oftentimes excusing of a fault doth make the fault the worse by the excuse, as patches set upon a little breach discredit more in hiding of the fault than did the fault before it was so patch'd.

— *Act 4, Sc. 2*

This day hath made much work for tears.

— *Act 2, Sc. 1*

What small things are boisterous there.

— *Act 4, Sc. 1*

How oft the sight of means to do ill deeds make deeds ill done!

— *Act 4, Sc. 2*

He that stands upon a slippery place makes nice of no vile hold to stay him up.

— *Act 3, Sc. 4*

Thou monstrous injurer of heaven and earth!

— *Act 2, Sc. 1*

. . . on the winking of authority.

— *Act 4, Sc. 2*

Thou hast sworn to do amiss . . .

— *Act 3, Sc. 1*

Is there any cause in nature that makes these hard hearts?

— *King Lear, Act 3, Sc. 6*

. . . undivulged crimes, unwhipp'd of justice.

— *Act 3, Sc. 2*

. . . this unnatural dealing.

— *Act 3, Sc. 3*

Makest thou this shame thy pastime?

— *Act 2, Sc. 4*

He weeds the corn, and still lets grow the weeding.

— *Love's Labour's Lost, Act 1, Sc. 1*

Too bitter is thy jest.

— *Act 4, Sc. 3*

This is not generous, not gentle, not humble.
— *Love's Labour's Lost, Act 5, Sc. 2*

I have seen the day of wrong through the little hole of discretion.
— *Act 5, Sc. 2*

My lord, his throat is cut; that I did for him.
— *Macbeth, Act 3, Sc. 4*

Bloody instructions, which being taught return to plague the inventor.
— *Act 1, Sc. 7*

Unnatural deeds do breed unnatural troubles.
— *Act 5, Sc. 1*

Left her in her tears, and dried not one of them with his comfort.
— *Measure for Measure, Act 3, Sc. 1*

. . . bite the law by the nose.
— *Act 3, Sc. 1*

It is too general a vice, and severity must cure it.
— *Act 3, Sc. 2*

. . . a dangerous courtesy.
— *Act 4, Sc. 2*

Alack, when once our grace we have forgot, nothing goes right.
— *Act 4, Sc. 4*

The villany you teach me I will execute, and it shall go hard but I will better the instruction.
— *Merchant of Venice, Act 3, Sc. 1*

By yonder moon I swear you do me wrong.
— *Act 5, Sc. 1*

Whose own hard dealings teaches them suspect the thoughts of others.
— *Act 1, Sc. 3*

A stony adversary, an inhuman wretch uncapable of pity, void and empty from any dram of mercy.
— *Act 4, Sc. 1*

. . . unweighed behaviour . . .
— *Merry Wives of Windsor, Act 2, Sc. 1*

He hath wronged me in some humours.
— *Act 2, Sc. 1*

. . . share damnation together.
— *Merry Wives of Windsor*, Act 3, Sc. 2

I believe we must leave the killing out.
— *Midsummer Night's Dream*, Act 3, Sc. 1

For thou, I fear, hast given me cause to curse.
— Act 3, Sc. 2

I see you all are bent to set against me for your merriment.
— Act 3, Sc. 2

Thou drivest me past the bounds of . . . patience . . .
— Act 3, Sc. 2

. . . sent with broom before to sweep the dust behind the door.
— Act 5, Sc. 1

What's the matter, that you unlace your reputation thus?
— *Othello*, Act 2, Sc. 3

I therefore apprehend and do attach thee for an abuser of the world . . .
— Act 1, Sc. 2

Guiltiness will speak, though tongues were out of use.
— Act 5, Sc. 1

. . . err against all the rules of nature.
— Act 1, Sc. 3

An index and obscure prologue to the history of lust and foul thoughts.
— Act 2, Sc. 1

Every day thou daffest me with some device . . .
— Act 4, Sc. 2

Heaven stops the nose at it.
— Act 4, Sc. 2

Your present kindness makes my past miseries sports.
— *Pericles*, Act 5, Sc. 3

Such a piece of slaughter the sun and moon ne'er looked upon!
— Act 4, Sc. 3

Of all the faults beneath the heavens, the gods do like this the worst.
— Act 4, Sc. 3

. . . sets seeds and roots of shame and iniquity.
— Act 4, Sc. 6

Serve by indenture to the common hangman.

— *Pericles, Act 4, Sc. 6*

The earth is throng'd by man's oppression, and the poor worm doth die
for 't.

— *Act 1, Sc. 1*

Shalt have thy trespass cited up in rhymes,
And sung by children in succeeding times.

— *Rape of Lucrece*

The rough beast that knows no gentle right, nor aught obeys but his foul
appetite.

— *Rape of Lucrece*

The shame and fault finds no excuse nor end.

— *Rape of Lucrece*

A happy gentleman . . . by you unhappied.

— *Richard II, Act 3, Sc. 1*

. . . the very book indeed where all my sins are writ.

— *Act 4, Sc. 1*

If thy offences were on record, would it not shame thee . . . to read a
lecture of them?

— *Act 4, Sc. 1*

By bad courses may be understood that their events can never fall out
good.

— *Act 2, Sc. 1*

Have stoop'd my neck under your injuries . . .

— *Act 3, Sc. 1*

No beast so fierce but knows some touch of pity. — But I know none, and
therefore am no beast.

— *Richard III, Act 1, Sc. 2*

Faith, some certain dregs of conscience are yet within me.
— Remember our reward, when the deed is done.
'Zounds . . . I had forgot the reward.
— Where is thy conscience now?
In the . . . purse.

— *Act 1, Sc. 4*

The sorrow that I have by right is yours, and all the pleasures you usurp
are mine.

— *Act 1, Sc. 3*

Conscience is but a word that cowards use, devised at first to keep the strong in awe.

— *Richard III, Act 5, Sc. 3*

. . . some offence that seems disgracious . . .

— *Act 3, Sc. 7*

Tut, tut, thou art all ice, thy kindness freezeth.

— *Act 4, Sc. 2*

The world is grown so bad, that wrens make prey where eagles dare not perch.

— *Act 1, Sc. 3*

Tyrants themselves wept when it was reported.

— *Act 1, Sc. 3*

The secret mischiefs that I set abroach I lay unto the grievous charge of others.

— *Act 1, Sc. 3*

This deep disgrace in brotherhood . . .

— *Act 1, Sc. 1*

Thyself thyself misusest.

— *Act 4, Sc. 4*

That foul defacer of God's handiwork, that excellent grand tyrant of the earth.

— *Act 4, Sc. 4*

Thou shamest thy shape, thy love, thy wit . . . digressing from the valour of a man.

— *Romeo and Juliet, Act 3, Sc. 3*

Mischief, thou art swift to enter in the thoughts of desperate men.

— *Act 5, Sc. 1*

. . . this general evil they maintain.

— *Sonnet 121*

I will comment upon that offence.

— *Sonnet 89*

Making a famine where abundance lies.

— *Sonnet 1*

Tricks eleven and twenty long.

— *Taming of the Shrew, Act 4, Sc. 2*

Such an injury would vex a very saint.

— *Act 3, Sc. 2*

Thus strangers may be haled and abused.
— *Taming of the Shrew*, Act 5, Sc. 1

. . . in no sense is meet or amiable.
— *Act 5, Sc. 2*

. . . snip and nip and cut and slish and slash.
— *Act 4, Sc. 3*

He's composed of harshness.
— *The Tempest*, Act 3, Sc. 1

. . . mischiefs manifold . . .
— *Act 1, Sc. 2*

Religion groans at it.
— *Timon of Athens*, Act 3. Sc. 2

Now breathless wrong shall sit and pant in your great chairs of ease.
— *Act 5, Sc. 4*

Their knives care not, while you have throats to answer.
— *Act 5, Sc. 1*

Dishonour traffics with man's nature . . .
Act 1, Sc. 1

. . . like a boar too savage, doth root up his country's peace.
— *Act 5, Sc. 1*

Canst thou say all this, and never blush?
— *Titus Andronicus*, Act 5, Sc. 1

Tut, I have done a thousand dreadful things as willingly as one would kill a fly.
— *Act 5, Sc. 1*

. . . your honour . . . spotted, detested and abominable . . .
— *Act 2, Sc. 3*

By whom our heavy haps had their beginning.
— *Act 5, Sc. 3*

Chief architect and plotter of these woes.
— *Act 5, Sc. 3*

. . . some device of further misery, to make us wonder'd at in time to come.
— *Act 3, Sc. 1*

A deed of death done on the innocent . . .
— *Act 3, Sc. 2*

This was but a deed of charity to that which thou shalt hear of me anon.
— *Act 5, Sc. 1*

. . . some notorious ill; as kill a man, or else devise his death; ravish a maid, or plot the way to do it; accuse some innocent, and forswear myself; set deadly enmity between two friends; make poor men's cattle break their necks; set fire on barns and hay-stacks in the night.
— *Titus Andronicus, Act 5, Sc. 1*

. . . the spring whom you have stain'd with mud . . .
— *Act 5, Sc. 2*

What hast thou done, unnatural and unkind?
— *Act 5, Sc. 3*

These wrongs, unspeakable, past patience, or more than any living man could bear.
— *Act 5, Sc. 3*

No, I warrant you, he will not hear of godliness.
— *Act 3, Sc. 4*

In nature there's no blemish but the mind; none can be call'd deform'd but the unkind.
— *Twelfth Night, Act 3, Sc. 4*

I am one of those gentle ones that will use the devil himself with courtesy.
— *Act 4, Sc. 2*

. . . harsh, untuneable and bad.
— *Two Gentlemen of Verona, Act 3, Sc. 1*

Perversely she perseveres . . .
— *Act 3, Sc. 2*

'Tis an ill office for a gentleman.
— *Act 3, Sc. 2*

Which the hot tyrant stains and soon bereaves, as caterpillars do the tender leaves.
Venus and Adonis

What studied torments, tyrant, hast for me? What wheels? racks? fires? what flaying? boiling? in leads or oils? what old or newer torture . . .?
— *Winter's Tale, Act 3, Sc. 2*

. . . that forced baseness which he has put upon 't.
— *Act 2, Sc. 3*

The prince himself is about a piece of iniquity . . .
— *Act 4, Sc. 4*

. . . all thy by-gone fooleries . . .
— *Act 3, Sc. 2*

42

ANGER

Why, look you, how you storm!

— *Merchant of Venice, Act 1, Sc. 3*

In his rages, and his furies, and his wraths, and his cholers, and his moods, and his displeasures, and his indignations . . .

— *Henry V, Act 4, Sc. 7*

We cannot call her winds and waters sighs and tears; they are greater storms and tempests than almanacs can report.

— *Antony and Cleopatra, Act 1, Sc. 2*

Do you dare our anger? 'Tis in few words, but spacious in effect.

— *Timon of Athens, Act 3, Sc. 5*

What, angry, . . .! Do you change colour?

— *Two Gentlemen of Verona, Act 2, Sc. 4*

Give me leave to curse awhile.

— *Henry VI, Part I, Act 5, Sc. 3*

If I be waspish, best beware my sting.

— *Taming of the Shrew, Act 2, Sc. 1*

I have a heart as little apt as yours, but yet a brain that leads my use of anger to better vantage.

— *Coriolanus, Act 3, Sc. 2*

To be furious is to be frighted out of fear.

— *Antony and Cleopatra, Act 3, Sc. 13*

For young hot colts being raged do rage the more.

— *Richard II, Act 2, Sc. 1*

God's bread! it makes me mad . . .

— *Romeo and Juliet, Act 3, Sc. 5*

They say, my lords, "Ira furor brevis est," but yond man is ever angry.

— *Timon of Athens, Act 1, Sc. 2*

He did provoke me with language that would make me spurn the sea, if it could so roar to me.

— *Cymbeline, Act 5, Sc. 5*

With too much blood and too little brain . . .

— *Troilus and Cressida, Act 5, Sc. 1*

For more is to be said and to be done than out of anger can be uttered.
— *Henry IV, Part I, Act 1, Sc. 1*

High-stomach'd . . . and full of ire, in rage deaf as the sea, hasty as fire.
— *Richard II, Act 1, Sc. 1*

Stamp, rave and fret . . .
— *Henry VI, Part III, Act 1, Sc. 4*

Spend'st thou thy fury on some worthless song . . .?
— *Sonnet 100*

Never anger made good guard for itself.
— *Antony and Cleopatra, Act 4, Sc. 1*

. . . whose rage doth rend like interrupted waters . . .
— *Coriolanus, Act 3, Sc. 1*

Who can speak broader than he that has no house to put his head in? such may rail against great buildings.
— *Timon of Athens, Act 3, Sc. 4*

Her fume needs no spurs; she'll gallop far enough to her destruction.
— *Henry VI, Part II, Act 1, Sc. 3*

. . . may haply be a little angry . . .
— *Cymbeline, Act 4, Sc. 1*

Violent fires soon burn out themselves.
— *Richard II, Act 2, Sc. 1*

. . . hare-brained . . . govern'd by a spleen.
— *Henry IV, Part I, Act 5, Sc. 2*

You look angerly.
— *Macbeth, Act 3, Sc. 5*

Desire not to allay my rages and revenges with your colder reasons.
— *Coriolanus, Act 5, Sc. 3*

. . . your health; the which, if you give o'er to stormy passion, must perforce decay.
— *Henry IV, Part II, Act 1, Sc. 1*

How impatience loureth in your face!
— *Comedy of Errors, Act 2, Sc. 1*

. . . the appertaining rage to such a greeting . . .
— *Romeo and Juliet, Act 3, Sc. 1*

Why art thou then exasperate . . .?
— *Troilus and Cressida, Act 5, Sc. 1*

The brain may devise laws for the blood, but a hot temper leaps o'er a cold decree.
— *Merchant of Venice, Act 1, Sc. 2*

My blood begins my safer guides to rule.
— *Othello, Act 2, Sc. 3*

. . . whose bosom burns with an incensed fire of injuries.
— *Henry IV, Part II, Act 1, Sc. 3*

Is your blood so madly hot that no discourse of reason, nor fear of bad success in a bad cause, can qualify the same?
— *Troilus and Cressida, Act 2, Sc. 2*

Who can be patient in such extremes?
— *Henry VI, Part III, Act 1, Sc. 1*

I thought thy disposition better temper'd.
— *Romeo and Juliet, Act 3, Sc. 3*

Bait not me; I'll not endure it . . . Urge me no more; I shall forget myself. Have mind upon your health; tempt me no farther.
— *Julius Caesar, Act 4, Sc. 3*

His incensement at this moment is so implacable, that satisfaction can be none but by pangs of death and sepulchre.
— *Twelfth Night, Act 3, Sc. 4*

Small showers last long; but sudden storms are short.
— *Richard II, Act 2, Sc. 1*

Disguise fair nature with hard-favour'd rage.
— *Henry V, Act 3, Sc. 1*

. . . a wayward son, spiteful and wrathful.
— *Macbeth, Act 3, Sc. 5*

A good mouth-filling oath . . .
— *Henry IV, Part I, Act 3, Sc. 1*

Well could I curse away a winter's night, though standing naked on a mountain top, where biting cold would never let grass grow, and think it but a minute spent in sport.
— *Henry VI, Part II, Act 3, Sc. 2*

When that rash humour which my mother gave me makes me forgetful.
— *Julius Caesar, Act 4, Sc. 3*

Anger is like a full-hot horse, who being allow'd his way, self-mettle tires him.
— *Henry VIII, Act 1, Sc. 1*

Seal up the mouth of outrage for a while, till we can clear these ambiguities.
— *Romeo and Juliet, Act 5, Sc. 3*

I understand a fury in your words, but not the words.
— *Othello, Act 4, Sc. 2*

And men ne'er spend their fury on a child.
— *Henry VI, Part III, Act 5, Sc. 5*

43

LISTEN!

Hast thou never an eye in thy head? canst not hear?
> — *Henry IV, Part I, Act 2, Sc. 1*

Lay thy finger thus, and let thy soul be instructed.
> — *Othello, Act 2, Sc. 1*

It is the disease of not listening, the malady of not marking.
> — *Henry IV, Part II, Act 1, Sc. 2*

Till then, my noble friend, chew upon this . . .
> — *Julius Caesar, Act 1, Sc. 2*

Then patiently hear my impatience.
> — *Richard III, Act 4, Sc. 4*

You are very sensible, and yet you miss my sense.
> — *Taming of the Shrew, Act 5, Sc. 2*

Wisdom cries out in the streets, and no man regards it.
> - - *Henry IV, Part I, Act 1, Sc. 2*

List to this conjunction . . .
> — *King John, Act 2, Sc. 1*

He nor sees, nor hears us what we say.
> — *Henry VI, Part III, Act 2, Sc. 6*

And now, . . . listen great things.
> — *Julius Caesar, Act 4, Sc. 1*

What shall be done? he will not hear till feel.
> — *Timon of Athens, Act 2, Sc. 2*

Your betters have endured me say my mind, and if you cannot, best you stop your ears.
> — *Taming of the Shrew, Act 4, Sc. 3*

Win her with gifts, if she respect not words.
> — *Two Gentlemen of Verona, Act 3, Sc. 1*

Many a time and often I ha' dined with him, and told him on 't, . . . and yet he would embrace no counsel, take no warning . . .
> — *Timon of Athens, Act 3, Sc. 1*

Hear me more plainly.

     — *Henry IV, Part II, Act 4, Sc. 1*

Be not obdurate, open thy deaf ears.

     — *Titus Andronicus, Act 2, Sc. 3*

Stand at her doors, and tell them, there thy fixed foot shall grow till thou
have audience.

     — *Twelfth Night, Act 1, Sc. 4*

I beseech your honour, vouchsafe me a word; it does concern you near.

     — *Timon of Athens, Act 1, Sc. 2*

If it will please Caesar to be so good to Caesar as to hear me . . .

     — *Julius Caesar, Act 2, Sc. 4*

Have done with words, my lords, and hear me speak . . . give no limits to
my tongue.

     — *Henry VI, Part III, Act 2, Sc. 2*

Dost thou scorn me for my gentle counsel?

     — *Richard III, Act 1, Sc. 3*

Construe my speeches better, if you may.

     — *Love's Labour's Lost, Act 5, Sc. 2*

Let them hear what fearful words I utter.

     — *Titus Andronicus, Act 5, Sc. 2*

Much he spoke, and learnedly, for life, but all was either pitied in him or
forgotten.

     — *Henry VIII, Act 2, Sc. 1*

I fear my Julia would not deign my lines, receiving them from such a
worthless post.

     — *Two Gentlemen of Verona, Act 1, Sc. 1*

I were best to leave him, for he will not hear.

     — *Henry VI, Part I, Act 5, Sc. 3*

According to the fair play of the world, let me have audience.

     — *King John, Act 5, Sc. 2*

Softly, my masters! if you be gentlemen, do me this right; hear me with
patience.

     — *Taming of the Shrew, Act 1, Sc. 2*

. . . you recount your sorrows to a stone.

     — *Titus Andronicus, Act 3, Sc. 1*

Bestow on me the sense of hearing.
— *Love's Labour's Lost, Act 5, Sc. 2*

To my unfolding lend your prosperous ear . . .
— *Othello, Act 1, Sc. 3*

. . . you hear now, too late . . .
— *Timon of Athens, Act 2, Sc. 2*

I have said too much unto a heart of stone.
— *Twelfth Night, Act 3, Sc. 4*

44

CRITICISM

Mark now, how a plain tale shall put you down.
— *Henry IV, Part I, Act 2, Sc. 4*

If I were covetous, ambitious or perverse, as he will have me, how am I so poor?
— *Henry VI, Part I, Act 3, Sc. 1*

. . . all find-faults . . .
— *Henry V, Act 5, Sc. 2*

. . . the carping censures of the world.
— *Richard III, Act 3, Sc. 5*

I would not, as they term it, praise her.
— *Troilus and Cressida, Act 1, Sc. 1*

. . . make mouths upon me when I turn my back.
— *Midsummer Night's Dream, Act 3, Sc. 2*

As a bear, encompass'd round with dogs, who having pinch'd a few and made them cry, the rest stand all aloof, and bark at him.
— *Henry VI, Part III, Act 2, Sc. 1*

. . . may perhaps call him half a score knaves or so . . .
— *Taming of the Shrew, Act 1, Sc. 2*

. . . aught that I can speak in his dispraise.
— *Two Gentlemen of Verona, Act 3, Sc. 2*

Turn then my freshest reputation to a savour that may strike the dullest nostril where I arrive . . .
— *Winter's Tale, Act 1, Sc. 2*

What tongue shall smooth thy name, when I . . . have mangled it?
— *Romeo and Juliet, Act 3, Sc. 2*

Such carping is not commendable.
— *Much Ado about Nothing, Act 3, Sc. 1*

. . . breathe his faults so quaintly . . .
— *Hamlet, Act 2, Sc. 1*

Yourself and all the world that talked of her have talked amiss of her.
— *Taming of the Shrew, Act 2, Sc. 1*

. . make pretence of wrong that I have done him.
— *Pericles, Act 1, Sc. 2*

Let them accuse me by invention, I will answer in mine honour.
— *Coriolanus, Act 3, Sc. 2*

Be thou as chaste as ice, as pure as snow, thou shalt not escape calumny.
— *Hamlet, Act 3, Sc. 1*

This, and all else this talking lord can lay upon my credit, I answer, is most false.
— *Henry VIII, Act 3, Sc. 2*

. . . public accusation, uncovered slander, unmitigated rancour.
— *Much Ado about Nothing, Act 4, Sc. 1*

A blasting and scandalous breath . . .
— *Measure for Measure, Act 5, Sc. 1*

Do not cast away an honest man for a villain's accusation.
— *Henry VI, Part II, Act 1, Sc. 3*

She did call me rascal fiddler and twangling Jack, with twenty such vile terms, as had she studied to misuse me so.
— *Taming of the Shrew, Act 2, Sc. 1*

Done to death by slanderous tongues.
— *Much Ado about Nothing, Act 5, Sc. 3*

No might nor greatness in mortality can censure 'scape; back-wounding calumny the whitest virtue strikes.
— *Measure for Measure, Act 3, Sc. 2*

They do but jest, poison in jest.
— *Hamlet, Act 3, Sc. 2*

Nay, but speak not maliciously.
— *Coriolanus, Act 1, Sc. 1*

Men's evil manners live in brass; their virtues we write in water.
— *Henry VIII, Act 4, Sc. 2*

Drown the sad remembrance of those wrongs which thou supposest I have done to thee.
— *Richard III, Act 4, Sc. 4*

I will speak daggers to her, but use none.
— *Hamlet, Act 3, Sc. 2*

Look how we can, or sad or merrily, interpretation will misquote our looks.
> — *Henry IV, Part I, Act 5, Sc. 2*

Not able to produce more accusation than your own weak-hinged fancy.
> — *Winter's Tale, Act 2, Sc. 3*

To follow still the changes of the moon with fresh suspicions?
> — *Othello, Act 3, Sc. 3*

Spoke scantly of me . . .
> — *Antony and Cleopatra, Act 3, Sc. 4*

Hath he not twit our sovereign lady here with ignominious words?
> — *Henry VI, Part II, Act 3, Sc. 1*

The complaints I hear of thee are grievous.
> — *Henry IV, Part I, Act 2, Sc. 4*

. . . spoke such scurvy and provoking terms against your honour . . .
> — *Othello, Act 1, Sc. 2*

. . . satire, keen and critical . . .
> — *Midsummer Night's Dream, Act 5, Sc. 1*

Malicious censurers, which ever, as ravenous fishes, do a vessel follow . . .
> — *Henry VIII, Act 1, Sc. 2*

Mere suspicion in that kind will do as if for surety.
> — *Othello, Act 1, Sc. 3*

Had his great name profaned with their scorns.
> — *Henry IV, Part I, Act 3, Sc. 2*

What have I done, that thou darest wag thy tongue in noise so rude against me?
> — *Hamlet, Act 3, Sc. 4*

Their tongues rot that speak against us!
> — *Antony and Cleopatra, Act 3, Sc. 7*

Throw your vile guesses in the devil's teeth, from whence you have them.
> — *Othello, Act 3, Sc. 4*

Causeless have laid disgraces on my head.
> — *Henry VI, Part II, Act 3, Sc. 1*

His backward voice is to utter foul speeches and to detract.
> — *The Tempest, Act 2, Sc. 2*

. . . wind of blame . . .

— Hamlet, Act 4, Sc. 7

. . . thrown such despite and heavy terms upon her, as true hearts cannot bear.

— Othello, Act 4, Sc. 2

. . . was made a wonder and a pointing stock to every idle rascal follower.

— Henry VI, Part II, Act 2, Sc. 4

Volumes of report run with these false and most contrarious quests upon thy doings.

— Measure for Measure, Act 4, Sc. 1

He speaks most vilely of you, like a foul-mouthed man as he is.

— Henry IV, Part I, Act 3, Sc. 3

Thou monstrous slanderer of heaven and earth!

— King John, Act 2, Sc. 1

A vulgar comment will be made of it.

— Comedy of Errors, Act 3, Sc. 1

Believe me, there's an ill opinion spread then, even of yourself.

— Henry VIII, Act 2, Sc. 2

. . . a sharp wit, . . . whose edge hath power to cut, whose will still wills it should none spare that come within his power.

— Love's Labour's Lost, Act 2, Sc. 1

They are prepared with accusations, as I hear, more strong than are upon you yet.

— Coriolanus, Act 3, Sc. 2

We in the world's wide mouth live scandalized and foully spoken of.

— Henry IV, Part I, Act 1, Sc. 3

'Tis slander, whose edge is sharper than the sword.

— Cymbeline, Act 3, Sc. 4

A most singular and choice epithet.

— Love's Labour's Lost, Act 5, Sc. 1

Rotten opinion, who hath writ me down after my seeming.

— Henry IV, Part II, Act 5, Sc. 2

. . . lines that wound . . . to the quick.

— Titus Andronicus, Act 4, Sc. 2

Traduced by ignorant tongues, which neither know my faculties nor
person.
— *Henry VIII*, Act 1, Sc. 2

For slander lives upon succession, for ever housed where it gets possession.
— *Comedy of Errors*, Act 3, Sc. 1

. . . seeking tales and information against this man . . .
— *Henry VIII*, Act 5, Sc. 3

These reproachful speeches . . . that he hath breathed in my dishonour
here.
— *Titus Andronicus*, Act 2, Sc. 1

. . . speech of insultment . . .
— *Cymbeline*, Act 3, Sc. 5

An old lord of the council rated me the other day in the street about you, sir.
— *Henry IV, Part I*, Act 1, Sc. 2

. . . takes exceptions at your person.
— *Two Gentlemen of Verona*, Act 5, Sc. 2

They are scoundrels and substractors that say so of him.
— *Twelfth Night*, Act 1, Sc. 3

Remove your thought; it doth abuse your bosom.
— *Othello*, Act 4, Sc. 2

. . . the shrug, the hum or ha, these petty brands that calumny doth use.
— *Winter's Tale*, Act 2, Sc. 1

Ill will never said well.
— *Henry V*, Act 3, Sc. 7

. . . slander Valentine with falsehood, cowardice and poor descent.
— *Two Gentlemen of Verona*, Act 3, Sc. 2

. . . drunken prophecies, libels and dreams.
— *Richard III*, Act 1, Sc. 1

45

DREAMERS

He is a dreamer; let us leave him, pass.

         — *Julius Caesar, Act 1, Sc. 2*

I reckon this always — that a man is never undone till he be hanged.

         — *Two Gentlemen of Verona, Act 2, Sc. 5*

The miserable have no other medicine but only hope.

         — *Measure for Measure, Act 3, Sc. 1*

Feeds on his wonder, keeps himself in clouds . . .

         — *Hamlet, Act 4, Sc. 5*

, . lined himself with hope, eating the air on promise of supply.

         — *Henry IV, Part II, Act 1, Sc. 3*

The task he undertakes is numbering sands and drinking oceans dry.

         — *Richard II, Act 2, Sc. 2*

Their thoughts do hit the roofs of palaces . . .

         — *Cymbeline, Act 3, Sc. 3*

. . . the golden time I look for . . .

         — *Henry VI, Part III, Act 3, Sc. 2*

. . . the star-gazers . . .

         — *Venus and Adonis*

Hope to joy is little less in joy than hope enjoy'd.

         — *Richard II, Act 2, Sc. 3*

Thy wish was father . . . to that thought.

         — *Henry IV, Part II, Act 4, Sc. 5*

We may boldly spend upon the hope of what is to come in . . .

         — *Henry IV, Part I, Act 4, Sc. 1*

Lambkins, we will live.

         — *Henry V, Act 2, Sc. 1*

An army have I muster'd in my thoughts . . .

         — *Henry VI, Part I, Act 1, Sc. 1*

. . . thoughts and dreams and sighs, wishes and tears . . .

         — *Midsummer Night's Dream, Act 1, Sc. 1*

45

DREAMERS

He is a dreamer; let us leave him, pass.
— Julius Caesar, Act 1, Sc. 2

I reckon this always — that a man is never undone till he be hanged.
— Two Gentlemen of Verona, Act 2, Sc. 5

The miserable have no other medicine but only hope.
— Measure for Measure, Act 3, Sc. 1

Feeds on his wonder, keeps himself in clouds . . .
— Hamlet, Act 4, Sc. 5

. . . lined himself with hope, eating the air on promise of supply.
— Henry IV, Part II, Act 1, Sc. 3

The task he undertakes is numbering sands and drinking oceans dry.
— Richard II, Act 2, Sc. 2

Their thoughts do hit the roofs of palaces . . .
— Cymbeline, Act 3, Sc. 3

. . . the golden time I look for . . .
— Henry VI, Part III, Act 3, Sc. 2

. . . the star-gazers . . .
— Venus and Adonis

Hope to joy is little less in joy than hope enjoy'd.
— Richard II, Act 2, Sc. 3

Thy wish was father . . . to that thought.
— Henry IV, Part II, Act 4, Sc. 5

We may boldly spend upon the hope of what is to come in . . .
— Henry IV, Part I, Act 4, Sc. 1

Lambkins, we will live.
— Henry V, Act 2, Sc. 1

An army have I muster'd in my thoughts . . .
— Henry VI, Part I, Act 1, Sc. 1

. . . thoughts and dreams and sighs, wishes and tears . . .
— Midsummer Night's Dream, Act 1, Sc. 1

But shall I live in hope? — All men, I hope, live so.
                              — *Richard III, Act 1, Sc. 2*

An esperance so obstinately strong, that doth invert the attest of eyes and ears.
                              — *Troilus and Cressida, Act 5, Sc. 2*

Past and to come seems best; things present, worst.
                              — *Henry IV, Part II, Act 1, Sc. 3*

Such shaping fantasies, that apprehend more than cool reason ever comprehends.
                              — *Midsummer Night's Dream, Act 5, Sc. 1*

My dreams presage some joyful news at hand . . .
                              — *Romeo and Juliet, Act 5, Sc. 1*

Now sits expectation in the air . . .
                              — *Henry V, Act 2, Prologue*

Prove true, imagination, O prove true . . . !
                              — *Twelfth Night, Act 3, Sc. 4*

Here we wander in illusions . . .
                              — *Comedy of Errors, Act 4, Sc. 3*

Tomorrow, then, I judge a happy day.
                              — *Richard III, Act 3, Sc. 4*

Expectation fainted, longing for what it had not.
                              — *Antony and Cleopatra, Act 3, Sc. 6*

The world may laugh again; and I may live to do you kindness . . .
                              — *Henry VI, Part II, Act 2, Sc. 4*

This is the very coinage of your brain . . .
                              — *Hamlet, Act 3, Sc. 4*

. . . by the strength of their illusions shall draw him on to his confusion.
                              — *Macbeth, Act 3, Sc. 5*

So full of shapes is fancy, that it alone is high fantastical.
                              — *Twelfth Night, Act 1, Sc. 1*

The imaginary relish is so sweet that it enchants my sense.
                              — *Troilus and Cressida, Act 3, Sc. 2*

. . . dreaming of renown.
                              — *Henry VI, Part III, Act 2, Sc. 1*

True hope is swift, and flies with swallow's wings; kings it makes gods, and meaner creatures kings.

> — *Richard III, Act 5, Sc. 2*

Hope is a lover's staff; walk hence with that, and manage it against despairing thoughts.

> — *Two Gentlemen of Verona, Act 3, Sc. 1*

Against ill chances men are ever merry, but heaviness foreruns the good event. — Therefore be merry, coz, since sudden sorrow serves to say thus, "Some good thing comes tomorrow."

> — *Henry IV, Part II, Act 4, Sc. 2*

Oft expectation fails, and most oft there where most it promises.

> — *All's Well that Ends Well, Act 2, Sc. 1*

There is hope all will be well.

> — *Henry VIII, Act 2, Sc. 3*

. . . long'd-for change or better state.

> — *King John, Act 4, Sc. 2*

. . . the imagined happiness . . .

> — *Romeo and Juliet, Act 2, Sc. 6*

Chewing the food of sweet and bitter fancy . . .

> — *As You Like It, Act 4, Sc. 3*

He takes false shadows for true substances.

> — *Titus Andronicus, Act 3, Sc. 2*

I do spy a kind of hope.

> — *Romeo and Juliet, Act 4, Sc. 1*

Expectation, tickling skittish spirits . . .

> — *Troilus and Cressida, Prologue*

Imagination of some great exploit drives him . . .

> — *Henry IV, Part I, Act 1, Sc. 3*

. . . dreaming on this fond exploit . . .

> — *Richard III, Act 5, Sc. 3*

True, I talk of dreams, which are the children of an idle brain, begot of nothing but vain fantasy.

> — *Romeo and Juliet, Act 1, Sc. 4*

The ample proposition that hope makes in all designs begun on earth below fails in the promised largeness . . .

> — *Troilus and Cressida, Act 1, Sc. 3*

And let us . . . on your imaginary forces work.

— *Henry V, Prologue*

. . . the baseless fabric of this vision . . .

— *The Tempest, Act 4, Sc. 1*

Yet I know a way, if it take right, in spite of fortune will bring me off again.

— *Henry VIII, Act 3, Sc. 2*

When time shall serve, there shall be smiles . . .

— *Henry V, Act 2, Sc. 1*

Strong as a tower in hope . . .

— *Richard II, Act 1, Sc. 3*

As when the bird of wonder dies, the maiden phoenix, her ashes new create another heir as great in admiration as herself . . .

— *Henry VIII, Act 5, Sc. 5*

One that draws the model of a house beyond his power to build it.

— *Henry IV, Part II, Act 1, Sc. 3*

46

SUNDRY SCOUNDRELS, MISCREANTS, WASTRELS, ROGUES AND FOOLS

The owner of no one good quality worthy your lordship's entertainment.
— *All's Well that Ends Well, Act 3, Sc. 6*

Is it possible he should know what he is, and be that he is?
— *Act 4, Sc. 1*

We have our philosophical persons.
— *Act 2, Sc. 3*

A very tainted fellow, and full of wickedness.
— *Act 3, Sc. 2*

. . . all the learned and authentic fellows.
— *Act 2, Sc. 3*

A man who is the abstract of all faults that all men follow.
— *Antony and Cleopatra, Act 1, Sc. 4*

Every one fault seeming monstrous till his fellow-fault came to match it.
— *As You Like It, Act 3, Sc. 2*

. . . counterfeit to be a man.
— *Act 4, Sc. 3*

I see no more in you than in the ordinary of nature's sale-work.
— *Act 3, Sc. 5*

. . .motley-minded gentleman . . .
— *Act 5, Sc. 4*

. . . chide God for making you that countenance you are.
— *Act 4, Sc. 1*

And all the embossed sores and headed evils, that thou with license of free foot hast caught, wouldst thou disgorge into the general world.
— *Act 2, Sc. 7*

. . . a rude despiser of good manners . . .
— *Act 2, Sc. 7*

I think he be transform'd into a beast, for I can no where find him like a man.
— *Act 2, Sc. 7*

There is such odds in the man.

— As You Like It, Act 1, Sc. 2

I would sing my song without a burden; thou bringest me out of tune.

— Act 3, Sc. 2

They were all alike one another as half-pence are.

— Act 3, Sc. 2

. . . the most unnatural that lived amongst men.

— Act 4, Sc. 3

. . . a fortune teller, a needy, hollow-eyed, sharp-looking wretch, a living dead man . . .

— Comedy of Errors, Act 5, Sc. 1

Has the porter his eyes in his head, that he gives entrance to such companions?

— Coriolanus, Act 4, Sc. 5

. . . such a name whose repetition will be dogg'd with curses . . .

— Act 5, Sc. 3

. . . general louts . . .

— Act 3, Sc. 2

I need not be barren of accusations, he hath faults, with surplus, to tire in repetition.

— Act 1, Sc. 1

. . . too bad for bad report.

— Cymbeline, Act 1, Sc. 1

Ambitions, covetings, change of prides, disdain, nice longing, slanders, mutability, all faults that may be named, nay, that hell knows . . .

— Act 2, Sc. 5

. . . that irregulous devil . . .

— Act 4, Sc. 2

From whose so many weights of baseness cannot a dram of worth be drawn.

— Act 3, Sc. 5

He's a strange fellow himself, and knows it not.

— Act 2, Sc. 1

We had very many there could behold the sun with as firm eyes as he.

— Act 1, Sc. 4

. . . unvalued persons.

— Hamlet, Act 1, Sc. 3

How dangerous is it that this man goes loose!

— Act 4, Sc. 3

A dull and muddy-mettled rascal . . .

— Act 2, Sc. 2

The extravagant and erring spirit . . .

— Act 1, Sc. 1

These men — carrying, I say, the stamp of one defect, . . . their virtues else
. . . shall in the general censure take corruption from that particular
fault.

— Act 1, Sc. 4

Use every man after his desert, and who shall 'scape whipping?
— Act 2, Sc. 2

. . . muddied, thick and unwholesome in their thoughts and whispers.
— Act 4, Sc. 5

There lives not three good men unhanged in England, and one of them is fat
and grows old.

— Henry IV, Part I, Act 2, Sc. 4

He ambled up and down with shallow jesters . . .

— Act 3, Sc. 2

The more and less came in . . .

— Act 4, Sc. 3

You must needs learn, lord, to amend this fault . . .

— Act 3, Sc. 1

How agrees the devil and thee about thy soul, that thou soldest him on
Good Friday last for a cup of Madeira and a cold capon's leg?

— Act 1, Sc. 2

I could brain him with his lady's fan . . .

— Act 2, Sc. 3

. . . tickle-brain.

— Act 2, Sc. 4

That reverend vice, that grey iniquity, that father ruffian . . .

— Act 2, Sc. 4

. . . a true face and a good conscience. — Both of which I have had, but their date is out.

— *Henry IV, Part I, Act 2, Sc. 4*

. . . every beardless vain comparative . . .

— *Act 3, Sc. 2*

. . . impudent, embossed rascal . . .

— *Act 3, Sc. 3*

. . . tattered prodigals lately come from swine-keeping . . .

— *Act 4, Sc. 2*

He may keep his own grace, but he's almost out of mine, I can assure him.

— *Part II, Act 1, Sc. 2*

I grant your worship that he is a knave, sir, but yet, God forbid, sir, but a knave should have some countenance at his friend's request. An honest man, sir, is able to speak for himself, when a knave is not.

— *Act 5, Sc. 1*

An you do not make him hanged among you, the gallows shall have wrong.

— *Act 2, Sc. 2*

. . . muddy rascal . . .

— *Act 2, Sc. 4*

Simon Shadow.

— *Act 3, Sc. 2*

A tame cheater . . .

— *Act 2, Sc. 4*

. . . courageous Feeble! . . . most forcible Feeble!

— *Act 3, Sc. 2*

I cannot endure such a fustian rascal.

— *Act 2, Sc. 4*

. . . spirits of vile sort.

— *Act 5, Sc. 2*

It is certain that either wise bearing or ignorant carriage is caught, as men take diseases, one of another; therefore let men take heed of their company.

— *Act 5, Sc. 1*

Three such antics do not amount to a man.

— *Henry V, Act 3, Sc. 2*

By Cheshu, he is an ass, . . . I will verify as much.
> — *Henry V, Act 3, Sc. 2*

They sell the pasture now to buy the horse.
> — *Act 2, Prologue*

What is the trust or strength of foolish man?
> — *Henry VI, Part I, Act 3, Sc. 2*

Contaminated, base and misbegotten . . .
> — *Act 4, Sc. 6*

. . . base and humble mind.
> — *Part II, Act 1, Sc. 2*

Tut, these are petty faults to faults unknown, which time will bring to light . . .
> — *Act 3, Sc. 1*

. . . thy face is . . . made impudent with use of evil deeds . . .
> — *Part III, Act 1, Sc. 4*

You show'd your judgement, which being shallow . . .
> — *Act 4, Sc. 1*

Thou art no Atlas for so great a weight.
> — *Act 5, Sc. 1*

Yonder is the wolf that makes this spoil.
> — *Act 5, Sc. 4*

Abusing better men than they can be . . .
> — *Henry VIII, Act 1, Sc. 3*

. . . a man sorely tainted . . .
> — *Act 4, Sc. 2*

. . . his means, if he improve them, may well stretch so far as to annoy us all.
> — *Julius Caesar, Act 2, Sc. 1*

A peevish schoolboy . . . join'd with a masker and a reveller.
> — *Act 5, Sc. 1*

. . . inferior eyes, that borrow their behaviours from the great.
> — *King John, Act 5, Sc. 1*

A stone-cutter or a painter could not have made him so ill, though he had been but two hours at the trade.
> — *King Lear, Act 2, Sc. 2*

O, the difference of man and man!

— *King Lear, Act 4, Sc. 2*

Some good I mean to do, despite of mine own nature.

— *Act 5, Sc. 3*

To wilful men the injuries that they themselves procure must be their schoolmasters.

— *Act 2, Sc. 4*

. . . a reproveable badness in himself . . .

— *Act 3, Sc. 5*

. . . subdued nature to such a lowness . . .

— *Act 3, Sc. 4*

This fellow pecks up wit as pigeons pease, and utters it again when God doth please.

— *Love's Labour's Lost, Act 5, Sc. 2*

Where will you find men worthy enough . . . ?

— *Act 5, Sc. 1*

You are attaint with faults and perjury . . .

— *Act 5, Sc. 2*

His humour is lofty, his discourse peremptory, his tongue filed, his eye ambitious, his gait majestical and his general behaviour vain, ridiculous and thrasonical. He is too picked, too spruce, too affected, too odd, as it were, too peregrinate, as I may call it.

— *Act 5, Sc. 1*

. . . none at all in aught proves excellent.

— *Act 4, Sc. 3*

I dare not call them fools, but this I think,
When they are thirsty, fools would fain have drink.

— *Act 5, Sc. 2*

. . . instruments of darkness . . .

— *Macbeth, Act 1, Sc. 3*

. . . this ignorant present . . .

— *Act 1, Sc. 5*

I . . . abound in the division of each several crime, acting it in many ways.

— *Act 4, Sc. 3*

Renown and grace is dead.

— *Act 2, Sc. 3*

The close contriver of all harms . . .

— *Macbeth, Act 3, Sc. 5*

All the particulars of vice . . .

— *Act 4, Sc. 3*

. . . the worst rank of manhood . . .

— *Act 3, Sc. 1*

. . . a temporary meddler.

— *Measure for Measure, Act 5, Sc. 1*

How like you the young German . . . ? — Very vilely in the morning, when
he is sober, and most vilely in the afternoon, when he is drunk.

— *Merchant of Venice, Act 1, Sc. 2*

. . . a soft and dull-eyed fool . . .

— *Act 3, Sc. 3*

It is the most impenetrable cur that ever kept with men.

— *Act 3, Sc. 3*

When he is best, he is a little worse than a man; and when he is worst, he is
little better than a beast.

— *Act 1, Sc. 2*

. . . thrust virtue out of our hearts by the head and shoulders . . .

— *Merry Wives of Windsor, Act 5, Sc. 5*

This spotted and inconstant man.

— *Midsummer Night's Dream, Act 1, Sc. 1*

. . . king of shadows . . .

— *Act 3, Sc. 2*

With the help of a surgeon he might yet recover, and prove an ass.

— *Act 5, Sc. 1*

I see, lady, the gentleman is not in your books. — No; an he were, I would
burn my study.

— *Much Ado about Nothing, Act 1, Sc. 1*

All disquiet, horror and perturbation follows her.

— *Act 2, Sc. 1*

Let me see his eyes, that, when I note another man like him, I may avoid him.

— *Act 5, Sc. 1*

He is then a giant to an ape, but then is an ape a doctor to such a man.

— *Act 5, Sc. 1*

Being no other but as she is, I do not like her.
— *Much Ado about Nothing*, Act 1, Sc. 1

They will not admit any good part to intermingle with them.
— *Act 5, Sc. 2*

. . . so bad a voice to slander music . . .
— *Act 2, Sc. 3*

She would infect to the north star . . .
— *Act 2, Sc. 1*

A kind of men so loose of soul . . .
— *Othello, Act 3, Sc. 3*

A likely piece of work . . .
— *Act 4, Sc. 1*

. . . such perdition as nothing else could match.
— *Act 3, Sc. 4*

. . . civil monster.
— *Act 4, Sc. 1*

A pestilent complete knave.
— *Act 2, Sc. 1*

Mark the fleers, gibes and notable scorns that dwell in every region of his face.
— *Act 4, Sc. 1*

Some busy and insinuating rogue . . .
— *Act 4, Sc. 2*

There's many a beast then in a populous city.
— *Act 4, Sc. 1*

. . . a practiser of arts inhibited and out of warrant.
— *Act 1, Sc. 2*

One unperfectness shows me another, to make me frankly despise myself.
— *Act 2, Sc. 3*

Hath all those requisites in him that folly and green minds look after.
— *Act 2, Sc. 1*

. . . false as water.
— *Act 5, Sc. 2*

. . . with the little godliness I have.
— *Act 1, Sc. 2*

A fixed figure for the time of scorn to point his slow unmoving finger at.
— *Othello, Act 4, Sc. 2*

There be souls must be saved, and there be souls must not be saved.
— *Act 2, Sc. 3*

He did not flow from honourable sources.
— *Pericles, Act 4, Sc. 3*

Here's them . . . gets more with begging than we do with working.
— *Act 2, Sc. 1*

If you were born to honour, show it now; if put upon you, make the judgement good that thought you worthy of it.
— *Act 4, Sc. 6*

Show me the strumpet that began this stir . . .
— *Rape of Lucrece*

Thou grant'st no time for charitable deeds.
— *Rape of Lucrece*

Thou liest in reputation sick . . .
— *Richard II, Act 2, Sc. 1*

The more fair and crystal is the sky, the uglier seem the clouds that in it fly.
— *Act 1, Sc. 1*

A sort of vagabonds, rascals and runaways.
— *Richard III, Act 5, Sc. 3*

Thee, that hast nor honesty nor grace . . .
— *Act 1, Sc. 3*

. . . subtle, false and treacherous.
— *Act 1, Sc. 1*

One . . . that God hath made for himself to mar.
— *Romeo and Juliet, Act 2, Sc. 4*

. . . that same banish'd runagate . . .
— *Act 3, Sc. 5*

Among a number one is reckon'd none . . .
— *Sonnet 136*

Now this ill-wresting world is grown so bad . . .
— *Sonnet 140*

. . . three-inch fool!

— Taming of the Shrew, Act 4, Sc. 1

One unworthy all the former favours that I have fondly flatter'd her withal.

— Act 4, Sc. 2

Now I well perceive you have but jested with me all this while.

— Act 2, Sc. 1

I will leave him; I have no long spoon.

— The Tempest, Act 2, Sc. 2

Misery acquaints a man with strange bedfellows.

— Act 2, Sc. 2

A very ancient and fish-like smell.

— Act 2, Sc. 2

Rid me these villains from your companies.

— Timon of Athens, Act 5, Sc. 1

'Tis honour with most lands to be at odds.

— Act 3, Sc. 5

The strain of man's bred out into baboon and monkey.

— Act 1, Sc. 1

. . . to the woods, where he shall find the unkindest beast more kinder than mankind.

— Act 4, Sc. 1

He's opposite to humanity.

— Act 1, Sc. 1

Bastard begot, bastard instructed, bastard in mind, . . . in every thing illegitimate.

— Troilus and Cressida, Act 5, Sc. 7

The primitive statue and oblique memorial of cuckolds . . .

— Act 5, Sc. 1

Thou dost not use me courteously . . .

— Act 4, Sc. 4

For honour travels in a strait so narrow where one but goes abreast . . .

— Act 3, Sc. 3

The plague of Greece upon thee, thou mongrel beef-witted lord!

— Act 2, Sc. 1

Heavens, what a man is there! a very horse, that has he knows not what.
— *Troilus and Cressida, Act 3, Sc. 3*

What sneaking fellow comes yonder?
— *Act 1, Sc. 2*

. . . his virtues . . . do in our eyes begin to lose their gloss.
— *Act 2, Sc. 3*

. . . a very land-fish, languageless.
— *Act 3, Sc. 3*

And mighty states characterless are grated to dusty nothing.
— *Act 3, Sc. 2*

If he were opened, and you find so much blood in his liver as will clog the foot of a flea, I'll eat the rest of the anatomy.
— *Twelfth Night, Act 3, Sc. 2*

The cur is excellent at faults.
— *Act 2, Sc. 5*

Nought enters there, of what validity and pitch soe'er, but falls into abatement and low price, even in a minute.
— *Act 1, Sc. 1*

. . . borrows his wit . . . and spends what he borrows.
— *Two Gentlemen of Verona, Act 2, Sc. 4*

How now, . . . are you crept before us?
— *Act 4, Sc. 2*

Thou common friend, that's without faith or love . . .
— *Act 5, Sc. 4*

. . . is nor of heaven nor earth.
— *Act 5, Sc. 4*

. . . wants but something to be a reasonable man . . .
— *Winter's Tale, Act 4, Sc. 4*

I see this is the time that the unjust man doth thrive.
— *Act 4, Sc. 4*

Should all despair that have revolted wives, the tenth of mankind would hang themselves.
— *Act 1, Sc. 2*

. . . negligent, foolish and fearful . . .
— *Act 1, Sc. 2*

There are cozeners abroad; Therefore, it behoves men to be wary.
— *Winter's Tale, Act 4, Sc. 4*

I cannot tell, good sir, for which of his virtues it was, but he was certainly whipped out of the court.
— *Act 4, Sc. 3*

Having flown over many knavish professions, he settled only in rogue.
— *Act 4, Sc. 3*

INDEX

233

Act 2, Sc. 1	27, 35 (3), 43, 59, 74
	140, 170, 194 (2), 205
	211
Act 3, Sc. 1	14, 52, 82, 88, 90, 92
	103, 127, 130 (2), 137
	158, 194
Act 3, Sc. 3	122, 148, 158, 165, 175
Act 3, Sc. 4	4, 35, 59, 103, 109, 194
Act 4, Sc. 1	70, 179, 194
Act 4, Sc. 2	12, 52, 59, 79, 90, 94
	110, 133, 134, 138, 140
	141, 150, 158, 173, 193
	194 (3), 215
Act 4, Sc. 3	59, 70, 93, 94, 104, 133
	167, 193 (2)
Act 5, Sc. 1	59, 64, 112, 145, 221
Act 5, Sc. 2	35, 95, 123, 178, 186
	194, 206
Act 5, Sc. 4	104
Act 5, Sc. 7	76, 111, 193

King Lear

Act 1, Sc. 1	27, 104, 141, 117, 194
Act 1, Sc. 2	94, 120 (2), 169
Act 1, Sc. 4	40, 65, 72, 113, 136, 144
	177
Act 1, Sc. 5	10
Act 2, Sc. 1	50
Act 2, Sc. 2	80, 104 (3), 158, 221
Act 2, Sc. 4	115, 117, 194, 222
Act 3, Sc. 1	104, 109
Act 3, Sc. 2	13, 35, 82, 150, 194
Act 3, Sc. 3	194
Act 3, Sc. 4	16, 25, 111, 222
Act 3, Sc. 5	222
Act 3, Sc. 6	185, 194
Act 3, Sc. 7	158
Act 4, Sc. 1	15, 92
Act 4, Sc. 2	104, 122
Act 4, Sc. 3	2, 46
Act 4, Sc. 4	188, 194
Act 4, Sc. 6	3, 22, 88, 120, 125, 158

Act 4, Sc. 7	52, 111
Act 5, Sc. 1	18, 22, 137, 175
Act 5, Sc. 3	3, 32, 41, 104, 119, 222

Lover's Complaint
18, 25, 141, 175

Love's Labour's Lost

Act 1, Sc. 1	20, 21 (2), 28, 47, 55, 65
	70, 86, 89, 90, 145 (2)
	146, 158, 164, 165, 183
Act 1, Sc. 2	7, 48, 136, 158, 165
Act 2, Sc. 1	31, 97, 133, 135, 211
Act 3, Sc. 1	21, 39, 126
Act 4, Sc. 1	12, 183
Act 4, Sc. 2	11, 14, 22, 53, 83, 176
Act 4, Sc. 3	7, 19, 26, 27, 68, 76, 90
	94, 113, 147, 158, 186
	222
Act 5, Sc. 1	53, 104 (2), 140, 146
	149, 211, 222 (2)
Act 5, Sc. 2	7, 20, 21, 35 (2), 36, 48,
	52, 53, 69, 91, 104 (3),
	115, 125, 138, 139, 143,
	148, 151, 173, 177,
	195 (2), 206, 207, 222 (3)

Macbeth

Act 1, Sc. 3	60 (3), 111, 222
Act 1, Sc. 5	59, 149, 222
Act 2, Sc. 1	111
Act 2, Sc. 2	59, 175
Act 2, Sc. 3	7, 92, 149, 153, 163, 173
	222
Act 2, Sc. 4	60
Act 3, Sc. 1	44, 104, 223
Act 3, Sc. 4	7, 60, 93, 166, 173, 195
Act 3, Sc. 5	20, 202, 203, 214, 223

Rape of Lucrece

17, 25, 36 (2), 42, 65, 69, 70, 71, 79, 88, 113
138 (2), 146, 150, 151
165, 181, 197 (3), 225 (2)

Richard II

Act 1, Sc. 1   128, 129, 136 (2), 141
202, 225
Act 1, Sc. 3   44, 47, 63, 216
Act 1, Sc. 4   8, 12, 106, 116, 152, 160

Act 2, Sc. 1   3, 39, 51, 109, 118, 166
176, 197, 201, 202, 223
225
Act 2, Sc. 2   65, 92, 94, 123, 175, 213
Act 2, Sc. 3   1, 118, 125, 151, 213
Act 2, Sc. 4   74

Act 3, Sc. 1   197 (2)
Act 3, Sc. 2   75, 80, 142, 177

Act 4, Sc. 1   45, 66, 77, 112, 121, 153
197 (2)

Act 5, Sc. 1   165
Act 5, Sc. 3   117, 166
Act 5, Sc. 5   78, 95, 132

Richard III

Act 1, Sc. 1   18, 20, 64, 106, 120, 153
160, 198, 212, 225
Act 1, Sc. 2   8, 106, 138, 150, 178, 183
197, 214
Act 1, Sc. 3   36 (2), 80, 97, 98, 106
150, 160, 197, 198 (3)
206, 225
Act 1, Sc. 4   131, 136, 142, 150, 197
Act 1, Sc. 5   120

Act 2, Sc. 1   173
Act 2, Sc. 2   1, 94
Act 2, Sc. 4   75, 94

Act 3, Sc. 1   44, 75, 127, 149, 160
Act 3, Sc. 2   92
Act 3, Sc. 4   118, 214

Act 3, Sc. 5   91, 148, 149, 208
Act 3, Sc. 6   170
Act 3, Sc. 7   145, 198

Act 4, Sc. 2   114, 115, 124 (2), 142
160 (3), 198
Act 4, Sc. 4   8, 13, 26, 40, 74, 75, 76
90, 106, 114, 122, 138
185, 198 (2), 205, 209

Act 5, Sc. 2   215
Act 5, Sc. 3   147, 188, 198, 215, 225
Act 5, Sc. 5   137

Romeo and Juliet

Prologue   3

Act 1, Sc. 1   21, 22, 85
Act 1, Sc. 2   92
Act 1, Sc. 3   83, 84
Act 1, Sc. 4   42, 70, 71, 88, 132, 163
177, 215
Act 1, Sc. 5   16, 30, 39, 86, 132

Act 2, Sc. 1   21, 85
Act 2, Sc. 2   61, 117
Act 2, Sc. 3   41, 61, 91, 170
Act 2, Sc. 4   20, 22, 36, 84, 121, 178
225
Act 2, Sc. 5   66, 184
Act 2, Sc. 6   215

Act 3, Sc. 1   106, 137, 202
Act 3, Sc. 2   28, 86, 93, 208
Act 3, Sc. 3   14, 109, 171, 198, 203
Act 3, Sc. 4   168
Act 3, Sc. 5   8, 36, 106, 132, 153, 201
225

Act 4, Sc. 1   36, 81, 215
Act 4, Sc. 5   40, 188

Act 5, Sc. 1   110, 198, 214
Act 5, Sc. 3   204

Two Gentlemen of Verona

Venus and Adonis

Winter's Tale